Sojou

A Tale of A Legal Immigrant

By

Norbert Jacobs

Table of Contents

Dedication

I want to dedicate this book to my father. Even though my relationship with him was stormy at best, I can't deny that he is responsible for instilling in me the determination and grit that has served me for most of my life.

About The Author

The author was 9 years old when his father and mother emigrated from Belgium to the United States and settled in San Antonio, Texas. Following High School he joined the US Navy and served on a submarine. When his 4-year stint ended he joined the San Antonio Police department and retired after a 34-year career. He and his wife live in the Hill Country North of San Antonio and spend time with their kids and grandchildren. He also enjoys time spent in his woodworking shop at home.

Foreword

My wife, Jeanette, and I are social people, and we are blessed with living in a friendly community that provides a lot of opportunities to mingle with our neighbors. We attend a regular card game and are part of an active wine club that gets together for several months of the year.

Funny, but once people find out I was a Police Officer, they often want to hear a police story. Like my father, it seems that I have a knack for telling a story, and after a 34-year career, it's not hard to come up with material. The good thing is that I don't have to make up anything because human beings are an endless source of funny, sad, tragic, and horrible stories.

Quite a few times, people suggested that I ought to write a book about my experiences, and I admit that the idea appealed to me. I love to read and often find my mind wandering off and changing the script to suit myself. I wondered if I could develop a fiction hero character and then work on my true-life police-related stuff. The problem with a fictional hero was that it could cause people to question whether the events were real. As far as I am concerned, the reality of the stories that I tell is what makes them interesting. So a fictional hero wasn't going to work, and as other "stuff" would come up in daily life to occupy my time, I would forget about a book. So why now?

Well, strange as it sounds, I got serious about writing a book because of an invitation I received from my then 3-year-old granddaughter, Rainy. Roughly eight years ago, my wife and I were visiting her oldest son, Doug, and his family at their home south of Stephenville, Texas. They have two daughters named Reese and Rainy, and my wife and I make the 3-hour drive up from our home in the Hill Country to spend a few days with them from time to time.

Back then, they would insist that we stay with them at their house. When it was time for bed, Reese (who is the older of the girls and the apple of her Mamaw's eye) would want Mamaw to stay in her room. Rainy was four years younger, and, for reasons unknown, she and I had formed a bond almost from the time she could crawl. So when it was time to go to bed, I would end up on a bunk bed in Rainy's room.

Right before one of our visits, the girls had been combined into one bedroom. When we got there, they wanted us to see how they had fixed it up. When Jeanette and I walked in, we were complimenting them on how nice everything looked when Rainy grabbed my hand and asked me to get under the bed with her! Her mother said, "Now Rainy, he doesn't want to get under there," but Rainy insisted. She asked me again, pulling on my hand, then dropping to the floor and scooting under the bed. Coming from under the bed, I heard, "Come on, Papaw!" So what could I do? I got down on the floor and crawled under the bed!

When I scooted under the bed, I was surprised and amazed! Rainy and her momma had strung little twinkling Christmas lights all around the wooden framework of the bed. There were various figures, dolls, and other precious things that Rainy had put here and there in every little spot available! She and her momma had created a special place… just for Rainy!

I was the guest of honor and got treated to a personal tour. Watching Rainy's excitement as she shared her magical place with me was enough to make my day. Instead of a scary place with a "boogie-man" under the bed, it was a safe haven where Rainy could entertain herself whenever she desired...night or day. We left a couple of days later and returned home, but that invitation, "Come get under my bed with me," wouldn't leave my mind.

A few days later, I was out in *my* special place (my wood shop) when I realized what Rainy's invitation had really meant to me. As proud as I am of my shop, I don't want just *anyone* coming in. I invite people I trust and those I know will appreciate the things I feel are special. When Rainy asked me to "get under the bed with her," she unknowingly had, through her trust in me, believed that I would appreciate how special her place was to her. I needed to tell her that she was the one who made it special for me, although I have to admit that the lights and the things that she had put there helped!

As the years have gone by, I have never forgotten that day when I crawled under the bed with Rainy. Several times I started thinking about writing a book with that title, but something would always come along that would keep me from the beginning.

Two years ago, I celebrated my 75th birthday, and I recalled that my father died when he was 77 years old. Another influence was that I often get e-mails from one of the guys who stays involved with our retiree organization and provides updates that involve retirees. These updates include the recent deaths of policemen. Of course, a lot of them are people I knew and worked with, but a lot of them are also younger than me.

I don't want to get morbid here, but I started thinking that my time here on earth is getting short. Since my sister, brother, and I are first-generation immigrants to America and are all that remain of our family tree here in America, chances are slim that my kids and grandkids will ever know the whole story of who I was or how I came to be part of their lives. So I decided to write this account of my life, and if any of them were interested, they could read it if they wanted.

For anyone who may come across this book that is not related to me and would ask why it should interest them, let me say this. Even though this is *my* personal story, we all share some similarities in our lives as we interact with probably hundreds (if not thousands) of people throughout our lifetimes. Maybe parts of this book will bring to mind your personal experiences and cause you to reflect on your journey.

As a Christian, I believe that God creates every person as a unique individual, and He has mapped out our lives –up to and including– the day we die. God purposely didn't create robots; we are allowed to make choices along the way, and we have to live with the consequences (good or bad) of those choices.

I titled this book "Sojourner," a word found in the Bible. It means "wanderer", "temporary resident", or "one who stays for a while." In the Bible, "Sojourner" was used to describe Abraham as he was ordered to leave his family and home, but I find it fitting to apply this term to each of us because we are all here on this earth for just a temporary time.

Let me add that God created Adam first, but He knew that it wouldn't be good for man "to be alone," so He created a helpmate for him. Adam named her "Eve." The bond they shared became the precursor to all of humanity. And that is because our God is all about relationships. This book will point out how the relationships that have been placed in my path have been instrumental in shaping and influencing my life. There is no way I could include everyone that has impacted my life, but rest assured that even if some of you are not specifically listed, you are not forgotten.

Much of the content in this book is based on my memory of how the events took place. It was not my intent to overly glamorize or minimize any of the stories contained here, but I can assure you that I tried as well as I could to portray them as I lived them. If a mistake was made, it was unintentional, and I claim full responsibility.

I invite you to "come and get under the bed with me," and maybe *you* will discover something about yourself in the process.

Norbert Jacobs

August 4, 2022

Chapter 1

Sojourner

(A temporary resident, a wanderer, a stranger)

"In the beginning..."

The very first verse in the Bible starts with "In the beginning God created...." As I started seriously thinking about writing this book, I felt that it would make sense to start from the beginning: with my appearance in this world. June 2, 1945, that's the day that Yours Truly made his grand entry. Following the chaos and noise of WWII, which ended a few months prior to this, my first cry wasn't noted in any significant history books; there were no parades, no cheering in the streets.

As the first born of three children, I became a part of the new generation to restock the population that was killed during the Great War. Apparently, I wasn't convinced that I was ready to leave the security of my mother's womb since the doctor had to use metal forceps to grab my head and help me out. The slight scars on either side of my forehead were visible for many years but have now faded with time. Wouldn't it be nice if *all* scars faded with time? But some scars seem to stay with us for as long as we live. The thing about scars is that we all have them...some are visible, but a lot of them are not. Some are physical, and a lot more of them are emotional, but surely *all* of them are evidence of the one experience we have in common...life!

I guess I should mention where all this took place. I was born in Belgium, in a hospital in Ghent, to a young couple named Robert Jacobs and his wife, Johanna De Mulder Jacobs. We lived in a small town called Wetteren, located northeast of Brussels, not far from the North Sea.

Wetteren is still a small town today (around 23,000 people) but was even smaller in 1945. The German occupation during the war years had increased the population, but my people probably would have preferred to be spared that dramatic growth spurt! My father was in the military and became a prisoner of war, but unlike political prisoners, and partisan fighters, he was allowed to remain in Belgium.

The rare times that he and my mother spoke of the occupation, I was surprised to learn that they feared the allies more than the Germans! Apparently, at the onset of the war, the Germans overran Belgium so quickly that not a lot of damage was inflicted. But as the tide began to turn in the allies' favor and the Germans started retreating, the allies began bombing military targets. As is sometimes the case, civilian locations were often hit. But Belgians have always praised the American soldiers and were grateful for their intervention and sacrifices. None-the-less, when you're running for your life to get into a bomb shelter, those grateful thoughts are often put on hold.

Because my father had no money, he and my mother lived with my mother's mother and father. Unlike my father and his family, my mother's family was considerably better off. They lived in a large multi-story house that a bakery, a store, and a large tract of land with an orchard joined.

The property also had several other buildings: one housed two tenants, and the other was a large horse stable. They also raised chickens and hogs. This was the hustle and bustle that I was introduced to on my arrival at what would be home for the first nine years of my life!

Fourteen months after I was born, my mother brought home my baby sister, Jeanine Marie, and two years later, I was introduced to a little brother named Rafael ("Ralph"). I am often told that my name (Norbert) is an unusual name, and a lot of times, people hearing it for the first time want to call me Robert. I correct them and tell them that I am called Norbert because when the doctor pulled me out of the womb, he held me up by the ankles, popped me on the behind, and said, "Look, no butt!"

Even though I was a little kid, I realized that everyone around me worked and worked hard. My grandfather ran the bakery, which meant he was generally up all night. The bread they baked was destined for markets everywhere around Wetteren and was delivered by a horse-drawn wagon or a bicycle cart. I later learned that these deliveries were one of the many jobs that my father performed for the family business.

Loading the bread loaves for daily delivery would begin at three or four o'clock in the morning so that the bread could be in the shops when they opened for business. As I mentioned, my grandmother also had a store where she sold meats, cheeses, eggs, bread, and other staples. Since we didn't have refrigerators, much of the meat was salted, cured, and stored in the cellar. Vegetables such as potatoes were also kept layered in straws in the cellar.

One of my fondest memories was the potato harvest. When the potatoes were being dug up in the fields, they were pitched into horse-drawn wagons. Many of the farmers used big Belgian draft horses to pull the loaded wagons. I remember those magnificent animals since I was sometimes taken to the edge of the fields and allowed to watch as the horses strained in their harnesses to pull the wagons--often in the mud!

The man on top of the wagon seat would be calling out-- urging the animals to pull harder, and, as the wagons began to pick up momentum, he would be almost singing as he called them by their names, praising their efforts. The horses would turn their ears back to him, and you knew they understood because they would nod their heads and strain even more. Just standing off ways, you could see, feel, hear, and even smell the effort of both men and animals as they worked as a team!

I guess because everyone could work, we kids were allowed the freedom to roam, much of the time on our own, but I expected that there was always someone who would have an eye on us as we explored. I have already mentioned all the available buildings, but much of the exploring took place in the orchard at the rear of the property.

At the right time of the year, the cherries began ripening, and when I was old enough to climb, I would be in the tree eating the cherries as I pulled them from the branches. It didn't take long to realize that you made sure the cherries were ripe before you tried to eat them! (My underwear provided proof of that a time or two when I tried to eat them too green).

I remember a cherry story that involved my grandmother's chickens. I will tell you a little more about my grandmother later, but for now, let me say that she had a real fondness for her chickens, her medium-sized dog named Markie, and her cat. I think that these three critters ranked ahead of almost any human being she was around.

The orchard was at the back of the property, and the chickens were usually in a coop more to the front, although they could go to the back if they wanted to. One day my grandmother went out to feed her chickens, and in no time, she was back at the house yelling for help. My grandfather and uncle ran outside, and she told them that something was wrong with the chickens.

They followed her, and when she stopped and started pointing, they could also see these chickens acting really strange! Some of them were falling down and getting back up, others were wobbling around on their feet, and others were running into each other and various objects in the yard! A few of them were making weird noises, and some of them were lying on the ground and couldn't get up.

My grandmother started yelling that someone had poisoned her chickens! She was trying to stand some of them up, and as soon as she would let one go, it would fall back down! My uncle noticed a few chickens on the path toward the orchard and started walking that way. As he walked along, he could see a few more chickens and some of them were scattered under one of the cherry trees. When he got to the tree, he noticed the ground was covered with overripe cherries that had fallen out of the tree.

My uncle started putting two and two together. He figured out that the chickens who had been scavenging around the orchard, had found the cherries on the ground. It seems that some of the fruit had begun to ferment when it ripened, and those cherries were in that stage when the chickens started eating them. Long story short, the chickens were drunk! Though they all recovered, I don't remember if the eggs were affected. So I guess you probably couldn't get drunk eating scrambled eggs.

There was a walking/bicycle path along the property that had a hedge bordering it which was used by people traveling to town. Somebody had told me that the hedge was a good place to hide and then scare kids as they walked by. I found out there was some truth to that, but I also found out that some people don't like being scared; thankfully, I was fast on my feet.

While the walking path was mostly quiet, the cobble stone streets would loudly ring with the sounds of horses' hooves pulling wagons mixed in with the occasional automobile. When you added the tinkling bells of bicycles and wheeled carts of vendors peddling fresh-caught fish brought in from the North Sea, it seemed the noise was non-stop.

As the oldest, I was in charge of organizing games and adventures for me and my brother and sister, or at least I *thought* it was my responsibility. One afternoon the adults were in the house visiting, and I came across one of the large darts that belonged to my uncle's dart set. The three of us were outside throwing the dart up in the air and watching it come down, trying to hit a "target" on the ground. Because of its weight, you could take and fling it way up in the air, and it would right itself and hit point first.

We had all been taking turns, and I don't remember who flung it up in the air, but we watched it come down toward us, landing with a loud Smack!! Right in the middle of the top of my sister's head! Oh boy! She reached up and, when she felt it stuck in her head, she yelled and started to run toward the house. Of course, as the designated organizer of this event, I knew that I was in deep trouble and would probably not live long enough to come up with a reasonable explanation.

Think about it, we walked into the house with this dart stuck in the top of my sister's head. How do you explain something like that? Let's see, "I don't know what happened; we were out in the yard, and all of a sudden, this dart came down out of the sky and landed on her head." Well, I did the only logical thing I could think of: I grabbed her before she got near the house.

I stopped her yelling and took her to the outhouse with my little brother following along, staring at the top of her head. I have to admit it was impossible not to stare at that big dart standing straight up like it sort of grew there! When we got to the outhouse, I had her sit down, and she asked me what we would do, and I told her that we would pull it out!

My sister is tough and said OK, but I could tell she was concerned. I stood up behind her on the bench, grabbed the dart, and yanked that thing right out. I don't recall it bleeding much, and after waiting for a while to see if there were going to be any problems, (and she didn't start acting funny), we snuck back in the house, and I put the dart back. We never played that game again!

When we were not in school, almost all of our time was spent outside, weather permitting. Since there was no television, outside was the only option, and that was where we met our friends. Once my brother was old enough to tag along, we were expected to look after him and some of the other younger kids. Because our community was small, I imagine we were not as "on our own" as we believed ourselves to be.

I discovered that the world was full of "snitches," and often, I would come home and be immediately confronted with questions about something that happened (that I had felt my parents should not be troubled with.) Heck, they had enough to worry about without wondering if forcing someone to eat grass (lawn) would affect their digestive system. It didn't seem to have much of an impact once the kid threw up! (Although a couple of the other kids also got sick just watching him puke!)

I don't want to give the impression that we were not included in the adult's social life. Although we were Catholic, we didn't attend church on a regular basis. But, when I became old enough, I was forced to go when my parents went, which fortunately wasn't too often.

It's amazing the way our lives are impacted in so many different ways as we grow up. My negative view of the church started the first time I was taken there by my parents, and I walked into this huge, imposing building. It was constructed of stone and had high arched ceilings with stained glass in the walls and behind the altar. There were individual chairs (not pews), and the rear of the chair in front of you had a fold-down wooden step which was flipped down when it was time to kneel. The person who designed the seating and kneeling arrangement must have been left over from the inquisition era, and I am certain he never used that kneeling step himself!

At the beginning of the service, the priest and altar boys would enter from the rear and slowly walk their way up the center aisle, burning incense as they made their way up to the altar. This was all pretty mysterious for a six-year-old boy, especially since much of the service was spoken in a foreign language (which I later learned was Latin.)

But the scariest part of the whole service was the men who walked the side aisles. They made sure that everyone behaved and that no one fell asleep. They each held a large wooden staff with a pointed metal spear on the top. As they passed by, they would look down the row of chairs, and if anyone needed correction, they would loudly tap the staff on the floor. Of course, all eyes would be directed to the offender, who would either be poked in the ribs by someone next to him or her, or, as in the case of Yours Truly, an ear could be twisted! All in all, the church was a scary place for me back then, and I avoided it for a large part of my life as I grew older.

The more enjoyable socializing took place at the local tavern. The tavern should not be confused with the drinking bars/sports bars that we have today. The tavern we visited was a place for young and old men, women, and kids. Pipes and cigarettes were smoked, and beer and other spirits were consumed along with food. But, more importantly, the tavern was a place for visiting with neighbors and catching up on all the latest gossip. The women would often sit at tables by themselves, and the men sanother group. There was a dart board (darts were a big deal there and, as I mentioned earlier, could be used for games other than the one originally intended.) There was also a billiard table, shuffleboard, and lots of places for kids to run around… playing while still being under the watchful eyes of their mom and dad.

There was also a Movie Theater in town, and I remember one time when I went there with my cousin Eddie and three other boys. Eddie was one of those guys who was always daring younger kids to do something stupid. From where we lived, we had to cross a cable car track with a rolling gate that would roll across the street, blocking anyone from getting in the way of the trolley. On this particular day, as we got close to the trolley crossing, the caution lights began to flash bright yellow, letting everybody know that a streetcar was coming and that the gate was starting to close.

Eddie began daring one of the younger boys to put his foot on the track which the rubber wheel ran on and leave it there until just before the wheel would run over his foot. This boy said heck no, and then he dared Eddie to do it *himself* so we could all see that he wasn't scared. Well, Eddie was trapped, so he put his foot out, and just as he was going to pull back, somebody nudged him, and he was too late! The wheel ran over his foot, and we found out just how loud Eddie could yell! People were wondering what had happened, but all they could see was Eddie hopping around, holding his foot. Luckily, nothing was broken; we went to the theater, although Eddie was really walking funny.

We were supposed to see an animated movie, but when we got there, Eddie decided that we should see a movie about the life of John the Baptist. This was a great movie until it got to the part of John's head being cut off! It was as graphic as you could get, and the people who made the movie spared no expense to make sure that you saw the stump of his neck and his severed head on the platter! That part stuck with me, and when I got back home, my mother could tell that there was something wrong. It wasn't too long before I spilled the beans, and Eddie (my cousin), was on the receiving end of some heavy corporal punishment. It just wasn't Eddie's day.

Like almost everywhere else, daily life in our community was for the most part repetitive, filled with work, school, and play. But I remember a day when everyone got excited because the Circus was coming to town! When I found out that we were going, I could hardly wait. The day arrived, and that evening the family set out to go where the tents had been erected. We had tickets for the show, and we sat through the acts under the big top, watching in awe at the people on the trapeze and constantly laughing as the clowns entertained us.

After the show, we started walking around the grounds, looking at various games and exhibits. We came to a big tent with a man out front of it who was inviting people to come in (for a price) to see the 'Wild Man of Africa!' Well, my uncle decided he wanted to see the "wild man," so we went along, hustling to get front-row seats. I was intently looking at the curtain that had been lowered down across the stage. It had a painting of a very dark, wild-looking man with crazy, long, kinky hair, and pointy teeth. It was scary!

I thought the front row might not be the best place to sit because we were just a few feet from the curtain. The tent was full of people, and as the lights began to dim, the front tent flap was pulled closed, and we started hearing grunts and growls from the other side of the curtain. Then the curtain started going up very slowly, and you could see the steel bars of a cage. The growls were now lower and louder! Soon you could see feet and legs pacing from side to side behind the steel bars!

When the curtain was completely up, I was looking at the scariest thing I had ever seen. This black creature had nothing on his body but a short skirt made of animal skin. His body was dark, but it was painted with stripes and other designs of bright colors. His face was painted, too! He had a bone pierced through his nose, and his teeth were filed to those sharp points! Other people were making screaming noises, but I was completely locked-in on this person because he seemed to be staring *right at me*. As I continued to stare at him, he jumped up onto the bars and began to roar and violently shake them! I began to realize that it was a *gate* that he was shaking, and it now appeared to be *moving*! I was already holding on to my father's arm when Wild Man let out another scream, causing most of the crowd to scream even louder. (I admit: I might have been one of them.) About then, the gate seemed to open, and the stampede for the exit was on! Let me tell you, this boy was *not* the last to leave that tent! So much for circus entertainment!

When we got home, we were asked if it had been a good show since some friends of my parents were also planning on going the next day. We told them that it had been sort-of fun, but that they shouldn't waste their money on seeing the "Wild Man of Africa" since it hadn't been very good.

Chapter 2

"…you will all be killed…"

I am not sure when I began to realize that there was tension between my parents and grandparents. A child will usually pick up on that type of thing, and from the comments made, it was obvious that my mother's mother didn't like my father. The fact that we lived in my grandparent's house certainly didn't help matters.

My father's parents were not as prosperous as my mother's (as a matter of fact, they were downright poor), and I think that my grandmother felt that my mother had married beneath her. On the other hand, my grandfather never said a word (to my knowledge) that showed he wasn't happy with his son-in-law. My grandfather was a physically small man, and what I remember most about him was that he always wore white baker's clothes and constantly had a hand-rolled cigarette in the corner of his mouth. More often than not, the cigarette wasn't lit, and I found him several times standing asleep, leaning against the oven with the cigarette in the corner of his mouth! Remember that the bread baking took place throughout the night, so he had to be nearby to monitor the progress of the bread as it rose so he could then place it in the oven.

We always called my grandfather "Pitchen," which would be similar to "Pops or Daddy" in the United States. He was *almost* always in a good mood and generally welcomed our intrusions into the bakery. My little brother was his favorite, and he had a little white apron made for him along with a white cap which is how my grandfather dressed. The bakery was an important part of our lives. It generated a large part of the family income, and during the winters, it was one of the warmest places in the house. Since there was no central heat (air conditioning was non-existent there), the bakery was where we took our weekly bath! A large metal tub was placed in front of the ovens, water was heated on the stove, and the tub was then filled with hot water. Our water was drawn from a well outside our backdoor, and the water was really cold all year… *especially* cold in the wintertime!

When the tub was filled, it was time to wash-up. The problem from my point of view was that the line was formed from oldest (adults) to youngest (kids.) There was no change of water in-between washings, so you can imagine what I was confronted with when my turn came around. There was *no* soaking in water up to *my* chin. But thank God I wasn't last! This bakery-bath held another fond memory for me: it was the first place I saw a grown woman naked! The "peep show" didn't last long since I was run out of there so quickly, but man, the questions I had in my head!

I guess I was around six years old when I started school. I attended a Catholic school where French was the language spoken, and all the teachers were nuns. We went to school five days a week and a half day on Saturdays. I made it through the third grade, but I honestly don't remember much of school other than I wasn't fond of it! That attitude stayed with me all the way through high school.

I described my grandfather as a kind, good, quiet man; my grandmother, though, was the total opposite. She had a fiery temper that the whole community was familiar with. Where my grandfather would give you the shirt off his back, my grandmother would take the shirt off your back and charge you for the effort it took to get it! She was in charge and didn't like repeating anything more than once. If she told you to do something, and you weren't moving 2 to 3 seconds later, she would give you an assist...applied to your butt! As I grew up, my mother kept that same philosophy!

My grandmother treated everybody in the same manner – including her husband and (unfortunately) her son-in-law, my father. I am convinced that she was a large part of the reason that my father announced one day that he was going to immigrate to the United States of America.

I wasn't asked if I thought leaving Belgium and going to America was a good idea. I didn't get a vote, and I don't know the process my father followed to make it happen. I do know that my grandmother was absolutely convinced that my father had lost his mind, and she would loudly announce that to anyone who would listen.

He had been talking about America for several years and read all he could get his hands on about life there. Our family knew people who had immigrated there, and the letters they wrote back to relatives and friends back to us in Belgium were full of praise for their new country. I heard of only one man who eventually came back just because he was homesick for his home country.

Before my father would be allowed to immigrate, he had to have a sponsor in America that would vouch for his character and integrity. The sponsor also had to line up a job for him so that he could immediately go to work. He also had to have a Belgian medical exam with a copy of X-rays that showed he was in good health.

Then there was the crucial matter regarding the cost of a ticket on a ship bound for America. My father was a poor man, and his parents didn't have money, so his sponsor agreed to advance him in the cost of his ship's passage.

Let me add a few quick words about my father's sponsor. His name was Rudolph DeWinne, and he and his family had immigrated to the US several years prior to my father wanting to go. Rudolph still had relatives living near us in Belgium, and they knew my father personally. Since they were able to vouch for my father's character, Mr. DeWinne sent the money for his passage. As he would be living with them, he would begin to repay them as soon as he went to work. By the time I became aware of his plans, he was committed to leaving Belgium and coming to America. Final destination – San Antonio, Texas!

Chapter 3

"…he is loose on the train."

I believe that up until a couple of weeks before my father left to board his ship, most of our people believed he wasn't serious. As I grew older, I realized that when he made up his mind about something, he rarely changed it. Despite his family, friends, and acquaintances telling him what a terrible mistake he was making, in March of 1954, Robert Jacobs sailed from Rotterdam on the Dutch Coast of the Netherlands to the harbor of New York City, United States.

Not many people went to see him off, and I think that maybe my grandmother felt a sense of relief that he was gone! I don't remember what I felt. I guess being around so many people under one roof with the constant activity of baking and coming and going, it wasn't hard to overlook the fact that my father wasn't there. As I write these sentences, I find myself hoping that I just don't *remember* how I felt and that I probably really did miss him.

It wasn't long before my grandmother began to announce doom and gloom to my mother regarding my father. More specifically, she would point out the lack of her husband by virtue of his absence. Other people were glad to join in, so there was never a shortage of naysayers and "I-told-you-so's."

I can't imagine the strain that my mother was under…constantly being told that her husband had left her and would probably never be heard from again. Then the letters began to arrive! When my mother would receive a letter, our neighbors would hear of the letter "from America" and would come over to listen to my mother reading out loud what my father had to say about his (and eventually *our* new country.)

He was quite a storyteller; my father was. By that, I mean that he always had a gift for drawing people into whatever he was talking about. So when my mother would read his letters, folks listening to her were drawn into visualizing what he was describing.

The letters were big news, and it was common for people to stop by and ask if we had heard from America. Of course, my father shared the details of his voyage to New York and the train ride to San Antonio. He wrote about the cities, countryside, and people he encountered, and you could sense his excitement and wonder. I guess it was the beginning of summer in Texas when my mother received his letter. As she was reading, several people were sitting in the room, and she read my father's description of a fruit he had just encountered in the grocery store.

He wrote, "…Jeanie, they have this fruit here that you will not believe. It is sweeter than anything I have ever eaten; it's green on the outside but red on the inside. I could only carry one, and carrying it in a wheelbarrow was easier!" Everyone in the room immediately exploded into hooting and hollering, wondering what my father had to drink as he wrote this letter. (I later learned that my father had been describing a "Black Diamond" watermelon!)

Now, it was one thing to go to America, but my father had not only gone to America but also to Texas! My grandparents and neighbors all had this picture of Texas as a barren, violent place, still fighting savages from time to time, with everyone carrying a six-gun and riding horses as they searched for water and trees! This, of course, was more ammunition for my grandmother as she would tell my mother that we would eventually all be killed if we joined him there! Remember, we had no television, so this perception of Texas was the result of stories that were passed around, mainly from hearsay.

Well, time passed, and after about six months, a date was finally set for mom and us three kids to prepare for our move to America. My father had been sending money; the tickets had been bought, and the final arrangements were completed. I have never seen so much crying and wailing as it took place in the final month before our departure. We had our medical exams, and I had to go back for a second X-ray, as the first one showed some cloudiness in my chest. Leave it to Norbert to create a major problem. What were they going to do? Leave me behind? To live with my grandmother? No way! The second one came back clear, so we were good to go!

I was amazed at the number of people who came to see us off at the pier where we boarded our ship. I am sad to say that many of them I never saw again. That included both sets of grandparents and many family friends. Pictures of that day show my mother and us three kids lined along the ship's deck rail prior to us getting underway. I remember my mother doing something I rarely saw her do…she was quietly crying as we waved to our relatives while our ship pulled away from the pier. It was September 28, 1954.

We all shared one cabin on board the ship. We had some luggage with us, and the rest of the steamer trunks were stored elsewhere. The sea-faring adventure began, and everything was going well until we hit open water. Then, the ship began to move in a way that was other than forward! In other words, it began to sway and roll a little. Of course, we stayed on deck, and the fresh air was helping some. When we went down to eat that afternoon, I had never seen that much food in my life!

We all ate all that we could and later went to our cabin. This was going to be some kind of trip if every meal was like the one we had just eaten. When we got to the cabin, we were all tired, so it didn't take much persuasion for us kids to turn in and go to sleep. The next morning we were up and ready to go eat breakfast. Once again, when we entered the dining room, we were greeted with every kind of breakfast food we could imagine! After eating, it was time to explore our new surroundings. Mom warned us about safety and pointed out how the ship's crew were dressed in case we needed help. We began to go everywhere on the ship that we could go.

Things were looking up, except that the danged ship continued to sway and roll! After exploring, we decided to go to the cabin and see how mom was doing. She wasn't feeling well and was lying down. I decided I would lie down for a while too, and that is when I noticed that our towels hanging on a rack by the bunk were swaying back and forth!

I was lying on my back and could feel myself rolling a little side to side. I was starting to feel queasy and a little clammy, and it wasn't long before I felt that I should probably head to the bathroom. Made it just in time to begin a conversation with the toilet. It's funny that I didn't remember eating all that stuff for breakfast, but I was looking at the proof! To make matters worse, the stuff in the toilet bowl was rocking back and forth, too!

I am not a quiet-sick person, especially when I am throwing up. I mention this because everyone in our cabin could hear what was going on, and if you knew anything about the power of suggestion, you could guess what happened next. The restroom got awfully crowded! Everyone but my little brother was seasick. It never bothered him for one minute, the little turd! The ship's stewards were kind enough to bring us toast and some other stuff for the next two days. I am glad to say that once we recovered from that initial bout, we were never seasick again. Thank you, Lord!

The rest of the trip was consumed with us kids running over every inch of that ship and playing all day long. I don't know much about what my mother did to pass the time. My mother spoke Flemish and French, and I seem to recall that she had met some people who spoke French and would often join us at mealtime. None of us spoke

English, and that would become a concern when we landed in New York.

October 11, 1954. After fourteen days aboard the ship, we arrived in New York Harbor. While the ship was being maneuvered to the pier, we were all packing our things in our cabin; our other baggage would be unloaded when we were docked. It was the responsibility of the passengers to take it to the next leg of the journey, in our case, the train station. The travel arrangements that my father had made included our baggage being routed to San Antonio, so we didn't have to worry about handling those large trunks.

When we finished packing, we went on deck and watched as the ship was tied to the pier and the crew began making it ready for the passengers to leave. As a nine-year-old kid, I concentrated on the things happening immediately around me. My mother, on the other hand, was attempting to locate her French-speaking friends (who also spoke English) so they could tell her what to say to get us to the train station. She was also trying to keep us three children by her side while we were in the middle of a large crowd, with everyone desperately trying to be the first off the ship! My mother came up with the smart idea of tying a stout thread around our wrists so that we stayed together.

Fortunately, we found our way to a taxi stand, and with our train tickets in hand, we were able to show the driver where we needed to go next. As we settled in the cab for the ride, I felt that sense of adventure that most kids will experience in new circumstances. But that would change very quickly as we neared the New York train station!

I had been to train stations in Belgium a time or two, but when we reached our destination in New York, I determined that I had never been in a real train station in my life. There were millions of people!

Ok…, but there were thousands of people, and everybody except us seemed to know where they needed to go.

The taxi had dropped us off and left, so we started to walk, and we walked, and we walked, and we walked some more, and oh yeah, we walked some more. People were bumping into us, giving us dirty looks, and when my mother tried to ask someone where we needed to catch our train, they just ignored her and went on their way. Desperation was setting in, and my mother pulled us to the side, out of the way of the people rushing around, and I could tell she was worried. By now, my sister and little brother were tired and needed to use the bathroom; we were all hungry and scared! I guess we looked pretty darned forlorn and miserable.

About then, an angel dressed as a man stopped and came up to my mother and asked her if she needed help. The problem was he was speaking English, and my mother didn't understand a word. She then asked if he spoke French, and he answered her in French! (Today, we would say OMG!!!.) He had not only stopped, but he then walked us to the exact place where we needed to wait for our train to come in and board. I pray that this man was blessed beyond human measure!

Finally, on the train! In our proper seats, with the twine removed from our wrists, we began to unwind. I could feel my mother relaxing as we began our journey south to be reunited with my father. The conductor had come by and checked everyone's tickets, and we settled in for the ride. We had four seats, with two facing the other two.

I was sitting next to my mother and had the aisle seat. I could see the door going into the next car and had seen several people going and coming through the door. A little later, I saw the door open, and a person backed into the car and turned around, and I could see he was black! Panic set in, and I shook my mother, who had been looking out the window. I told her that a wild African man had just entered the car, and he was headed our way! And I am in the aisle seat!

She leaned over me, and sure enough, this black man was stopping and talking to passengers as he made his way toward us. He was dressed in a white jacket of some kind, carrying a tray, and seemed to be civilized! It turned out that he was a very nice man who worked for the railroad and sold sandwiches, snacks, and drinks. I was a little embarrassed to be clinging to my mother, halfway out of my seat, ready to run somewhere. That darned circus!

If you have never ridden a train from New York to Texas, it is a very long train ride. By day two, we were all pretty tired, and I don't remember exactly how long it took, but it seemed to us kids to be forever ("Are we there yet?".) We once again couldn't understand a word that was spoken, so we had to make do with sign language. We would point and then nod yes or no; that was about the extent of our communication skills. It was interesting the first time we had to ask where the bathrooms were. I will leave it to your imagination how we pointed out our need, but I was the guinea pig. We did manage to sleep while still sitting in our seats, but of course, I can't speak for my mother. At long last, we heard the conductor coming through our car announcing, "San Antonio!" We were in Texas! So far, not an Indian anywhere in sight.

Chapter 4

"...no whining, no excuses..."

The conductor announced that we were pulling into the station and everyone should remain seated until the train stopped. I was looking out the window and was really not sure what I was looking at. I didn't see all the trains, the huge terminal, the thousands of people that we had seen in New York, Central Station. Everything here was supposed to be bigger in Texas, right?

I also didn't see any Indians, cowboys, or horses. I didn't see anyone sporting a six-shooter and wearing a big hat, facing off with another guy. That was a relief on the one hand but a disappointment on the other. As the train stopped, I *did* see a group of people waiting on the platform, and then my sister spotted our father (we kids had been bragging about who would see him first.) It was then that I realized just how much I had missed him...a lot!

People all around us were up on their feet getting bags together, so we sat until the area cleared some. The group that my father was with was all still waiting and appeared to be anxiously looking at the door that the passengers were coming out of as they stepped from the train. When my mother stepped out on the platform from the train car, they all began to clap and cheer. I was a little overwhelmed by all the attention and the number of people coming to the station to meet us, but I understood that later.

Next thing I knew, my father was grabbing and hugging all of us, and I was happy because I could finally understand what was being said because we were *all* speaking Flemish! A person doesn't realize just how important language is when you are trying to become a part of a group... until you lose that opportunity to fit in. (This would become even more pronounced after I started going to school.)

After some time was spent greeting one another and being introduced to people we didn't know, we began looking for luggage. We had our carry-on with us, but all the rest of mother's trunks from the ship were being sent directly from the ship to the train station. The luggage area was packed, so we waited away from the crowd until it cleared out.

My mother and us kids were sitting on a bench with some of the people who had come with my father to welcome us to Texas. A few could speak Flemish and were talking to my mother, but I was suddenly not feeling well. My brother and sister were also not feeling good either. We, including my mother by this time, were all sweating up a storm, and I was lightheaded. One of the ladies with the group saw the change occurring and asked someone who spoke Flemish to ask us what was wrong. That person did, and we all said we were extremely hot and feeling sick.

Now, when we left the ship, my mother had included in our carry-on bags a change of clothes. These were our best little suits for my brother and me, and a nice dress for my sister. We also had shined shoes and clean underwear! We changed into these clothes as we got nearer to San Antonio. Since we brought all these clothes from Belgium, they were made from WOOL!

When we got to San Antonio and stepped off the train, the temperature was in the nineties! This was quite unlike the temperature in our hometown, where if the temperature even crept up into the mid-eighties, everyone there was ready to collapse-it was a heat wave!

Luckily for us, the same lady who had noticed our discomfort in the first place realized our problem. She told the people who were standing around that we needed to lighten up our clothes. After taking off jackets and opening shirt collars, my brother and I felt a little better. My mother and sister were taken to a restroom, and whatever they did there seemed to help.

A bigger problem was soon brought to my mother's attention. Our trunks and other baggage were not on the train! Everything my mother cherished and was able to bring with her was missing. Forms were filled out at the station, and we reluctantly left without our things to go to our new *home*.

I want to stop here and acknowledge the woman I knew as my mother. (I will get to my father later in this book, 'account, narrative, journal,' whatever.) Johanna Marie DeMuelder was born on Christmas day, 1918, in Wetteren, Belgium. She was the oldest child and was followed by a sister and brother. She went to school and finished the third grade. It was decided that she needed to stay at home to work, so her schooling came to an end.

My mother never spoke about her younger years; what I know I heard from my Aunt and Uncle (her sister and brother.) I remember seeing my mother on her hands and knees, scrubbing the floors in my grandparents' house, and pretty much working non-stop. I don't know when my aunt married and moved out, but I have the impression it was as soon as possible. I know my uncle left as soon as he could and moved to Paris to become a pastry chef. When he moved back home, he was married, and my grandmother wasn't overly fond of her new daughter-in-law. (Do you get the idea that, in my mind, my grandmother wasn't overly fond of much of anything?)

So with my aunt married and my uncle living and working in Paris, my mother had become the hired help. She and my father were married in 1944, but they stayed living with my grandmother, so mom's situation didn't change; she was still the hired help!

I have already described my grandmother from my personal relationship and perspective. Since my mother never spoke much about her mother, I want to be careful not to let my personal bias paint the picture I envision of their relationship.

It would be easy to draw the conclusion here that my mother was a slave, never smiled, never had fun, and was miserable most of her life while we lived in Belgium. That would be wrong, as I have pictures of her with her girlfriends on an outing in Paris and pictures of us as a family on vacation at the coast and elsewhere.

Predominantly, she worked hard, but then so did everybody else in the family. She probably didn't know it at the time, but she was being prepared for life with her husband in America! I am reminded that my parents and their counterparts were referred to as "The Greatest Generation." They survived a depression, had their home country occupied by the Germans, he was a prisoner of war, and they endured daily hard work and many hardships. They were *accustomed* to HARD! No whining, no excuses, no pity parties, no "woe is me; what are we going to do?" Their anthem was "Just get it done!"

My mother is a woman who spoke no English, but took her three young children, boarded a huge ship with all of her belongings, and left for a place called America! And Mother wasn't keen on emotional, touchy-feely, public displays of affection. Her ritual for expressing her love for me, my brother, and my sister was to take her thumb, place it on our foreheads, make the sign of the cross, and ask the angels to protect us. This usually occurred as we went to bed. She did this every day until I became a teenager. When I got older, she would do it when she was worried about me, which was much more often than it should have been. It's a wonder I don't have a dent in my forehead; I was a problem child, OK?

Now, back to going to our new home in San Antonio, Texas. My father had an old DeSoto sedan, and we all piled into the car. Of course, there was no air conditioning, and the car was like an oven, so when we got to the house, we were ready to pass out! Our first act was to get out of as much of our clothes as we could and still be decent. Personally, I would have been good with naked.

Our sponsors were an old couple named Rudolph and Mamie DeWinne, who owned a home and property on the Southwest side of San Antonio. The home had a cellar that was originally a bomb shelter but had been converted into a bar. To get into the cellar, you had to raise two metal doors that rested on the ground. The doors were heavy enough that a chain and pulley were used to lift them up. Once the doors were up, you walked into the darkness downstairs. With a lot of war souvenirs on the walls and hanging from the ceiling, it was like something you would see in a movie.

My father had moved in with Rudolph and Mamie when he arrived, and they made it possible for him to save his money to pay for our trip. Mamie was originally from Scotland and had a heavy accent. She was a physically big woman and had a heart twice as big as her size. When she hugged you, there was no doubt you had been hugged! She had a large bosom, and when she picked me up and pulled me in, I made sure I took a deep breath, hoping I could hold it in long enough to be back on the ground before I passed out. Her husband was a little smaller (but not by much) and had a cigar in his mouth pretty much non-stop!

These were the people that made it possible for our family to immigrate to America. There is no way to describe what they (as our sponsors) and everyone else who came out to the train station to show their support meant to our family when we arrived.

They made us all feel that we were welcome. They were genuinely glad that we had come to join my father. A few years later, I was told by one of these men that my father had confided in him that he felt that his mother-in-law would somehow prevent my mother from getting on the ship and that he would never see his wife and children again. I have no idea how many people were aware of my father's fears, but that may explain the large group of people who were at the train station when we arrived.

Chapter 5

"…why are they making fun of me?"

My father was full of surprises because, within a few days of arriving in San Antonio, he told us that he had rented a house on the Westside of downtown. This was behind a restaurant/motel known as DeWinne's Belgium Inn, located on West Commerce Street. *These* DeWinnes were close relatives of our sponsors and were Belgium immigrants themselves.

The house had only one window cooler, so much of the time, we had the windows open. Since the house was right behind the restaurant, there wasn't a lot of breezes. In addition to little wind, when air did come through, it was heated to the outside temperature, which was often in the upper nineties.

There was one other "little" problem. At the rear of the restaurant was a large shed where the restaurant barbecued on a cinder block pit. When I say barbecue pit, I am talking five feet wide by fifteen feet long! The restaurant had a popular catering business, and their specialty entrees were chicken and Belgian sausage. They used this outdoor pit when they had to cook a big bunch of barbecued food. I soon learned what a *bunch of food* was. I had personally helped when they cooked fifteen hundred chicken halves for one event!

This meant *a lot* of smoke! The smoke seemed to travel from the pit to our house and then settle throughout our house. Believe me, a person can get tired of the smell of chicken grilling pretty darn fast! Luckily, they only used this pit when they had an exceptionally large catering event.

I mentioned that I was given the chance to help with the grilling, and it was quite an experience. When you are going to cook fifteen hundred chicken halves for an afternoon event, you begin early, around 5 a.m.! The initial fire required to cook that many chickens meant it had to reach the coal stage, which took a lot of wood and time. The heat of the pit and the temperature of the air itself would combine to give you a sampling of what the hell could really be like on a bad day.

Once the coals were ready, the chicken halves would have to be placed on the grills, starting from the middle and working toward the outside edges. You had to extend your arm over glowing red coals to place the chicken in the middle without getting burned. To solve this problem, they gave us large rubber gloves that reached up beyond the elbows. We would then fill the gloves with some cold water which allowed us to reach across the pit without getting burned.

The heat would be so intense that we would have to periodically empty the water (because it would get too hot) and refill the gloves with cold water. Do that for several hours, and I can tell you that you will probably think long and hard before you decide if this is what you want to do for the rest of your life! (You might ask why they didn't use long forks to place and turn the chicken. The answer is that they didn't want to puncture the meat so that the chicken would stay moist.)

We had not been in our new house more than a couple of days before we came to the realization that my father had omitted some vital facts about life in Texas. He failed to mention the "Creepy Crawly from Hell," the cockroach! This darn bug was everywhere, and it had a large cousin that everyone called the "water roach." Hmmm…he failed to mention that one, too!

My mother was introduced to these *monsters* when she got up early one morning, went to the kitchen, turned on the light, and screamed! The battle was on! Those suckers were fast, and sometimes they came right at you! On top of everything else, we soon discovered that they could FLY! Holy S….!! Oh man, to this day, I *still* hate those evil suckers! Even if you managed to step on one and kill it, it *still* won because of what was left on the bottom of your shoe.

It was almost two weeks later when my parents were informed that the rest of our luggage had arrived at the train station. My mother was excited to finally get the rest of our belongings, especially her prized personal possessions. My father brought the steamer trunks home, and we put them down in the living room. From the outside, they looked like they had been around the world, dragged behind a team of horses!

If I remember correctly, there were three large trunks and several suitcases. Opening the suitcases, everything seemed to be OK, although you could tell that they had been inspected since the pieces of clothing were just wadded up and crammed back inside.

Then the trunks were opened, and my mother began to cry! She had carefully packed her wedding gift China only to discover that much of it was broken. The same fate was for her crystal and a lot of other mementos and knick-knacks. She was devastated, to say the least, and it was something that grieved her for as long as I can remember. (There have been exposes that showed how the New York stevedores handled the baggage of immigrants, and that explained what happened to my mother's baggage. A lot of today's airline baggage handlers are direct descendants of those stevedores!)

The new school year had already started when we arrived in San Antonio, so my sister, brother, and I were enrolled at Sacred Heart Catholic School. The school was within walking distance of our house, so we walked to and from school. On my first day, I discovered that no one at school spoke Flemish or French, and I didn't speak English.

I mentioned previously that we were living on the Westside of San Antonio, which had a large population of Mexicans. They spoke

Mexican and English, and I soon found out that they were not overly fond of white boys who spoke a funny language. (For whatever reason, they thought French was really funny.)

To make matters even worse, I was sent to school wearing my Belgium school clothes because we had not yet purchased any Catholic school uniforms. Kids in Texas dressed nothing like we did in Belgium, so I might as well have been wearing a clown suit!

I remember being walked into that classroom (which was already in session), being introduced by my name (which brought on giggles) and then escorted to a desk. I could see the smirks only third graders could display, and I wished I was anywhere but there. I sat at my desk with no paper, pen, or any idea of what was going on for the rest of the day. I didn't know it at the time, but I was introduced to "total immersion" in American culture and to the beginning of some of the most difficult days of my short life.

It didn't take long for me to realize that I wasn't going to be accepted or welcomed into school with open arms any time soon. It is hard to fit in when you don't know what is being said. I went to school every day and was present in my body, but I was absent in every other way. During lunch recess, I would go to a swing set and swing or just sit and watch the other kids.

The good thing about finally getting my school uniform was that I could blend in with everyone else and could easily be ignored! Ignored wasn't bad. The problems started when someone would try to talk to me or ask me a question. I guess my face would make them laugh as I tried to figure out what they were saying, tried to respond in Flemish, or worse yet, tried to respond in English. It wasn't long until some of them made a game out of it and laughed as I tried to formulate the right words. I remember coming home one day, walking up to my mother in tears, and asking her why the kids were laughing at me. The only thing she could say was that it would get better. I wasn't so sure.

The laughing and being ignored turned into the pushing and shoving phase. That was easier to deal with than the ridicule since now I could do something. After all, I didn't need to talk to swing my fists! There were some days that I would be walking home, and two or three boys from school would be waiting for me. The race for home was on! Once or twice I made it to the front porch where the fight would begin. My mother would hear the ruckus and yell out the door as she grabbed a broom and ran them off.

On the other hand, my sister and brother seemed to transition into school much easier than I. I'm sure they had their moments too, but I don't recall them complaining about the ridicule and badgering I had to endure. I will give my sister credit in that she never had a problem standing up for herself, and I guess she was just more adaptable to our new circumstances.

The novelty of the "new kid in school" eventually wore off, and each day I became more familiar with the English language and American customs. But I *never* made any *real* friends with those kids or the schoolteachers. My resentment for school, as I have already stated, lasted all the way through high school, and it was most certainly reinforced there.

Looking back on my experiences at Sacred Heart School, I have formed the opinion that, despite the tough times of trying to fit in, "total immersion" is the best way to go if you want to learn a new language and assimilate into a new culture! Within four to six weeks, my sister and I caught on to the language by understanding, speaking, and reading. There was no bilingual education experience for us, by golly!

My father worked as a janitor at Butter Krust Bakery on Broadway Street, the job our new sponsors had arranged for him while he was still in Belgium. My mother was given a job at the DeWinne's Restaurant, baking biscuits, pies, and anything else that needed doing. Because we lived in a house owned by the DeWinnes, my mother's job helped pay for the rent. My mother would begin her baking around three-thirty every morning, and since she didn't speak English, my father would get up and go with her, staying until it was time for *him* to leave and go to his own job. (My father had a gift for languages: he spoke Flemish, German, and French. Because he had been in America for several months, he could now speak English fairly well, too.)

When it was time for us kids to get up and get ready for school, my mother would rush home, make us breakfast, and get us ready to go to school. I guess I was probably about ten years old when it became *my* responsibility to make breakfast and get everybody up and ready to go.

One of my favorite breakfasts was French toast and scrambled eggs. The good thing about this arrangement was that our mother was just a minute away and could check on us to ensure everything was going OK.

I want to back up to our first few days after arriving in San Antonio: I think my father had gone to work and usually got home around five in the afternoon. It was soooo hot, and we were all still trying to figure out how we could cool off when he came in the house carrying this big-green-oblong-thing.

We were all staring at it, and he was grinning like a Cheshire cat. We asked him what it was, but all he would say was, "You'll see." He took it into the kitchen and set it in the sink, and started cutting slices out of it lengthwise. On the inside, it was cherry red with hundreds of black seeds. Then he asked my mother if she

31

remembered him writing to her about a fruit that was so big he could barely carry it? She answered, "Yes," and he told her she was looking at it…a big Black Diamond watermelon! He started slicing off chunks, and my first taste was incredible. I had never tasted fruit so sweet in all of my short life! When we got through eating, my stomach was swollen, and I was covered with juice, just like my sister and little brother. At that moment, my father's decision to come to America seemed to make sense!

I also forgot to mention that we now had a television set. We didn't have televisions in Belgium when I was growing up. But not long before we left, one of the store owners in Wetteren had gotten one, and he would place it in the window of his shop so that people could stop and watch it as they walked by.

Our new "black and white TV" (which must have weighed at least 100 pounds) would begin programming in the morning and would then turn off sometime around 10 or 12 PM. A few years later, I remember that when they signed off at night, a voice would ask, "It's 10 PM; do you know where your children are?"

I remember being mesmerized by that bulls-eye test pattern… waiting for the programming to begin. We also got pretty good at moving the "rabbit ears" so we could try to bring in a clearer picture. We lived at this house for a year, but it was still not *our house*, so they began to make plans to buy one.

My brother, sister, and I were not worrying about buying a house. We were adjusting to a completely new culture and new living arrangements with just the five people who made up our family. In Belgium, my father had been gone much of the time, but now he was home after work every day. Odd to say, but this created a problem for me and my relationship with him.

Remember, in Belgium, we lived with grandparents and very near to uncles, aunts, and boarders. Everyone in our part of the community knew everyone else and knew who the kids belonged to. It wasn't unusual for a kid to be yanked up and taken to their house by someone who witnessed bad behavior. Our parents would be told what happened, and justice was administered as needed!

I came to realize that the consequences of bad behavior were going to be completely different after we moved to America. Across the street from our house was a Woolworth store. One day my brother, who was six years old at the time, stole a pair of Lone Ranger and Tonto rubber figures from the store while he was shopping with our mother. When they got home, he started playing with them on the front porch. I came out, saw what he was playing with, and asked him where he had gotten them. He told me what he had done, and I knew he was in trouble.

I told him he would probably be killed if our mother found out, and we had to take them back. He agreed, so we each put one under our shirt and went back to the store. We were inside, headed toward the toy aisle when the store manager stopped us and lifted our shirts, and pulled out the toys. He then grabbed us both and took us to the office, where he called our house and told our mother what we had done. All our attempts to convince him that we were actually bringing them *back* fell on deaf ears!

Our embarrassed mother showed up and tried to apologize, and then we went back home. We tried again *to* explain to her what had happened, but all she would say was that we could explain it to our father. When he came home, mom told him what we had done, and all hell broke loose! He took us back to the store, and we had to apologize to the manager.

I still don't know how I got to be part of the crime, but by the time we walked back to the house from the store, my father had convinced himself that I should have known better. He said that I was more to blame than my little brother! This was probably the first time that my father was personally involved with disciplining us. I had been spanked a lot of times by my mother or grandmother, but this frantic, loud, terrifying man scared the crap out of me! This set the pattern for the relationship that would develop between my father and me. The good thing that came out of all this was that all three of us kids were absolutely convinced that stealing was a capital offense!

Chapter 6

"…Who gets up at 4:30 in the morning?"

We hadn't been in Texas very long before we found out that there was an active "Belgian community" in and around San Antonio. They held an annual picnic at the Lone Star Brewery in San Antonio, and the turnout there was tremendous, with lots of adults and kids. There was a mix of businessmen and other trades, and there were lots of farmers.

My parents became really close to a farming family named VanDamme, who lived on a farm in the small town of Devine, Texas, located about 50 miles south of San Antonio. They had three sons named Rene, Julian, and Cyrill. All of them were older than I, with Cyrill being the youngest and a senior in high school.

Cyrill played football for the Devine Warhorses and was their running back and punter. Because Cyrill never wore shoes at home, his feet were so wide that they could not fit him with football shoes, so he played barefoot! The soles of Cyrill's feet were so calloused that one day I watched as someone took a Camel cigarette and put it out on the bottom of his foot!

The men in their family were all short and stocky, making Cyrill extremely hard to tackle. While he played for them in High School, the Warhorses were a force to be reckoned with, and I think they went on to State within their division. (I spent a little time introducing the Van Dammes here because…they never knew this… they were instrumental in awakening in me a desire to live in the country, or in other words, "out of the city.")

I guess I was a freshman in high school when the Van Dammes suggested to my parents that I spend part of my summer vacation working with them on their farm. It was arranged, and in the summer of 1959, I was introduced to life on the farm. But who gets up at 4:30 AM to get ready for work? A FARMER! For Pete's sake!!!

That first morning when the light came on, I thought there was something wrong. I stumbled around and got some clothes on, and when I got into the kitchen, everybody was already drinking coffee and…seemed happy! I looked outside, and it was pitch black. I finally looked at a clock and saw the time, yep, 4:30 AM. Now, I had been raised not to question my elders, so I said nothing, but I thought, "OK, this is some unusual occasion that has come up, and we have to deal with it."

It then dawned on me that I could smell a breakfast of eggs, bacon, coffee, and homemade bread; we sat down to eat. And did I eat! Well, I thought I ate, and then I watched Cyrill and his two brothers eat, and I could not believe what those boys could put away. I don't know how many eggs we ate, but I was surprised that the chickens didn't run away from home! One thing was for sure, if a hen didn't produce eggs, she literally got the axe! We ate what seemed like *a lot* of chicken on the farm. I think maybe some of the chickens felt being eaten was better than trying to lay all those eggs every day!

After breakfast, the boys started heading outside, but their mother, Leona (which means Lion), held me back. She told me to be sure to use the bathroom before we headed out, as there would be no break until lunch. Thankfully, I followed that advice and went outside to join the others.

When I walked out, everybody was standing by the barn next to a truck with a flatbed. The flatbed had empty bushel baskets stacked on it, along with hoes, shovels, and other stuff. Cyrill and his middle brother smoked, so they were smoking a cigarette while their father, Emile, and the oldest boy, Rene, talked over the day's schedule. It was still dark, with just a tinge of gray beginning in the East, and I couldn't help but wonder why we were standing out there. So I asked

36

Cyrill, and he told me (like I am a little slow), "Why, we're waiting for it to get *light*." What? And he thinks *I'm* a little slow?

When it was light enough to see, we headed out to the fields, and when we stopped, everybody jumped down and began to grab implements. I was given a hoe and told to begin hoeing a row, chopping out the weeds. I asked how far I should go, and after they stopped laughing...they told me to go to the end. Once I got there, I could step over to the next one and start working my way back. I looked off into the distance, and it seemed to me that I was being teased because there would be no way to finish the one I started and finish before the day was over! Little did I know....

We started evenly lined up, with everybody joking and laughing, but it didn't take long for me to be left behind. That was hard work, and before long, the blisters showed themselves on my hands. I was convinced that I would likely not see another day, and I didn't think this was farming. Farming meant driving a tractor and bringing crops to the market! What was wrong with these people?

I could still hear them laughing, and once in a while, one of them would call back, asking me why I was so slow. I quit looking up and just kept my eyes on the ground. Before too long, I was meeting them coming from the other way! Well, I just kept on hoeing, and eventually, I came to an end, and I could turn around and start back. Since they irrigated their crops, the furrows were moist, and the weeds were not that hard to chop out. So I kept at it.

By noon I could see a pick-up headed our way. It pulled up to us, and Leona got out of the truck, honking the horn. Everybody put down their hoes and headed for the truck. It was lunchtime! Thank you, Lord! Leona had a big thermos of coffee, sandwiches, and fruit. Everybody grabbed something, plopped down, either sitting on the ground or on the back of the flatbed and ate.

My hands were hurting, but I found out I was *really* hungry, and the homemade bread was as good as anything I could remember eating since leaving Belgium. As soon as we finished eating, we all stretched out in the shade of the trucks and took a nap. It seemed that lasted only about thirty seconds, and then everybody was up and ready to go. I had to wonder again what was *wrong* with these *people.*

It was probably five or six that evening when we called it a day, and boy, I was beat. We picked up our stuff, headed back to the barn, where everything was put back in its place, and we cleaned up. Supper was ready almost as soon as we came into the house, and everyone sat down and dug in. Even though I hurt all over, I ate as if it was my last meal, which I felt was a real possibility. Leona could really cook, and like my mother, she derived pleasure by watching people enjoy a good meal.

My first-day thoughts of that early start being just a special occasion were dashed at 4:30 the very next morning. I came to learn that this was their working routine. It was followed every day of the week except Saturdays and Sundays unless the crops were ready to come out of the fields. When harvest time began, the Van Dammes worked non-stop until they were done. I stayed there for a month, and I was never able to keep up with the boys, but I got better. More importantly, I began to appreciate standing out in the yard waiting for daylight so we could head out to the fields! Crazy, huh?

As I mentioned at the beginning of this chapter, this opportunity of getting up early and watching a new day begin, smelling the earth, hearing that first chirp in the pecan trees as the birds started waking up (they might have been bitching that we woke them up), all created within me a love for the sunrise. To this day, I look forward to seeing the sky begin to lighten up as the Lord paints a brand-new day. I wish I could call and thank the Van Dammes, but they have all passed on.

There were many other Belgian people that we became friends with, but it was through the friendship of another farmer that my father was able to buy our first house. Since he had no credit history (he had no history in America, period,) it was impossible for him to get a bank loan. Then one day, one of the older Belgian men spoke with my father and told him to find a house. They would go to look at it, and if it seemed like a good buy, this man would loan my father the money. That was it. No contract, just a handshake and my father's promise to pay it back.

The house my parents bought was north of downtown San Antonio in a nice residential neighborhood. It was around 1200 square feet in size, had two bedrooms, one bathroom, kitchen, and living room, plus a detached, one-car garage. It cost five thousand dollars and was the best place we had ever seen. It was *our* home! Think of it, my father and mother had never possessed a house of their own, and now, this was *theirs!*

Chapter 7

"I don't know who put that sandwich there…"

As we settled into our new home, which had been built sometime in the early 1940s, life immediately improved. No more barbecue smoke or noise of busy streets, and we had a large grassy backyard to play in. There were also neighbors with children our age who became our new friends.

One of these kids was a girl named Kay, and she was my first official girlfriend. Unfortunately, she was sitting on the front handlebars of my bicycle one day, and I wrecked it! She was skinned with road rash and crying when I walked her home. That budding romance ended right then; her parents deemed me unsafe.

The move to our new house also meant a change to a new school. All three of us kids were now enrolled in St. Mary Magdalen's Catholic School. But I *still* hated school!! I will not blame my attitude solely on the priest and nuns who ran the school, but in my mind, they were responsible for creating the change in my relationship with my father. This was really complicated, but let me spend some time here to try to explain what I mean.

I will acknowledge that I was a daydreamer. When the weather was nice, I found that things going on outside the window were a lot more interesting than fractions, verbs, or adverbs that were being taught inside. The problem was that I was often caught looking out. This resulted in my being brought up to the front of the room, ridiculed, and punished. One of the older nuns (I *still* remember her name) was the worst. She seemed to be eager to break out the wooden ruler and apply it to the back of my hand. After a couple of times applying that ruler, the next time, I yanked my hand back just as the ruler was coming down, causing her to miss me. Not good! The class laughed, and she got mad and tried to swat me anywhere she could. When that didn't work, she sent me to the office to await further action.

The principal (a priest) brought me into his office and administered some licks to my butt. He sent me back to class, but from then on, I did nothing in school unless I absolutely had to. I didn't do homework, nor did I participate in any classroom assignments. And, if forced, I even did my best to screw things up.

Of course, this led to a request for my parents to come to school for a conference with the teachers. When we got home after the meeting, my father lost his mind! He wanted an explanation, and I could not provide one, so I guess he thought a beating would provide the needed explanation. It didn't work, but it made me hate school even more than ever. When report card day arrived, I opened mine and saw that I had received "Fs" all the way down every category…in every single subject, including Citizenship! To this day, I don't know how a person can flunk citizenship; my father even asked me that very question.

We were required to take our report cards home. There was a place for parents to sign to prove that they had seen the card. I figured I could probably forge my father's signature, but my sister and brother were also bringing their cards home as well, so that wouldn't work. I was toast! To make things even worse, my sister and brother were pretty much straight A&B students. I had to decide whether I should show mine first and get the beating over with or wait until he saw theirs, putting him in a good mood and hopefully diminishing the severity of the beating. Anyway, I looked at it; a beating was in my future. Well, I was right; I got a beating!

If there is anything good about getting all "Fs," it's that there is no place to go but up! I guess I probably figured that if I wanted to see my next birthday, I was going to have to make some changes about school. I began trying to complete some of my assignments and stopped telling everybody how much I hated school. Another thing that was going to work in my favor was that the new semester included Literature. I hated Grammar, but I really did like to read especially fiction. I also found that I liked Writing and that, despite my dislike for the Grammar courses, I made good grades in Writing.

There was one subject that I could not improve on, and that was Math. However, I knew that one way I could raise my grades was to start turning in my homework assignments. This meant that I would bring my books home and work on various subjects after supper. We only had one place to work, and that was the kitchen table.

When I got to the Math work, I was stumped much of the time. My father was really good at Math, so he would try to help me, but the problem was that neither one of us had a lot of patience. As he would go over and over the problem and show me the solution, I could not get it! He would get frustrated, and before long, I was frustrated, and then the situation would become explosive. He would say something along the lines of "anybody" could see the solution because it was as plain as the nose on your face, blah, blah, blah.

Before long, I didn't ask for his help, and if he asked me if I had Math homework, I would lie and tell him that I had knocked it out earlier. I found out that lying about Math spared us a lot of aggravation and me from being yelled at and sometimes getting slapped on the head. The lesson I did learn really well was…never to ask him for help!

I am not going to say that my lying about Math had anything to do with it, but about this time in my life, I started lying about everything. Seriously! I would lie about the school, about what I had been doing outside, about homework, and even about what I was thinking. Maybe I felt like it was a form of self-preservation. The problem was that I wasn't very good at it, and I was often caught in my lies! It seemed that I was fully on board with that old saying that "I would lie even if the truth would serve me better." I can't think of a better story to illustrate what I mean by that than "The Sandwich Incident."

Each morning my mother would fix us kids lunch to take to school. Usually, a sandwich, fruit, and a cookie... all put in a paper bag. One morning I didn't feel like taking my lunch, so I threw the bag behind the stove in the kitchen (don't ask me why.) It was probably a couple of weeks later when a funny smell became obvious in the kitchen, and the bag was discovered. My parents asked all three of us who had thrown the sandwich bag behind the stove, and we all denied it.

After threatening us all with a spanking, we *still* denied it. We were sent to our room (all three of us shared the same bedroom) and told to talk it over and have the guilty party admit the deed. I am ashamed to this day to say that I refused to confess. A few minutes later, we were called out and asked again who was responsible. Again, we all denied it, so the spanking began.

The first was my brother, then my sister, and they each got spanked on the butt. Then it was my turn. Like them, I was asked again if I had put the sandwich bag behind the stove. I denied it *again*, but then I had to add fuel to the fire and blurted out, "What's the big deal about a stupid sandwich?" That did it. My father began slapping, punching, and hitting me everywhere he could; the whole time were both yelling and screaming. We started in the *kitchen*, and he hit me the last time in the *bathroom*, knocking me ass over a teacup into the *bathtub*.

The only reason he stopped was because my mother pulled him off, yelling that he was going to kill me. He had bloodied my nose, blackened my eye, and bruised me up all over. It was the most severe beating I ever received from him, and I think it was probably the last time he ever went off like that with me. It was also the moment that he stopped being my father and became "The Old Man."

Chapter 8

"…it was the size of a golf ball with large legs…"

I guess this is as good a time as any to give my father a little more of an introduction based on his background and not just on my personal relationship with him. What kind of a man gets up and leaves home, country, family, friends, and all that he is familiar with to go to a completely foreign place with nothing but his name?

There are many answers to that, but in the case of my father, he wanted something better for himself and his family than what he could see in his future in Belgium. He wasn't afraid to try anything, and he was always determined to finish what he started. He smoked, and he drank, and when he cursed, which wasn't all that often, it was mostly in Flemish. But all the while, he always worked his ass off! And, oh yeah, as I have already pointed out… he had an explosive temper that he inherited from *his* father.

Robert Jacobs was born in his family's home in Wetteren, Belgium, on August 25, 1919. I regret that I wasn't able to spend much time with his mother and father, although the brief visits that I had with them were certainly memorable. My father had a younger sister, and twenty-plus years after she was born, his parents welcomed another boy. My grandfather wasn't pleased with the news that his wife was pregnant, and he made no bones about his feelings. I was told that he tried to convince my grandmother that she had a tumor!

My grandfather was a small, short man. He had a bad temper which I saw firsthand when I was visiting their house one day. Because my father's younger brother was only six to eight years older than me, we usually spent time together when I visited. I was spending the night on one visit, and it was late afternoon when my grandfather came home from work. My grandmother had been cooking and had soup prepared on the stove for supper. He had walked in from the backdoor into the kitchen and was taking his shoes off when he asked my grandmother what she had fixed for supper. She told him we were going to have soup, and he came unglued.

He started yelling and cursing, and the next thing I knew, he took the wooden shoe that he was holding and threw it into the pot of soup! I didn't know what was happening, but it was scary. I also don't remember what we had for supper, but I can tell you for certain that it wasn't soup!

Many years later, I was struggling with trying to fix something on our small tractor, and it wouldn't come together. I got so frustrated that I threw the large wrench I was holding clean out of sight. I stood there, and after I calmed down and realized that I was going to have to go looking for the wrench, I thought back to the soup incident. The thought popped into my mind, "Like father, like son." I apparently had inherited that same tendency to fly off the handle; I struggled with that for most of my life.

As I said earlier, when describing my father's parents, they were poor but hardworking people getting by as best they could. I want to add that despite my grandfather's temper, he could be fun to be around. He was the first person that I could remember who took me fishing, and I guess he took his son (my father) fishing too because as I grew up, my father would often take us fishing. My grandmother was the opposite of her husband as she was a kind, quiet woman who always wore an apron when I was around her. They lived in a small house, and by the time I was old enough to spend time there, my father's sister was already married and living elsewhere.

Getting back to my father in Belgium, he finished what we would call "High School." He worked any job he could find, including delivering bread for his mother-in-law, working for his uncle, who was a well driller, and even working for a confectioner making sweet rolls and other desserts. He was on a soccer team and belonged to an archery club.

He loved to swim when he was younger until he and his best friend decided to swim across one of the rivers nearby their home. About halfway across, his friend started to cramp up, and he drowned. That had such a profound effect on him that I cannot ever remember my father swimming or getting in the water with us at a lake or at the ocean beaches. He liked getting in a boat and fishing, but he stayed as dry as much as possible. He also liked hunting, and those were probably the times when he and I got along the best.

I have already mentioned that he had a job as a janitor at the huge, commercial Butter Krust Bakery when he arrived in San Antonio. This had been prearranged by his sponsor, so within just a few days after he arrived in Texas, he went to work. Like my mother and us kids, he didn't speak English. I later learned that he had a very similar experience as I had in school trying to fit in.

One day at the bakery, a couple of men began to confront my father on the shipping dock, and a fight began. It was broken up, but of course, *only their side* of the story was told since he could not communicate in English. He was fired and told to go home. Well, he left for the day, not quite sure of what was going on, but he went back to work the following morning. The boss was notified that he was back, so he was called to the office, and once again, he was told he was fired and to go home. My father went home once again, but the next morning he was back at work!

This time one of the upper managers approached him and told him he was fired and to go home. My father left, but he was back the next morning, grabbing his brooms, mops, etc., starting to work. Management was *again* notified that he was back, but *this* time Herman Richter, one of the owners of the bakery, was informed of what was taking place. Mr. Richter's response was that if a man was so devoted to his job that you could not run him off... just leave him alone and let him work. My father never told us of the incident, but one of Mr. Richter's sons told me the story during the brief time that I also worked there. My Father worked for Butter Krust Bakery(s) for over 40 years, and when he retired, he was the Head Mechanical Engineer responsible for the operations and automation of their four commercial bakeries in Texas.

He was a smart man who, as I have already mentioned, loved Mathematics and everything mechanical. He taught himself to repair TVs, and he would make service calls to make extra money. I would sometimes go with him so I could help him move the sets when needed and hand him parts and tools so he wouldn't have to get up and down from behind the TV. He was also one of the very few repairmen who would venture to answer service calls in the so-called "bad parts of town."

While I was with him one night, I witnessed a terrible knife fight out on the street. In spite of what was going on a short distance away, my father continued with his service call as if nothing was going on. Thank God the police arrived and took care of the situation before we ended the call.

He wasn't scared of much... except spiders! It didn't matter whether it was big or small; if he spotted a spider, my mother would have to come and kill it. If she wasn't around, one of us kids was called up to deal with it.

I remember one evening, we were home and watching TV in our small living room. My father had his usual spot at the end of the couch with his feet up on an ottoman. He happened to look down, and walking on the floor from the back of the couch was this HUGH chocolate-colored creature! He let out a yell which turned into a Flemish curse word (which sounded like "potferdomme"), and he jumped from the couch and was clear across the room in one leap. We all jumped up,

47

not knowing what was going on, and he pointed to the "monster" as he hid behind my mother.

I have to admit that I have a little of his fear of spiders myself, but none of us had any idea then what we were looking at. It was scary and hairy and was the size of a tennis ball with large, hairy legs. (I am getting goosebumps as I write this some sixty-plus years later.) This was a small room, but all five of us had managed to crowd into one corner while we watched this creature slowly crawl across the floor. This thing wasn't scared of anybody!

My father turned to my mother and said, "…what are **you** going to do?" "Well," she said, "watch it while I go to get the broom." He then turned to us kids and said, (yep, you guessed it) "Watch it while your mother gets the broom!" We had all moved to the doorway leading into the kitchen when my mother returned with the trusty broom. The Monster was now in the middle of the room and had gone beyond the coffee table, moving like a sloth. This lulled us into a false sense of security about its ability to move with any significant speed. My mother approached it with my father close behind, and we were behind him.

She raised the broom, and I swear, I could see this creature's glittering, dark eyes stare at us as it came to a stop. It then raised itself up on its hind legs and prepared for battle! She swatted down with the broom once and then raised the broom to come down again…but she missed it, and it jumped three feet straight up off the ground!

We all cursed in Flemish and English, and my father darned near knocked us all down, vacating the room! My mother hung in there and subdued it with several more swats of the broom while my father, from the doorway, urged her to "Smack it again!" several more times "just to make sure." With the help of our neighbor, we learned that we had encountered the mighty Tarantula spider! I think that might have been one time that my father thought seriously about his decision to emigrate to America.

Chapter 9

"…just bend over and grab your ankles…"

Getting back to school, I started improving my grades somewhat, if for no other reason than for survival. I was never anything but a C or D student except for spelling and literature. I almost always received As or Bs in those subjects. When I finished the eighth grade, my parents decided it was time to move me to a Public School.

I was elated to get away from those nuns and priests and the Friday confessions we were required to make each week! It always made me mad that I was forced to go to "confession," which meant I was supposed to tell a priest all the things I had done wrong during the week prior. Once I was done, he would give me my "penance" (which I preferred to think of as "my sentence".) This usually meant reciting numerous Hail Mary's and Our Father's, all the while kneeling on a narrow wooden step!

This seemed so silly because there was no way that I was going to tell him the really good stuff; remember my first look at a fully naked woman in the warm bakery back in Belgium? I remembered that really well! There was no way that a priest, who I had been *led to believe* was completely free from sin, was going to understand the thoughts of a thirteen, fourteen, and fifteen-year-old boy about things such as naked ladies. If I had told him all of my thoughts, I would have *never* gotten off that kneeling pew!

The other reason that confession made no sense was that as I was kneeling there, praying my penance (serving my sentence), I was already in the hole for the coming week because naked women would creep into my thoughts while I was praying! It was a no-win situation!

Another major difference at Mark Twain was that kids would bring all sorts of things to school, including cigarettes, firecrackers, dirty magazines, and knives! Some kids there were even being held up for their lunch! Dorothy was no longer in Kansas, and I was no longer in St. Mary Magdalen's Catholic School.

While at St. Mary Magdalen's school, I had been in scuffles, but I had an awakening at Mark Twain. One day between classes, I was in the boys' bathroom at a urinal when another boy walked in and asked if he could use my comb. I said sure and gave it to him. When I finished, I walked over to the sink, and while I was washing my hands, he finished, said thanks, and threw my comb into the urinal! He stood there looking at me, grinning, and that was when the fight started.

We fought for a couple of minutes and decided it would be better if we finished the fight behind the gym. We both headed out and when we got behind the gym, we started fighting again. I was bigger than the other guy, and I was also very mad, and I guess "The Old Man" came out in me. I pounded on this guy's head and face, and I had him in a headlock, beating him in the face when he bit a chunk out of my left wrist.

I was still wailing away when the shop teacher and a couple of kids out of his class ran up and started pulling us apart. He was bleeding from his face, and they took him to the School Nurse. What I didn't realize when we agreed to finish the fight behind the gym was that it was in full view of the shop classroom.

The teacher and his students could see us fighting, and not knowing what had happened in the bathroom, figured that I was beating the crap out of this guy for no reason! That wasn't a stretch because it happened *a lot* at Mark Twain.

The shop teacher took me to his classroom and bandaged my wrist. He then proceeded to bend me over and gave me 5 licks with the wooden paddle. You may or may not remember the wooden paddles with the holes drilled in them to cut wind resistance (you'd remember them if you were ever on the receiving end). He couldn't deal with the other guy because he had been taken to the nurse.

When he finished the whipping, he sent me to my next class, where I walked in late. The teacher never asked what happened but sent me to the office, where I was taken in to see the vice-principal. He told me that the rules for tardiness were three licks with his freakin' paddle. No further conversation; just bend over, grab your ankles, and get three *more* licks! I was sent back to class, where I *stood* for the rest of the hour, ignoring the smirks of students *and* the teacher.

If this had ended there, I could have lived with it, but oh no! Apparently, the school nurse decided that Comb-guy had a broken nose, and his eyes and face were swelling up, so his parents were called to pick him up and take him to the doctor. This was relayed to the school principal, who had me called back into his office. When I got there, he told me that he was going to call The Old Man, at work no less, and tell him that he would have to come to school to pick up his son.

I tried everything I could to persuade him that he didn't want to do that (including offering him the opportunity to give me *his* licks.) But no luck; he called The Old Man. I thought about running off, but the principal saw the thoughts in my head and made me sit in his office. I suddenly knew how people must feel on death row: time moves slowly…and yet way too fast!

I heard the voice in the outer office, and the principal walked out, closed the door, and spoke with The Old Man. A few minutes later, they both walked in. The Old Man said, "Let's go," and we walked out. I didn't know the nature of the conversation he had with the principal, but as I walked out and looked back at him, I think I saw regret on the Principal's face. I thought, "A little too late to do the right thing now."

We got into the car, and the muscles in his jaw were sticking out like he was trying to break walnuts. Not a word was spoken all the way home. (Think "The Green Mile.") We walked into the house, and even though my mother had no clue about what had happened, she knew immediately that it was going to be bad.

All three of us sat down at the table, and The Old Man began to tell her about the fight and about the kid having to go to the doctor. He then surprises her and me and tells us that I have been kicked out of school! The Old Man is starting to get even madder at the re-telling of the story, but my mother sees the bandage wrap on my left wrist. She asked me what happened, so for the first time, I was given the opportunity to tell *my side* of the story.

Then an amazing thing happened: The Old Man became my father. He is now getting mad at the people at school because *no one* has given me the chance to tell my side of the story. My mother took off the bandage, and it was ugly. This made them *both* even madder. It was decided that my father (for the time being) would take me to school the next morning and speak with the principal.

The next morning at school, I remained sitting outside in the hall; I was called in when they were through talking. The principal told me that now, having heard additional details, and that since I had already received licks with the paddle (my butt was still bleeding), he would rescind the expulsion, and I could go back to my class.

My father's sticking up for me meant more than he would ever know! He now became "My Old Man," as opposed to The Old Man, and I guess that was a definite improvement. The other boy also came back to school, and he never asked to borrow my comb again. Thinking back, I should have made him buy me a new one.

That physical scar on my wrist stayed with me for many years, but it is hardly noticeable now. The lack of opportunity to present my side of the story stayed with me a hell of a lot longer than that scar. Another nail in the coffin of my fondness toward school....

Chapter 10

"…a job"

It was obvious that the public schools had no clue how lax their school discipline was in comparison to the Catholic Schools. This lack of supervision was evident in the classrooms, with kids talking and acting up and a total lack of respect for the teacher. But it *was really* obvious in the cafeteria.

Fights were not uncommon, especially at the beginning of the school year. During the 1959 -1960 school year, a fight broke out in the cafeteria of Edison High School. This is where I would attend High School when I finished at Mark Twain Jr. High. The fight involved boys that were in a gang and members of the school football team. The fight started with fists flying, but in no time, knives were produced, and several football players were cut and stabbed. I wasn't there, but local news stations covered it for several days, so everyone had a good idea of what happened. The result for us junior high kids was that we were banned from bringing pocket knives to school, and searches became a common occurrence. Since it wasn't unusual for guys to have knives, it took a while before they realized that they had to hide them or leave them at home.

I was never in a gang, but it was common knowledge that certain parts of town should be avoided. Like all gangs, their primary objective was guarding their "turf," and trespassing was dangerous. I didn't have any interaction with these people until I started going to high school and got my first car. It was while I was driving home with some friends one day that a scary event happened that changed my life. (But that's for later!)

The rest of my time at Mark Twain Jr. High passed by without too much more drama, and as summer arrived, I turned in my books. The wise guys checking in the books made the remark that they looked brand new! If they could have seen my report card, it would have become instantly clear why my books looked new. Oh well, time to enjoy summer, go fishing, swimming, play ball in the neighborhood, meet some girls, and simply forget about everything else.

But now a job!? Really?

Yep, my mother and My Old Man had conspired to get me a job helping my mother where she now worked at the new Belgium Inn restaurant that had recently opened at San Pedro and Oblate Streets. This was located about five miles north of where we lived. My mother never drove a car her whole life, so My Old Man would load us up at about 5:00 AM and drop us off as he went on to work. This was almost as bad as my farming internship! The good thing about her going in early was that she was generally finished by about noon or shortly thereafter. The bad thing was that we needed a ride home, and we would sometimes have to wait an hour or more for the lunch crowd to finish so that someone could break free and bring us home. This left the rest of the afternoon for me to do some of the things I wanted to do.

What I liked doing was riding my bicycle to the Alamo Heights recreation center and swimming in their pools. The swimming part was OK, but the girls were the real reason I was there every chance I could get. (You probably figured that out on your own.) I had two friends of mine that liked "swimming" as much as I did, so it was usually the three of us that would go. We had to pay the admission fee of twenty-five cents plus a locker fee of twenty-five cents. We didn't always have the money, so one or two of us would sneak in, and we would spring for one locker. The problem was that the locker had a key that was attached to a large industrial safety pin, and you were supposed to pin the key to your swim trunks so that the lifeguard could see it and know you were legit. We figured out that if we wrapped our towel around our waist often enough, the lifeguard would leave us alone… as long as we behaved.

This pool was the premier swimming center in San Antonio, and part of the pool complex had a diving pool with a diving tower. The tower had a 7 1/2-meter platform and a 15-meter platform. (15 meters is 45 feet tall for those of us who are metrically challenged!) The diving pool was also a good place for sunning as it had a grassy lawn not far from the edge of the pool. There was also a diving board which was used a lot. I mentioned the lawn because that is where the girls would go to lay down and tan and watch the boys dive and jump from the platforms!

What better way to draw attention to yourself than to go to the top of the platform and jump off and make a big splash? My problem was I didn't know how to swim! I could be in the big pool and stay in the 5-foot part of the pool and *act like* I was swimming, but I would have to put my foot on the bottom to give me a boost. The diving pool was too deep for that to work, so I had to come up with some other option.

I found that I could swim underwater, so I started practicing holding my breath to see how far I could swim before I had to come up for air. I got to where I could swim from edge to edge without coming up until I could grab the edge of the pool. I was ready, and my friends and I had been daring each other to tackle the top of the platform. They had been jumping off the 7 1/2 meter, but I had not. I figured, what the heck… 15 meters wasn't *that* much higher. Wrong!

The day came when we decided it was time, and we walked to the tower, got in line, and climbed to the top. There were a lot of people that day, so it took a while to get to the top. As I kept climbing, I realized that I could see really far when I got that high. I also realized that 45 feet was really, really far up!

Well, with one of my friends in front of me and the other behind me on the narrow ladder, there was no backing out. I think they had it planned that way. It was finally my turn, and as I walked to the edge and looked down, I realized how FAR DOWN 45 feet up was! I think it's moments like this that shape us forever. I wanted to go back down the stairs, I was scared s_____less, but I jumped!

I learned a lot that day. First, use just one hand to hold your nostrils closed; second, use that other hand to hold your crotch; third, keep your legs tightly clenched together; fourth, don't jump off the 45-foot tower! I neglected all four of the pointers and almost drowned getting to the edge as all the wind had been knocked out of me. I thought that my testicles were lodged somewhere in my sinuses! Despite all that, by golly, I had jumped, and I was so glad that I didn't chicken out and go back down the ladder.

My job at DeWinne's Belgium Inn was to help my mother and do any other odd jobs that had been assigned to me by the boss. This was a formal restaurant and could seat two hundred people or more, so there were lots of employees, including cooks, waitresses, busboys, and my mother and me. This was the place where I became introduced on a personal level to black people.

Of all the cooks, busboys, dishwashers, and cleaning staff, I was the lone white boy. I was around these guys all the time, and it wasn't long before they figured out that even though my parents were friends of the DeWinnes, I was no snitch! As a result, I became part of the group. But there was no getting around the fact that I was white.

My parents and I would get there around 5:30 in the morning, and if no one else was there yet, my father would unlock the door, go in and begin turning on the lights, making sure everything was secure. Often the janitor, Mouton, would already be there preparing to begin sweeping, mopping, and buffing the floors. Mouton was a young black guy, and I would often help him put the chairs back down after the floors were clean. He would also stay over for the lunch run bussing tables, which I started doing, too, when I finally got my own car, so he and I became friends. After being around these men for a short time, I thought back to "The Wild Man of Africa" and was embarrassed for myself!

These guys always treated my mother with respect, and the rare times one of them would slip up and drop a word that might have offended her, they would immediately apologize. They always offered to help with anything she needed; all she had to do was ask. The time frame I am talking about here took place in 1958 – 1962. "Coloreds" had to use their own bathrooms and drinking fountains, and they were not allowed to eat in the main dining area. Despite these circumstances, they showed no animosity toward me or my mother. It proved to me that "color" is not an issue when we are all just trying to make a living.

While my mother was around, everybody tried their best to act right. When she wasn't, it became a different story! These men were always "messing" with each other, and the language became quite colorful. They introduced me to the "N" word, and they were not shy about using it *often* when referring to one another.

The "N" word wasn't something my parents were familiar with, so we didn't use it at home. As a matter of fact, I don't recall my mother *ever* using that word. My father probably did once in a great while, but that was rare. I dwell on the use of this word because the guys taught me a lesson as they used it with one another.

Like a lot of young boys, I tried to talk like I felt an adult would talk. Our dishwasher was named Leroy. He was a small-statured man, very dark-complected, who could get really worked up if things started getting screwed up. His dishwasher station was set up with a large counter across the front where the busboys would bring in the large trays full of dirty dishes and off-load the trays. The dishes and silverware were put into containers that Leroy would then put on a conveyor- type of table that would take them into the washer. It was hot, steamy work, and Leroy would glisten with the sweat running off him.

One Sunday during the lunch Rush Hour, one of the new busboys brought in a tray and started screwing up… placing the dishes and silverware where they didn't belong. Leroy started hollering at him, and the busboy called him a "stupid N..!" The next thing everyone knew, Leroy had climbed over the counter and had that boy on the ground on his back, beating the crap out of him! They pulled Leroy off and sent him home.

Another boy and I had to fill Leroy's spot for the remainder of the rush hour run. It didn't take us long to understand what made Leroy mad when the dishes and silverware were not put in the proper spots for washing. It was hot and steamy, and the demand for clean dishes was constant. I didn't know what Leroy was paid, but I decided right then and there that *it wasn't enough*!

That same afternoon after we had cleaned the kitchen, several of us were sitting around, and Leroy's name came up. We were all talking about what happened when someone mentioned that the busboy should not have called Leroy an "N…." They all nodded yep; that was a no-no. This was when I learned that talking like an adult was a little more complicated than I had thought.

I was confused, but I kept my mouth shut until I was able to talk to one of the older cooks when it was just the two of us alone. I reminded the cook that they called each other the N-word all the time, so why did Leroy get mad *this* time? He told me that the young busboy had not earned the right to call Leroy that name: because of the boy's youth, because he was new on the job, and because he was light-skinned, as opposed to Leroy's dark complexion.

Apparently, back then, skin color (dark vs. light) was sometimes used to demean or enhance a person's worth. Dark skin color was more esteemed than light color! So I was left with a lot to think about, but I had the good sense to realize that I didn't need to be using the word. Leroy came back to work the next day, but the busboy *was finished* working there if you know what I mean.

The summer ended, and it was time to get registered at Edison High School. From the moment I started school there, I could feel the tension everywhere. The cafeteria brawl from last year was still very much on everyone's minds, and teachers were constantly patrolling the halls (and especially the cafeteria) during lunch hour. The police department had assigned police officers in their police cars to park on the campus throughout the day.

With everyone as tense as they were, it wasn't unusual for a one-on-one fight to break out at any time and anywhere. The good thing about those fights (more pushing and shoving than fighting) was that they ended quickly. The word was out that the school authorities were determined to suspend anyone caught fighting, so as soon as something started and a teacher was spotted heading in the direction of the tussle, someone would warn the offenders, and everyone would head in opposite directions.

The parking lot was probably the most fight-prone area since that was where the kids would try to finish something that had started during school. I didn't have a car yet, so I had to ride the bus, which allowed me the opportunity to avoid a lot of those confrontations.

My parents had managed to pay off the house on Wildwood St. and began to look for a bigger house since all three of us kids were still sharing one bedroom. They found a new brick house on Dawnridge Drive, several miles north of where we currently lived. This house had three bedrooms and two bathrooms, and an attached garage. It was beautiful.

My sister finally got her own bedroom, and my brother and I continued to share the larger second bedroom. We all felt that we had finally made it to the big time, and we were proud of what our parents had accomplished. Our house was also two blocks from Robert E. Lee High School, home of the Lee Volunteers! I transferred from Edison to Lee in January of 1961, and my first day at my new school was a total culture shock!

Here at "Lee," almost everyone was white, almost no one dressed in gang clothes, and no one challenged me in the parking lot, the hallways, the gym, or the bathroom! When they found out that I had transferred from Edison, they looked at me like I should have a tattoo or, at the very least, some sort of healed-over scar. Edison had quite a bad reputation, and the kids at Lee acted like Edison should probably be a part of the penal system!

I didn't know how much tension I was under at Edison until I got to Lee. Even though I was around a completely new group of kids, most of them had gone to a different junior high school, and it was a calmer atmosphere. Don't get me wrong, there were still problems, but they didn't seem quite as severe. I guess what else really made a difference was that I knew this was going to be my last school, and I became part of the class of 1963.

Chapter 11

"That is the ugliest car I have ever seen!"

The spring semester came to an end, and summer arrived. I had been driving my father's car whenever he would let me, and when I turned sixteen on the 2nd of June, it was time for me to take my driver's test. My Old Man took me to the Driver's License office, where I took the written test and passed with no problems.

The actual driving test was administered by Texas State Troopers in uniform. When my guy came out to our car with his clipboard, he took a walk around to make sure the car was safe, and then he got in the passenger seat. I was already stressed, but the fact that he was wearing a gun on his hip, had handcuffs, plus a cowboy hat… all that notched up the pressure on me even higher. He introduced himself and asked me if I was ready to go. I was surprised that my voice worked, although I sounded like I was just starting to go through puberty.

I was breezing through all of the various obstacles, but I knew that the parallel parking test was rapidly approaching. Then a really weird thing happened as we drove up to that part of the course. The way that the test was set up was that they put two large poles into position, and the object of the test was to park the car between the two poles without hitting or bumping them. Since the poles just sat on top of the street, no damage was done to your car since the poles would just move.

When my trooper and I arrived at the location, a woman was ahead of us, and she was trying to park. It was obvious that she had made several attempts and was still not parked properly; you could tell that she was upset. Her trooper had gotten out of the car and was trying to help her park back into the space when she backed completely *over* the pole *despite* him yelling for her to stop! I wanted to laugh, but it didn't seem like a good idea, and besides, I was getting even more nervous myself.

My trooper got out and went over there because we could see that the other guy had totally lost his composure. He kept yelling for her to stop even though she *was* stopped. The troopers walked off a few feet, and I guess they came up with a plan on how to get the pole out from under her car.

My trooper went to the back of the car, bent over, and grabbed the pole that was sticking out from under the car. The other trooper stood by the driver's side door and started telling the driver to slowwwwly drive forward. (I think I forgot to mention that, like me, this woman was driving a standard shift car.) I imagine that later on, the troopers probably looked back on their plan and decided to *never* use it again in the likelihood that they should *ever* have to get another pole out from underneath- the- car-event.

Anyway, the trooper was directing the driver to ease forward using his hands to signal for her to *go slow*. Well, I think everything would have been OK if it hadn't been for the woman's foot slipping off the clutch. Because when that happened, the car became an animal; it growled, hopped up, and dove forward, which made her trooper jump back! As the car hopped forward, the back pole that my trooper was holding on to bounced out from under the car, caught him upside the head, knocked off his hat, and knocked him down!

Before I could react (I was still sitting in my car,) my trooper jumped up and got his hat back on his head (apparently, wearing your hat as a trooper was of utmost importance). Her trooper was screaming at the woman to cut off the ignition, and I could hear the woman screaming back that she didn't know what had happened! The woman was told to *get out* of the driver's seat and *into* the passenger seat as the trooper got behind the wheel, and they drove off. My trooper set the poles back where they belonged, got into the car, and asked me if I knew how to parallel park. I said, "Sure," and he said, "Good." He directed me to drive back to the license office and told me I had passed with flying colors!

When my father saw me come back into the office waiting room, he had a concerned look on his face, and he asked me why it had taken so long. I told him that I would tell him on the way home. He told me he was getting worried because a woman had been brought in with a trooper, and she was crying as the trooper told her she should *never* be behind the wheel of a car! I told him the story, and we both had a good laugh, but he *stopped* laughing when I mentioned that since I had passed my test, I guess it was time to get me a car!

I guess a month had passed when my father came in one day and proudly told me and the rest of the family that he had found me a car. We were going to pick it up on the following Saturday. I had all kinds of questions as to make, model, and so on, but he told me he wanted it to be a surprise. *That* should have been a warning.

On Saturday afternoon, he and I loaded up and drove out to the westside of San Antonio and pulled up in front of a small house. An old Mexican man came out and greeted my father, and he and I shook hands. My father told him to show me the car, and we went to the backyard. When I turned the corner, the man proudly pointed to the ugliest car I had ever seen! It was a 1947 Studebaker, 2-door sedan, hand-painted battleship grey.

When I say hand painted, I mean hand painted with a paint brush!! The other thing about the car was that the back looked a lot like the front, so it was hard to tell if it was coming or going. It had a flat-head six-cylinder motor and standard shift transmission with the shift-stick on the steering column. I was speechless, but I think my father thought it was pure joy!

It was already a done deal since my father had paid the man earlier in the week, and I had no say so in the matter. There was nothing left to do but drive it home! This was now my car, the one I drove all the way through high school, and I know for a fact that there wasn't another one like it in all of San Antonio or probably even in the whole state of Texas and beyond.

I eventually got used to the car, and fortunately, since school was out, I didn't have to worry about anyone seeing it and me having to explain that it really *was* my car! You might recall when I mentioned that Robert E. Lee High was a far cry from Edison High regarding culture… well this also included *economic* standing in the city. What I am trying to say is that a lot of the kids that attended Lee had parents who had money, and this translated to the types of cars you would find in the student parking lot.

There were nice new cars, sports cars, muscle cars, foreign cars, and hot rods, but there was only one hand-painted, grey Studebaker by God! Looking back, I now realize that once the novelty wore off, no one really cared what I drove… especially since I seldom mingled in their social circles.

I learned at an early age that there are upsides and downsides to everything, and this held true with owning a car. I finally became sort-of proud of my car (despite hearing remarks like, "Hey, I saw you at the drive-in, but I couldn't tell if you were coming or going !"). With the help of my father, I did all the upkeep myself, which included changing the oil, washing it, and even working on the motor. I tried compounding and waxing it, but I found that to be a total waste of time since *nothing* would remove those brush strokes.

Another major upside was that I didn't have to rely on any of my friends to go on a date, and the days of my father driving us to a movie were over! Remembering being driven by my father brings back an especially horrible memory for me. On my first real date, my father was going to take me by her house and then drive us to the show. We were getting ready to leave, and I was waiting on him when I remembered something and started to get back out. I grabbed the edge of the door, and at the same time, my father was walking by. Seeing the door partially open, he slammed it shut with my fingers still in the door! My middle finger caught the worst of it, and it was already bleeding when I got the door open. I was hopping around, trying hard not to cry.

My Old Man had not seen what happened, and he asked me what the problem was. I screamed that my fingers had been caught in the door! His reply was something along the lines of "what did you do that for?" He then asked me if we should call the girl and cancel the date. I was convinced at that moment that he had *never* been a young guy but that he had just *completely* skipped over that part of a *normal* person's life and had gone right to being an *asshole*!

We put a bandage on my finger and drove over to pick up my date. When I knocked on the door (using my left hand), her father opened the door and immediately wanted to know what had happened to my finger. I told him what had happened, and he asked if I wanted to cancel the date. Did he and my father grow up together? Geez! I lied and said it didn't bother me and that I was good to go. The whole evening though, my hand felt like it was going to fall off, but I got to put my arm around her, and I never once groaned when my finger was accidentally bumped!

As I said, there are upsides and downsides to almost everything, and it didn't take long for the downside to show up. The whole family soon looked at me as the designated errand boy (remember: my mother didn't drive), so if she needed to go to the store, I had a car! When my brother or sister needed to go somewhere, I had a car!

It was understood from early on that when I got a car, and I would have to pay for the fuel and maintenance, and other expenses except for insurance. This meant that I was going to need a source of income. In other words, I needed a *regular* job. Working with my mother and bussing tables wasn't going to get it, so it was time to hunt for a real job.

Like a lot of teenagers, my first job was at one of the local grocery stores, with starting pay at fifty cents an hour. That lasted until several of us were caught smoking in the warehouse. The next job was at a family-owned grocery store, and that lasted until I got into an argument with the owner's wife. I was right; *everyone,* including the owner *knew* I was right. But I learned that arguing with the owner's wife is never a good idea. *She* obviously stayed, and *I* was out of a job.

Because of the relationship my mother and father had with the Belgium restaurant, I always knew that I would be welcomed back. This meant I would never have an excuse to sit at home because I could not find a job. But before I resigned to that idea, I finally found a job at a Gulf service station, and I stayed there all the way through the rest of my time in high school. I have to say that this job turned out to be an education in ways that I could have never imagined!

I was hired on a Saturday, and I found out that the only workers there would be just the owner and me with *me* being the only employee. It wasn't long before I realized that the owner (I will give him the name of Lowell) was a shady character. He had the morals of an alley cat and the integrity of a carnival con man. He was short and stocky, dark-complected, and had hair growing out of his ears and nose and coming out of the top of his T-shirt. I am not exaggerating!

I had been working there for about two weeks, going in after school during the week and all day on Saturdays. One Friday afternoon, about an hour after I had started, these two guys in suits drove up, parked to the side, went into the office, and started talking to Lowell. A few minutes later, Lowell called me in and told me I would have to close the station at the end of the day. The two men put handcuffs on him and started to walk him outside to their car. I followed them out, asking Lowell what the heck I was supposed to do with the money, and he told me to take it home with me. They put him in their car and drove off!

I had only been there a little over two weeks and had never closed at the end of the day. I was now faced with bringing in all the displays, counting the money, and putting Lowell's car into one of the bays. This all happened on a Friday. The service station was about two blocks away from the entrance to a drive-in movie theatre, so Friday was one of the busiest days of the week. The kids that were going to the show would pull in and get some gas, and since this was a full-service station, I was expected to wipe the windshield and check the oil, etc. We had two gas islands with four pumps, and I was jumping around like a frog dipped in scalding water.

When I finally made it through the rush, I had money in both shirt pockets, plus my pants pockets! These were mostly dollar bills since most of the requests for gas were for a dollar or two. (We sold regular gasoline in 1962 for about 20–23 cents per gallon. We would occasionally have "gas wars" and would lower our regular gas to 15-17 cents per gallon… Really!) But I finally had the chance to go into the office and put the money in the register. When I got through, I realized that there was *a lot of money* in there, and I started thinking about somebody coming in and robbing me. I ended up calling my father and explained that I was the only one at the station and would have to close by myself. I asked him to come over around closing time and stand-by for me. He agreed, and I felt a whole lot better.

Of course, when my father asked me what had happened, I told him what I knew, and he asked me what I was supposed to do the next day, which was Saturday. Well, I didn't even know how to contact Lowell, so I told him that I guess I would come in and open for business. My father agreed but told me he would follow me and make sure there were no further surprises. The next day I opened up, and I finally heard from Lowell's wife, who told me that I should keep regular hours, close that night, and drop the money at her house. When I arrived at the house that evening, she came to the front door, took the money bag, and thanked me. She also told me that her husband would let me know something by the following Monday.

When I got home from school on Monday afternoon, my mother told me that my boss had called; he told her to tell me that I should come to work. When I got there, he was already there, and we worked the rest of the day. Nothing was said between us until we closed. Well, there was no way that my father was going to allow me to work there unless Lowell would come up with some reasonable explanation of why he had been arrested. I told him that, and Lowell said that it was related to someone that had filed charges against him for an assault that had taken place months earlier. He went on to say that it was now taken care of and that I had nothing to worry about. When I got home, I passed on to my parents what had been said, and they asked me how I felt. I told them I was OK with it and that I still wanted the job.

The more I thought about what had happened along with his explanation, I knew the guy was lying to me. I couldn't see two detectives in suits coming out to arrest a guy on an assault charge. It got even more interesting when a couple of women drove into the station one day looking for Lowell. I told them he wasn't there, so they said that they would wait for him. They pulled to the side of the building and parked.

After a while, the woman called me over and asked if I knew where Lowell had gone and when he would be back. I honestly told them that I had no idea. My instinct began telling me that these were not people I wanted to mess with and that this wasn't a social call. They waited around a little longer and finally left after telling me to give the boss a message: that so-and-so had been by and needed to talk to him.

Lowell usually called me to see how things were going, and about an hour after the two women left, he called. I told him what had been said, and he asked me to describe them. When I gave him the description, he told me to close the station by myself again at the end of the day and bring the money to his house.

Well, I did as he asked, and he met me on his front porch, looking very nervous, while he thanked me. He said he would see me the next day. I was nervous driving home, but I had no idea why *I* should be nervous! I didn't say anything to my parents about this latest development because I didn't want to lose this job. Lowell was paying me twenty-five dollars a week, plus my gas, plus I could service my car anytime I liked for free! I was making more money than I had ever made before (even though I gave my parents half of what I made to contribute to the household), I had lots of girls coming through the station, and I pretty-much enjoyed the responsibility!

Despite my feelings about not wanting to lose this job, I was determined to get my boss to level with me about what was really going on. The next day I got there, and since business was slow, I confronted him and told him he needed to be honest with me about why the women were looking for him.

To my surprise, he agreed and told me that I deserved to know. Apparently, Lowell was a frequent visitor to a couple of brothels in San Antonio, and occasionally, the people running the brothels would ask him to take one of the girls to another brothel in Louisiana! I later learned this constituted a Federal Offense, but at the time, I figured Lowell was simply crazy. Anyway, he went on to tell me that the day he had been arrested, he had been charged with transporting a minor female across state lines for the purpose of prostitution! The two women who had come by the station also had a business interest in that same girl, and apparently, they felt that Lowell owed them some money for their lost earnings.

Talk about surprised! Fortunately, at this point in the conversation, a car had driven up to the pumps, and I went out to service the car. When I came back into the office, I asked Lowell where all this stuff was headed. He assured me that earlier in the day, he had contacted the women and that everything had been worked out. I guess, for once, he was telling the truth because I never saw them again, and the police never showed up anymore to haul him off... although they probably should have.

Lowell eventually hired another guy who was about four years older than me and was taking a semester off from college. We became friends, and he could buy the beer, which saved me from having to go to one of the out-of-the-way places to get the beer. I had three other friends of mine that also attended Lee High School, and we basically all ran around together.

When the new guy, Bill, was hired, he and I alternated taking Saturday evenings off, so I finally started having some time to go out. If we had dates, we would often double-date and go to the drive-in movies. The father of one of my friends was the projectionist at the drive-in, so we got in for free. I can tell you that we did spend a lot of time going to the movies, but I cannot remember a lot of the movies themselves because if we weren't drinking beer, we were "making out" with the girls.

Going to the drive-in movies was sometimes referred to as going to the "submarine races," which referred to activities that took place in the back seat of the car. (You know, as I write this, I just realized that some of that "activity" probably prompted my career choice as a submariner when I joined the Navy.) NOT!

I didn't have a steady girlfriend during high school but dated two or three girls off and on. I wasn't a Romeo and didn't claim to be one. But I was one hell of a kisser! (Or so they told me.) Shoot, we could do that for hours. This one girl that I went out with felt it was important to refresh her lipstick every twenty minutes or so, and I guess it gave us a chance to grab our breath and regain control.

This one particular cold night, we stayed at it right up to the time the movie ended, and it was time to go home. I would often stop by the concession stand and use the restroom as we left. But this night, we didn't stop by there, and I took her home, dropped her off, and then went straight home. When I pulled up and parked, I noticed that a light was still on in our kitchen.

When I walked in, My Old Man was sitting at the kitchen table. As I came in, he was staring at me with this bewildered expression on his face! I stopped and asked him what was wrong, and he asked me if I felt all right. I said sure. He asked me where I had been, and I told him that my date and I had gone to the drive-in movies.

He then told me that I probably ought to give some serious thought to dating this particular girl again because my face looked like she had tried to pull it off my head! He then told me to go directly to the bathroom before my mother saw me and clean up! When I got into the bathroom and looked in the mirror, I understood what he was talking about. My entire face was her shade of lipstick, and I had small suction marks on my neck!

The next morning was Sunday, and when I walked into the kitchen, he was already up and sitting at the table. My mother was cooking breakfast and asked me over her shoulder if I had a fun date the previous night. I was fixing myself a cup of coffee, and I could see My Old Man look at me and start to smile. I told her that I had a good time, and he chimed in that he was still up when I got home and thought I might have come down with something, but he guessed he was wrong since I looked OK this morning. Just then, breakfast was ready, and thank goodness, that was the end of that conversation!

Chapter 12

"He needs to work to do his share for the family."

Other than the three high school friends that I ran around with, most of the other people I associated with were older. As I mentioned previously, Lowell, the owner of the service station where I worked, treated me like an adult. I guess when you consider that after only two weeks on the job, I had closed the station at the end of the day and handled his money without ripping him off, I had proved myself, at least in his eyes. I was smoking and drinking beer, paying for my expenses, and still contributing to the family income.

I was making barely passing grades in school, but Math was still something I struggled with. I made a D in Math, but in my senior year, I had to take and pass Algebra to be able to graduate. There wasn't much use in asking My Old Man to help, as that would lead to frustration and anger. I had a couple of friends that tried to help, but it just wouldn't sink in, no matter how hard I tried.

I still loved reading, and some of my favorite reading was comic books! It would drive My Old Man crazy if he caught me reading comic books since he saw no redeeming value in spending time reading something like that. (I wished I had some of those comic books today, considering what some of them are now worth.) I liked to draw, and I liked to build things, mostly out of wood.

My Old Man was somehow convinced that since I wasn't good in Math, I wasn't very smart. The fact that I would waste my time reading comic books was further proof that I didn't have much of a future. I knew he felt that way, so consequently, I *behaved* like a guy with not much of a future ahead of him. As I have said, I ran with some guys who drank and smoked, and often we would go out to the drive-in theater and sit on the roof of the projection booth and drink. It wasn't unusual for us to get drunk and then drive home. After one of those nights, I was drunk and drove home and woke up the next morning with My Old Man banging on the door of my car, yelling at me to get up! I tried to get out, not really knowing what was going on, but he ended up pulling me out of the car, and I fell down on the lawn.

When I managed to stand up and I looked around, I found that instead of parking in the *street* in front of the house, I had driven *over* the sidewalk and stopped in the *front yard*! The next-door neighbor had two young boys and had brought them over to their front window so she could show them what *not* to do as they got older! (Years later, one of those boys told me that his mother would threaten him with turning out like me if he didn't straighten up. I never cared much for that woman.)

Given the tendency of my father to blow up when I made him mad, he didn't say much after he parked my car in the street, and we went inside. I didn't go into too much detail regarding him while we lived in Belgium, but he, too, liked to drink, and he pulled some stunts there that he was probably not too proud of himself. I guess he was reminded of some of those days as he helped me go into the house.

I know that he and I just never saw things the same way most of the time, but in fairness to him, there were lots of times that I would aggravate the situation just because I could. I am not excusing his terrible anger; I'm just saying that sometimes I could have probably cooled the situation and chose not to. (Don't ask me why).

I was not the only one who was expected to work when I got old enough; my sister and brother followed in my footsteps. But just as everyone worked, we also took an annual vacation which for the first few years meant loading up and driving south to Corpus Christi, Texas, on the Gulf of Mexico. There we would either rent a motel room or camp on the beach at Padre Island.

All we kids wore all day long was a bathing suit and suntan lotion. We did this for three years running, and the first two or three days, we always had a blast. We had a small fishing tackle, and we would fish in the surf or off the large Bob Hall Pier. My most memorable catch was a small catfish that everyone called a "hardhead." As I was trying to take it off my line, it flipped off, and one of its hard fins stuck me in the ankle! The pain was immediate, and I was on the ground thrashing around in obvious agony.

My father came over and had no idea what to do since we had no experience with something like this. Some other people had seen what happened and called for a lifeguard. The lifeguard had a medical kit and put some salve on the entry wound, and it began to feel better. We later learned that these "trash fish" had a notorious reputation for inflicting painful stab wounds with their spiky fins which are coated with some sort of slimy toxin.

The last year we ever went back to the coast for vacation was when we were once again camped on Padre Island. On the third day, we kids were complaining about the sand being in our sleeping bags, in our underwear, and in our food, and we all had bad sunburn!

It was after lunch, and suddenly The Old Man jumped up, cursed in Flemish, and announced that we were packing up and leaving! When he said that, we all began to fuss that we didn't want to go home, but he started throwing stuff in the station wagon and wouldn't say another word.

We had no choice but to pack up and get in the car while he finished yanking the tent apart and lashing it on top of our station wagon. As we pulled away from the beach, he stopped at a public rinsing station, and we got out and stood under the fresh water and rinsed ourselves off. We toweled dried and got back in the car, still in our bathing suits, and we drove off.

Some eight or ten hours later, we pulled into Lake Valecito Park in the state of Colorado and rented a cabin! We had gone from the Gulf of Mexico beach, temperature in high 90s, to the mountains of Colorado, the temperature at night in the low 40's. And we almost froze to death that first night! The people running the camp looked at us like we were from Mars, considering that we were still in bathing suits, and I glowed because of my sunburn!

The next morning we spent several hours taking everything out of the car, cleaning the sand out of the tent, and packing it properly. Most importantly, we started trying to find warm clothes! All of us agreed that we had found heaven! We never went back to the beach again. (Years later, I took my own family to Valecito Lake, rented a cabin, and spent a week fishing and hiking. It was just as much fun then as it was the first time I was there.)

When we weren't on vacation, my life consisted of school and going to work. Since school was mandatory, I endured it until I could enjoy myself at work. I was attracted to sports and thought I wouldn't have minded trying out for football, but an incident in my junior year put in perspective where sports would fit into my life…according to my father's thoughts about the matter.

Throughout high school, we were required to participate in gym class. One afternoon we were playing dodge ball in the gym since it was raining outside. Because of the weather, the football team was also going to be in there with us.

For those who have never played dodge ball, the rules are simple. Four or five rubber balls, the size of small soccer balls, are put on the floor of the gym between two teams of boys who are lined up across from each other with their backs against the bleacher walls. The object of the game is to hit an opposing player with a ball, and if he is hit, he has to leave the floor. The last guy standing wins for his team.

Normally you *pick* players for each side, but this time the football players were on one side, and we grunts were on the other.

The game began, and it was evident quite early that the grunts were extremely under-matched, athletically speaking. We were getting *killed,* but there were some of us who were doing well. There was one boy who had some disability issues, and we were trying to shield him as much as possible because he could barely run and had no coordination skills whatsoever. It was obvious that these football guys were targeting him from the start, and it was hard to keep him at the rear because he wanted to get out there in front.

One of the rules was that if the player you were throwing at *caught* your ball, *you* were "out", so we generally threw the ball at the body or legs because then the ball was harder to catch. It became obvious that this one football player was throwing at the head of the guy we were trying to protect, and it started to piss me off. It wasn't long before he got our man, and yep, he got him in the face!

The next time I got one of the balls, I started to stalk this one guy, and sure enough. I manage to hit *him* right in the face. Well, he knew what I had been doing, so instead of leaving, he charged across the floor, and we got into it. I am sure it was a lucky punch, but I nailed him and broke his collar bone.

Man, that felt good, but the coach didn't agree. His player now had a doctor's appointment, and I was sent to the showers. A couple of days later, the head football coach, Coach Drew, notified me that I would now be participating in football gym instead of my regular gym class. When I got to the football gym, I was told that since I liked to fight, I would now get a chance to expend some energy with his players in one of their drills.

The drill consisted of ten or twelve boys on the gym mat, forming a circle with everyone facing into the center. In the center, the coach placed a medicine ball. He then walked behind the boys and would suddenly tap a boy on the butt, and the selected boy would jump into the center of the circle, grab the medicine ball, and try to fight his way out of the circle with the rest of the boys trying to tear the ball out of his hands.

I don't know why Coach Drew bothered walking around the circle after about the third or fourth time because, by then, everyone knew that only *one boy* was going to get tapped on the butt. I would still like to know who kept grabbing my jock strap, but I hurt all over for several days.

I think it was early the following week when Coach Drew showed up at my house one evening and wanted to talk to My Old Man. Our next-door neighbor, Jack, was a big booster for our football team, and he came over with the coach to talk to my father.

I was at work at the time, but I later learned from the neighbor what was said. Coach Drew told my father the entire story beginning with the dodge ball incident in the gym and my participating in the medicine ball drill. He then went on to tell my father that he would like to see me try out for the team since I didn't seem to mind getting physical. Jack tried hard to convince my father that it would be a good thing for me personally (since he had probably seen the condition I was in sometimes when I got home around daylight), but my father's answer remained the same. His response was, "No, he needs to work to do his share for the family!"

(Let me set something straight here. My father was responding based on *his* background, and I am sure that my mother was in total agreement with his decision! Remember their background…to them, work was as natural as breathing, and work defined who they were to a large extent. They were living in the land of opportunity where you worked for what you had and were rewarded for your efforts. (Their life proved their argument as they could point to "their" house and their overall lifestyle. They were able to support their family and wanted nothing, and I am not talking about just money.)

I say this because I don't think back on this as some sort of lost opportunity for me. It was more of a validation of *my worth* to our family based on my meager contributions to our functioning as a family unit. When your family consists only of your mother, father, brother, and sister, you have a totally *different* perspective on family than those folks who can also interact with their uncles, aunts, nieces, nephews, and grandparents.

I guess what I am saying here is that I didn't resent my father for nixing my football career for whatever it may have become. Besides, I was still flunking Algebra and probably wouldn't have been eligible to play anyway.

My senior year in 1962-1963 was much like any other: I still needed to pass Algebra, and I still had not gotten a grasp of the Basics. I was still drinking and spending time with my friends and wasn't paying much attention to a conflict that was brewing in a place called Viet Nam. I continued to work at the Gulf station and had settled into that routine, but I was becoming more and more aware of what a totally despicable character the owner, Lowell, was. Soon, my real-life education was going to expand.

One day a man drove into the station driving a nice new car, and he wanted an oil change. He specified that he used a special blend of oil that was a significant upgrade from our bulk oil. We carried this upgrade, and it came in individual cans. I made a special note of it on our service order because it cost quite a bit more than the bulk. The customer left the car, and I pulled it into one of our service bays. I lifted it up and began to service the car.

While the oil was draining, Lowell came over and looked at the invoice. He told me that there was no need to use the high-dollar oil but to put in the *bulk* and *charge* him for the more expensive oil. I argued with him and told him that the guy was specific as to what oil he wanted to be used, and further told him that this guy didn't look like someone to mess with. When he insisted that I use the bulk, I flat-out refused and came out of the pit.

Lowell did the service himself and parked the car when he finished. A while later, the owner of the car arrived and asked me if his car was ready. I told him that Lowell had serviced his car and that he should talk to *him*. He went in, began to talk to the boss, and for some reason, he smelled a rat. He asked him if he had used the upgraded oil, and Lowell said sure.

The guy then asked for the empty cans! Oh, oh. Lowell tried dancing around the request, but the cat was out of the bag! The next thing I knew, the car owner punched out Lowell and then left without paying a dime! He also left Lowell nursing a bloody nose plus some other knots. To top it off, Lowell was mad at me for not backing him up!

I was never able to convince him that what he was doing wasn't right. He was mad that he had been caught and that I hadn't helped him while he was getting his butt kicked. The lessons I learned at that station were never taught at school! (I also didn't realize until later on that my mother and father had molded my character a whole lot more than I had realized – remember the Lone Ranger & Tonto toys my brother had stolen?)

As I mentioned earlier, San Antonio had a considerable gang problem in the 60s, and I became much more familiar with them than I should have. It was a Saturday evening, probably around midnight or a little later, and two friends of mine were with me in my Studebaker, driving north on San Pedro St., coming home from cruising downtown.

We stopped at the red light at San Pedro and Hildebrand, and a car with four guys in it pulled up alongside us. We glanced over, and they looked at us and gave us a sign that they wanted to fight. I put my car in neutral, and I and the guy sitting in the passenger seat beside me got out and started to go over to the other car, but they ran the red light and started speeding North on San Pedro. We hurried back into my car, and the race was on.

As we chased the other car still going out of town on San Pedro, we started closing the gap. We were now in the country, and we were passing the airport property with no one else on the road. (Today, this area is completely built up, and it looks *nothing* like it did in 1963.)

The fact that we were closing the gap should have alerted me that *something* wasn't right; my Studebaker didn't outrun anything! The thought that we were going to kick some ass as we closed the distance even further *immediately* left my mind when we saw someone leaning out of the rear seat window on the driver's side with a *shotgun*, and he began shooting at us! The first shot hit the hood of my car and bounced into the windshield. The second shot (which must have been a slug) blew a hole underneath my left headlight. I was laying as low as I could get in the seat and still see so that I didn't run off the road, and we came to a screeching stop! Thank God they kept going, so we turned around and started back to San Antonio. I dropped off my friends and headed home.

Since I saw no sense in waking my parents up at two in the morning, I decided to park my car in front of the house and go into bed. Wrong! I woke up when My Old Man started dragging me out of bed. He didn't stop dragging me until he had me on the floor and told me to get up and follow him outside. The next-door neighbor lady got an eyeful that morning since I was in my underwear while My Old Man was yelling at me, asking what had happened to my car!

The light of day left no doubt that someone had shot at me with bad intentions. You could plainly see the shots that had impacted my hood and bounced into the windshield and the hole under the left headlight, all on the driver's side! It was not surprising: I was told that the only place I could now drive my car was to school and work. My senior year soon came to an end, and I flunked Algebra *again*! Now I was going to have to go to summer school and take Algebra and *pass it* so that I could get my High School diploma.

I was enrolled at MacArthur High School for Summer School, and it was going to start in the middle of June. Just prior to the summer session starting, my father told me that he had *sold* my car effective at the end of the summer. He told me that the guys that shot at me were probably part of a gang and that my car would be easy to spot. There was no arguing with that. And then he added that if I stayed in San Antonio, I was going to end up getting killed, so as soon as school ended, I was destined for the military.

He was kind enough to give me a choice: the Navy or the Marines. I found that he had arrived at those two choices because both branches were recruiting at the same building on Arsenal St. in downtown San Antonio. I went for my exams and physicals, and I passed everything. My enlistment was put on hold pending my passing Algebra and getting my high school diploma.

The summer session started, and since I was working every day and getting home late, I would usually fall asleep during class. About a week in, the teacher told me he wanted to talk with me after class. He and I sat down, and he asked me what my future looked like if I got my diploma. I told him about my pending enlistment in the military, that I was working a job every day, that I was coming home late at night, and that these reasons were why I fell asleep during his class.

He thought for a few minutes, and then he told me that if I came to class every day, I could sit at the back of the room, go to sleep, and he would give me a D, and I would pass. We shook on it, and on July 31, 1963, I passed Algebra! On August 13, 1963, I took my first airplane ride to San Diego, California, and began Navy boot camp.

Chapter 13

"President Kennedy has been assassinated."

The airplane left San Antonio late in the evening of August 13, and I remember my parents, brother, and sister at the airport seeing me off. My mother cried, but everyone else held it together.

The plane stopped twice before arriving in San Diego, and by then, it was a late night, or maybe it could have even been early the next morning. We then had to wait for busses that eventually took us to the Navy training base. I had received instructions prior to my departure that I should bring nothing with me other than a toothbrush.

As I looked around at the other guys, I could see that a few of them had some large bags, and I was a little worried that I might have made a mistake not bringing some of my personal stuff. I soon found out I had made the right decision by traveling light! When the bus pulled into what I later learned was the receiving barracks, we were all ordered to get off the bus and form up. Form up??

Everybody was milling around, trying to figure out what forming up meant, when two of these guys started yelling at us, wanting to know why we were not forming up. Luckily, I was around two guys who had been in ROTC in high school, and they started to line us up, and I fell into line alongside them.

Some of the other guys were still running here and there, and the drill instructors continued to scream at them to form up. Everyone finally got into a semblance of three rows lined up, facing the building. The two guys in uniform, who had been doing the screaming and yelling, paced back and forth, looking at us. They began to call out guys who had bags with them to step out of the formation.

When they had everyone with a bag out in front of the rest of us, they began with the first guy and told him to open his bag and dump the stuff on the ground! They then started picking through the stuff, and when they got to items like fancy underwear, photos, medicinal ointments, and food stuff, especially cookies, they would have the guy holding them out so that we could see what it was.

After they had gone through all the bags and the guys were holding all of their special stuff, the ridicule began. "Mommy sent your favorite jammies with you?", "Tell everybody what this ointment is for", "This is a picture of your girlfriend?" "You know your buddy is probably going to wear that out in about a week or so, right?" And on and on…Man, was I glad I had nothing but my toothbrush!

It was about two-thirty in the morning when we were finally taken to a barracks and issued some soap, a wash rag and towel, and a toothbrush and paste. We were told that we would be allowed to sleep-in the following morning since it was so late, and they knew we were stressed out. I could smell a rat, and I picked a bunk, took a shower, and hit the sack.

As I started to go to sleep, there were several guys who were sitting around talking about everything that had taken place that day, and I guess they were just too wound up to sleep. Some of them had not showered yet when suddenly the lights went out, and they were in the dark! A couple of them started yelling that someone should turn the lights back on. They were quickly met with several replies that they shut the f___ up!

It was four-thirty in the morning (what was it with me and four-thirty?) when I figured that the world was coming to an end. A loud, metallic sound exploded, and the lights began flipping on and off, and some voices were screaming and asking us what we were doing in bed! Guys were yelling, and believe it or not, someone was crying and asking what was happening. The rat that I had smelled had arrived!

We were told we had ten minutes to be lined up out front of our barracks, dressed, and carrying our issued towel, washcloth, toothpaste, and brush. I guess some of those boys had no concept of time or were used to their mommas calling them two or three times, but at exactly the ten-minute mark, those of us who were lined up outside were treated to the sight of several guys running out in their skivvies, barefoot, carrying their clothes and issued items! Welcome to the United States Navy!

Almost from the time I arrived at boot camp, it became obvious to me that the objective of the military is to take individuals from a wide variety of backgrounds, with specific individual skills and tendencies, and mold them into a functioning unit. To achieve this goal, the first thing they must do is re-focus the importance of self and shift that focus to the well-being of the unit.

Navy boot camp (in my mind) achieved that "unit focus" by severing family ties and creating a new family. The new head of the family was the drill instructor, also referred to as the Company Commander. Each company had a Company Commander, and ours turned out to be a stern but fair man; I developed a great deal of respect for him. He had six assistants who were total assholes!

These were the guys who trained us each day and got into our faces, screamed, yelled, and did everything they could to convince us that we were totally worthless and the dumbest individuals that God ever gave life to! But none of them could hold a candle to My Old Man! As a result, dumb as this may sound, I enjoyed boot camp.

During the first two weeks after I arrived, we were held in a receiving barracks, and it was during this period that some of the obvious recruiting "mistakes" were eliminated. By "mistakes," I mean the bed wetters, the guys who could not stop crying for their mothers, and even the one who tried to hang himself in the shower! (Hard to believe, but I am not exaggerating.) There were forty-five of us from all different parts of the country when we finally became Company 331. We were eventually placed in our own barracks, which would become home for the next fourteen weeks.

It took no time at all for me to realize that I owed a great debt of gratitude to my mother and father and probably even my grandmother for my upbringing. Several guys in our company apparently had never been made to work or take care of their stuff or even pick up after themselves. They couldn't get used to the concept of authority, and as a result, they asked "why" a lot! This might not sound like such a big deal, but remember that we were being molded into a cohesive unit! Sometimes stopping to ask *why* could endanger *everybody*, so now, whenever somebody asked ''why,'' the entire company was made to pay the price.

As an example, we were required to form-up (remember form-up at our arrival?) at 0500 hours in front of our barracks. Once formed-up, we would send a Runner to the mess hall (cafeteria) to get permission from a drill instructor to bring our company up to be presented for our meals. The area in front of the cafeteria was a huge concrete slab where numerous recruit companies would line up to wait at "parade rest" until they could enter the cafeteria.

If the Runner presented himself, and he was inspected and found to be in violation of dress code or some *other* violation, he was rejected, and our company could not proceed to the mess hall until another Runner was sent.

One morning we sent our Runner to the mess hall, and he was rejected. He felt that he had been unfairly treated, so he asked "why." As a result, we were held back because they made him stay where he was while they decided who would answer his "why!" This meant that we fell behind, and when we finally entered the cafeteria, we had all of about 5 minutes to eat. Forty-five hungry young men were not something to be trifled with, so the position of Runner was deemed of extreme importance. This guy was never sent again!

At the beginning of 1963, the naval base in San Diego experienced a severe outbreak of Spinal Meningitis. By the time I arrived in August, the outbreak was over, but the base was still following protocols to make sure it didn't re-appear. One of the safety measures they had instated was for recruits to do their own laundry instead of taking it to the base laundromat. As a result, we did our laundry on outside scrub tables.

These tables were located outside, in front of our barracks. When you finished washing your clothes, they were put on clothes lines. But no clothes pins for us; we had to tie our stuff on the clotheslines with short strings that had to be tied with a "square knot." The Drill Instructors, commonly called the "DIs", would inspect your clothes, and if one piece was found not to be tied with the proper knot, they would cut your clothesline, and all of your clothes would hit the ground. You then had the pleasure of re-washing all your clothes! We had one guy who lost count of the number of times he washed his clothes after they hit the ground.

I became one of several squad leaders, and it took no time at all before I realized that I had not been done any favors. Now, I wasn't only responsible for my own behavior but also for the behavior of the seven or eight guys assigned to my squad! So, yes, it was an honor, but it also meant that if any one of the guys in my squad flunked an inspection, I got the same butt chewing as the guy who flunked the inspection, and we were often disciplined to the same extent that he was.

I won't name the guy who became my cross to bear, but I will never forget him. (You remember that Johnny Cash song where he talks about stealing car parts from the factory he worked in and building a car at his house over several years…combining all those different year model parts?) Well, that was the way this guy was put together. He proved that God definitely has a sense of humor!

He wasn't very tall, not very big, and wore glasses, but he had *big feet*. He walked like a duck, and five minutes after he finished dressing and was squared away, he looked like someone had picked him up and stuck him in a clothes dryer! His bunk *always* had to be redone, and his clothes locker was *never* completely right. Those of us who had started growing whiskers were required to shave every morning. This guy had maybe three hairs on his chin, but he was required to shave! I don't know how he managed it, but he always seemed to miss one of them and would flunk inspection.

When he flunked inspection, the rest of the squad and I would draw disciplinary duty, which could range from marching around one of the parade grinders (cement lots), standing guard outside the company commanders' quarters, policing the grounds looking for trash or cigarette butts, or a host of other tedious jobs, while the rest of the company enjoyed down time!

Needless to say, this got old quick! Finally, after costing my squad another inspection, the DI came up to me and asked me what I was going to do to remedy this situation. I asked permission to take my man back to the barracks to get him squared away before the conclusion of the inspection. Permission was granted, and I took him to the barracks bathroom and shaved him.

I did a "dry" shave which meant using no water or soap, just a safety razor! As I said, he wasn't very big or strong guy, so I held on to him as I worked on his face. He was bleeding from numerous cuts as I marched him back out to our formation. He fell in line, and the DI walked up while I stood by and looked him over. By then, he had blood dripping off his chin and looked like a mess. The DI turned to me and said, "Well done, Jacobs. He looks perfect!" I finally convinced the guy that it would go a whole lot smoother if he shaved himself, and he never flunked another inspection based on a bad shave.

For the first two months, we were not allowed to use the phone, but we could receive mail and could write letters to whom we wanted. We didn't have access to any food other than what was served at the mess hall! The food was excellent, and there was no junk food. That, plus daily exercise, everybody started getting into decent shape.

Most of us smoked, and we could buy cigarettes as we needed. Like everything else in boot camp, smoking was controlled. They would announce that the smoking lamp was lit, and only then were you allowed to light up. One afternoon I found out what the penalty involved for violating the smoking lamp.

Two other guys and I were outside of the barracks by the scrubbing tables, just shooting the breeze, and we decided to light up. We had forgotten about the smoking lamp and were enjoying our smoke when one of the DIs walked by and saw us. As he walked up, we stood to attention, and he asked for our names which we provided. He then told us that the smoking lamp wasn't lit and to put out our cigarettes. We did, and he left, and we felt that we had dodged a bullet. Not!

The next day our CO (Commanding Officer) had the company fall out to the scrubbing tables. He then called the other two smoking guys and me forward and instructed us to go back into the barracks and bring out our metal clothes-washing buckets. When we got back outside, we were ordered to stand up on one of the scrubbing tables with our buckets. He then had us take out our cigarettes and light one up and begin to smoke. We did as he ordered, but then he had us put cigarette number *two* in our mouths and lighted it up, and then numbers 3, 4, 5, and 6, quickly followed suit. It was a mouthful!

This was kind of funny, but that changed when he had us put the buckets upside down over our heads and told us to really start puffing. Everybody was laughing *except us* since the three of us were doing all we could to keep from throwing up. I don't know why I didn't stop my smoking habit right then and there! The CO then went on to explain that violating the smoking lamp rule was a definite no-no which I now understood. He went on to tell us that we were expected to be aware of what was going on around us at all times, and that eventually made sense. I didn't have to be reminded of that particular rule ever again!

Boot camp was three and a half months long, and by about the sixth week, we were beginning to function as a unit. I guess I felt that it was a good thing that my father had insisted that I join a branch of the military if for no other reason than it gave me an opportunity to be part of a group. I now had to compete with my peers and see for myself how I stacked up against my age group, and even more importantly, my father wasn't there to judge my performance.

Around two months into the training, we were told that we should start giving some thought to various career paths that would be available when we completed our basic training. There were a lot of choices, and we all knew that this would be an important decision that could affect our lives for a long time.

A few other guys and I were sitting around one day, kicking around ideas about what we thought we would like to do. Out of the blue, one of the guys says that he had heard that submarines fed their sailors the best food in the entire Navy! Don't ask me why, but I started giving a lot of thought to going into the submarine program. It wasn't the food (although the promise of good food didn't hurt), but I had read up on our submarine service and found out that the crew size was small compared to that of other ships.

As basic training began to wind down, we had to make our final choice. I stuck with submarines and passed the initial qualifying tests. I was set to attend submarine school in Groton, Connecticut, and had to report at the end of November 1963.

They held a nice graduation ceremony for us when we finished Basic with a lot of parents in attendance. I was given an airplane ticket that routed me to San Antonio and then on to Connecticut. The ticket was open to allow me to have two weeks of leave before I would fly on to submarine school.

I landed in San Antonio early one evening, and since my folks had no idea when I would arrive, I decided to take a cab to the house. The cab dropped me off, and as it was dark, the house lights were on, but I could not see anyone inside. I was more nervous about ringing that doorbell than arriving at the San Diego Naval base!

I think my sister answered the door, and she let out a yell, and everyone else came running. I knew I had changed mentally, but it was also apparent that I had changed physically as well. Somehow my mother had shrunk a little bit, and My Old Man wasn't quite as intimidating as I remembered. But most of all, it was good to be home!

About three days of being home, I could tell that my father wasn't treating me as a misdirected, uninspired idiot but more as an adult. Mom still felt that she needed to tuck me in when it was time for bed and give me the sign of the cross on my forehead while she prayed for the angels to protect me. And I didn't mind a bit! To say that I enjoyed those two weeks of leave at home is an understatement. Those Navy cooks are good, but they couldn't hold a candle to my mother's cooking.

My father and I got along as well as we ever had, and I think he was proud to show me off to a lot of his friends. The fact that I smoked and he could bum a cigarette off me didn't hurt either. A couple of times, I joined my brother and sister when they went out to go dancing. I have to say that I did the Navy proud when it came to drinking beer.

The three and a half months I was away in Basic wasn't a long time, and yet, a lot happened, and a lot changed. That became clear when I met up with some of my friends who were now going to college. We were still friends, but it seemed that we didn't have a lot in common anymore. Two of them had joined the Marines, and one of them had been killed in Vietnam after being "in country" for just two months.

The two weeks at home flew by, and on November 22, 1963, my folks took me to the airport and saw me off. I flew into Dallas, where I had to change planes to go on to Connecticut. As I walked from one gate to another in the Dallas airport, I started to see people standing around a TV, crying.

I stopped and asked someone what was going on, and they told me that earlier in the day, President Kennedy had been assassinated in Dallas! When I got to my departure gate, I was told that all flights coming and going were suspended until further notice. I wasn't a political guy at 18 years of age, but even I knew this was a big deal. I was also worried that I might miss my connections and arrive late for my reporting time at submarine school. There wasn't anything I could do, so I grabbed a chair at the departure gate and settled in for the long haul. Surprisingly, the airport reopened after about two hours, and I was on my way.

With my poor math skills, I didn't qualify for nuclear boats (submarines are referred to as boats and not ships), so I would eventually be assigned to a WWII diesel boat when/if I passed the school. This was a three-month school, and the classroom portion of it was taxing and intense.

I thought that one of the more interesting aspects of the school was the water tower escape training. This part of the training included simulating an escape from a disabled submarine that was sitting on the ocean floor. The base had a tall tower that resembled a grain silo. It was about 100 feet tall and was filled with water. The tower had several pressurized compartments that had 2 doors, with one of them that opened up to the main tank.

One of the instructors would take six of us at a time, wearing our bathing suits and a life vest, to the compartment at the bottom of the tank. When everybody was inside, the door (with steel hatches) was closed, and the round compartment started flooding with water until it reached above the hatches. The compartment was then pressurized so that we could open the other hatch that opened into the tower.

What was expected of us then was that one at a time, we would take a deep breath, hold it, kneel down in the water, and step through the hatch and into the tower. Once in the tower, you grabbed a handle and inflated your life vest and then let go; the vest would start taking you up to the surface a 100 feet up! There were a few other things going on then that I don't need to explain here, but the drill was meant to show that you could handle stress, that your ears could equalize, and that you weren't claustrophobic! Believe me when I tell you that this was *stressful*, and we each had to do it several times. A few guys couldn't do it, and they washed out then and there.

I am proud to say that I passed and graduated from submarine school. I was given orders to report to the submarine USS Sennet #408 for sea duty. The boat was stationed out of the Charleston Naval Base in South Carolina. The remainder of my three and half years of my four-year enlistment was spent on the Sennet, and I had a blast while, at the same time, I served my country.

Duty on a submarine is completely different than being on a large ship like a destroyer or an aircraft carrier. Because of a lack of space, the officers and enlisted men were always physically closer to one another compared to a large ship. The duties of both enlisted and officers overlapped in a lot of areas, and that was necessary to maintain safety and carry out the mission of the boats.

Primarily our mission was to provide practice for anti-submarine detection vessels such as destroyers and other ships. The nuclear submarine force was expanding, but the old diesel boats could still provide valuable training to surface vessels. The boat I served on did combat duty during WWII, and I cannot say enough for the men who fought in that war as they served on one of these boats.

Upon my reporting to the pier where the Sennet was tied up, I had to ask the pier guard where the Sennet was moored. I gave him my orders, and he asked me where I was from. I told him Texas, and he said, "I reckon you will probably fit in with that bunch of Rebel sons-of-bitches." He then showed me the proper boat, and I reported aboard. The first time I climbed down the forward torpedo room ladder was an experience that I would never forget! The smell of diesel was everywhere, and the space was crowded beyond belief.

I found the officer of the deck and gave him my orders; I was welcomed aboard. He took me to the chief-of-the-boat (COB), who then gave me a tour of the boat and introduced me to my boss, who oversaw the torpedomen. This is where I would spend my time for the next three and a half years.

In no time, I felt at home and a part of a close-knit group of men who served as a unit. We had a diverse bunch of guys that included white, black, Filipino, and Cherokee Indian men. The pier guard didn't lie because the biggest group *were* southern rebels. These guys came from Alabama, Georgia, Tennessee, and Mississippi and were proud of their heritage. We had some interesting times when Texas played Alabama, but I held my ground!

Chapter 14

"a raft ride…"

As I mentioned, my boat was active during WWII, and it was built around 1938 – 1940. It looked nothing like the nuclear boats that now make up the submarine fleet today. The Sennet was powered by four diesel engines as opposed to the nuclear reactor that powers nuclear boats. The Sennet was built to run on top of the water until it reached its destination or target, then, she would dive beneath the surface and operate below the water.

Nuclear submarines (they are referred to as "Nukes") are basically designed to operate below the water and do not spend much time on the surface. I don't want to bore you with all of the differences between Nukes and diesel boats, but in the final analysis, I just want to point out that, though they were both submarines, they were quite different, and the crews that manned them were different.

The crew on a Nuke had to be prepared to be under the water for long periods of time, while we diesel boat guys knew that we had to "surface" regularly so we could run our diesel engines. It takes a special mindset to remain in close quarters and not see daylight or night for weeks on end. I was happy to be right where I was and never looked back.

It didn't take long to confirm the talk about submariners having the best food in the Navy. One time while we were docked in a New England port, our cook somehow managed to have crates of live lobster waiting on the pier as we arrived! There were surface ships also docked by us, and those guys could not believe their eyes when they saw those lobsters. There is an old saying, "Don't mess with the cook!" and that tip was upheld by everyone, including our officers.

You might have heard about military pilots having to earn their "wings" by qualifying on their planes, well, submariners had the same requirement. For a submariner to be awarded his "Dolphins," he had to be qualified on the boat. Everyone was given a year to qualify and earn their Dolphins, or they were kicked out of the submarine service and re-assigned to a different ship in the fleet.

Qualifying meant that a sailor would have to start at the front of the boat (the forward torpedo room) and go all the way to the rear of the boat (the aft torpedo room) and identify every valve, whether water or air, or hydraulic, and explain its function and purpose. You were also required to identify *every* feature in all eleven compartments and explain what you would do to secure the room in the event of a water leak, fire, or other catastrophe.

Within a week of reporting for duty, I was given a schedule to work through the qualification process. This consisted of asking the senior person in a particular room if you could stand his watch with him. He would then begin to familiarize you with the room. You went back to him again and again until you had the functions down pat. This required that you stood your own watch and then stood another one, which left you time for only about 4 hours of sleep.

Periodically the Chief-of-the-boat would ask to see my schedule to make sure that I was on track to complete my qualification within the one-year time frame. If a sailor fell behind, days off were spent on board until he was caught up! I earned my Dolphins within the one-year time frame, and the beautiful sterling silver dolphin pin was pinned on me by the boat Commander during a special ceremony in front of the entire crew. It was one of the proudest moments of my life!

There was a tradition that you had not truly earned your Dolphins until you "drank them" at an informal ceremony usually held at a bar. The legal drinking age in Charleston was eighteen, but checking sailors' identifications was practically unheard of! A bunch of us went to one of our favorite bars for the informal ceremony.

The tradition dictated that a beer glass was filled with various alcoholic beverages, and the dolphin pin was dropped into the bottom of the glass. The newly qualified sailor then drank the entire glass of booze until he caught the dolphin pin with his teeth. This signified an emptied glass.

So, I qualified again and again and again! I wanted to be sure that I was truly qualified. They quit putting the dolphin pin in the glass after about the third qualifier since someone in the past had to be rushed to the hospital because he had swallowed the pin. Wow, talk about a major hangover; I think it lasted for three days.

Now, with having the burden of qualifying for my Dolphins over, I was finally part of the crew. We alternated our time docked at our home base in Charleston… performing upkeep on the boat and living in a barracks. Married men lived off base, and single men could choose to live off base as well, but our pay didn't include housing as the married sailors' did. I lived in the barracks until about the last year of my enlistment.

When we were not in Charleston, we were at sea, generally cruising to join up with a group of ships and participate in simulated war maneuvers. Since we were based on the East coast, we stayed on the Atlantic Ocean and the Caribbean Sea, and we spent a lot of time in Guantanamo Bay, Cuba.

I liked Guantanamo because we would be there for six weeks or so, and then we would visit Jamaica, Bermuda, or even Curacao, Venezuela. Haiti was off limits because of the danger presented by the widespread practice of Voodoo on the island. Apparently, an American tourist had once been killed while engaging in some sort of Voodoo ceremony. The Navy felt that it was in their best interest that we didn't lose any sailors to some sort of shrunken head ritual! Amen to that, Brother!

I got to know several ports in Jamaica, including Kingston, Montego Bay, and Ocho Rios, and we always had a great time there. But one of my most *memorable* trips was when we visited Curacao. We were at Guantanamo Bay when our captain (we sometimes referred to him as "The Skipper") informed us that we had been granted a rare honor. We would be the first US Navy vessel to be granted permission to visit Curacao in the past fifteen years! We would be representing the United States government, and we were expected to be on our best behavior.

We planned to be in port for a whole weekend, beginning on a Friday and pulling back out to sea on Monday morning. I was fortunate to be on deck as we approached the entrance to the port area, and the town came into my view. It was *beautiful* as it lay nestled on the hillside, with whitewashed houses and red roofs overlooking the crystal-clear deep waters of the bay!

The docks and marinas were filled with all types of watercraft, and as I later learned, this was a large merchant-vessel port with ships from all over the *world*. These large tankers were anchored out, away from the docks, waiting for their turn to tie up and unload their cargo.

The town had prepared a dock to be designated for our arrival, and there was a large contingent of dignitaries waiting on us as we tied up. The Skipper wanted to make a good impression and had part of our crew in dress whites to man the rails of the deck. We arrived and were treated to a band that played their national anthem and then played ours, and it was impressive all the way around! Once the festivities concluded and the boat was secured, the entire crew, including officers were brought to the deck for a briefing of how we would conduct ourselves while on liberty in town.

Our Executive Officer began by reminding us that we were guests of a foreign country. He emphasized how we should remain mindful of the customs that may differ from our own. He then went on to tell us of a very specific prohibition that he had been made aware of by the local law enforcement authorities.

He told us that Curacao had a 100 acre fenced compound located on the outskirts of town. This was populated by girls from all over the world who lived in individual cabins and sold their services to interested men. What was stressed was that the compound wasn't policed beyond the entrance gate, making it sort of a no-man's land. We were told that under no circumstances were we to go to the compound! The Skipper then added a few words again, reminding us that we were representing the U.S. Government and, just as important, the United States Navy!

It was a little early to head for the compound, so several of us decided to go downtown and check out the sights. I was immediately impressed with the cleanliness of the city, and the local people were friendly and helpful. Being sailors, we were soon sitting in a large bar that had a good crowd of locals, merchant seamen, and various tourists. I was sitting and drinking a beer when I suddenly heard someone talking in Dutch/Flemish at a table next to ours. I looked over and saw a group of merchant seamen drinking and talking in my old language! I couldn't believe it, so I got up and went over to their table.

They stopped talking and looked up at me with that curious "What's going on?" look, and then I spoke to them in Flemish. Mouths dropped open, and they were speechless until one of them asked me who I was and where I was from. I told them, and before anyone from my bunch knew what was going on, we were all sitting together and having a good time! Who would have figured that I would come across old countrymen so far from my birthplace in such an unlikely spot?

We went to a couple of other bars, and by then, it was late enough to get a couple of taxis, and we headed to the compound (What did you expect?). We were dropped off at the front gate, where some guards had a small building, and we were given a list of warnings about what we should or shouldn't do once we went in. They counted the number of guys in our group, made a note of that on a sheet, and opened the gate.

We split up into three groups of twos and took different paths that were lit with lamps in front of small cabins. Girls who were not busy stood or sat outside their cabin if they were available, but they were not aggressively trying to get anyone inside. We spent time walking around, and one of us would stop and begin to talk to one of the girls. It didn't really matter if they spoke English or not. Everybody seemed to be able to communicate well enough to come to an agreement. Funny how that works!

After all the talk about what a bad place this was supposed to be, I found it comfortable (don't laugh) and interesting. There was one brief incident where a guy (not one of us), who had way too much to drink, got loud and abusive with one of the girls. Two guys came out of nowhere and had a quiet conversation with him, then walked him toward the entrance and out of the compound. Apparently, there was some private security group that protected the girls and made sure they were taken care of. Other than that incident, everyone seemed well-behaved, and I realized that you couldn't call 911 if your alligator mouth overloaded your hummingbird butt!

It was no exaggeration when we were told that there were girls from all over the world at the compound. The girls that I saw seemed to be of age and were probably in their late teens to late twenties. On our next liberty trip into town, some of us were sitting in a bar, and we asked the bartender for some history on the place. He then explained that some of the girls were there to make a living and were natives of Venezuela. A lot of the foreign girls were there to work off debt for their families!

Apparently, there are parts of the world where the father of a family in debt could send his daughter here, and through her income, she could pay off the debt. Even though we were told that there was no stigma attached to this arrangement, I would not have been surprised to learn that the girls themselves had a different viewpoint about the whole deal. During the time period (2022) that I wrote this book, human trafficking has been constantly in the news. I don't know how much that had to do with the girls' presence at this camp, but looking back now, I imagine it played a large part in some of the girls being there.

All in all, the crew behaved appropriately as ordered by the fleet command. There was one *exception:* our Captain was brought back to the boat in handcuffs, *drunk* as a skunk, wearing *wet* clothes, and still wanting to *fight* the police who had him in custody! Apparently, the Skipper had been booked into a fancy hotel in town, and during the evening, he had been required to attend several social functions, which all involved the drinking of alcohol.

The last function took place at a different hotel, and our Skipper was being escorted by the wife of one of the town bigwigs. We were never told why our Skipper decided that he and his escort should jump into the hotel pool with their clothes on, but he did. She had not signed on with his idea, and that was the start of the problem. Needless to say, he was deposited at our boat and taken on board, where he remained in his private room for a day or two. He was our hero!

You should have picked up by now that there was a lot of drinking going on, and I was doing more than my share. Whether we were on liberty in a foreign port or at home or some other port on the eastern seacoast of the United States, we were drinking! When we went to Cuba or hit one of the towns in Jamaica or Bermuda, we always bought liquor by the *case* to bring back to Charleston. It was duty-free, which meant we paid no taxes, and it was cheap. Those that drank, including the officers, would stock up, and we found that we could store a lot of booze in some of the *torpedo tubes*. This was common knowledge around the navy base, and unfortunately, it came back to bite us on one of our trips.

We were coming back from Cuba and had stocked up on a boat load (ha ha) of cases of liquor that we had shoved in our forward torpedo tubes. We were getting close to Charleston when the Skipper received a radio message that we would rendezvous outside of Charleston and pick up an Admiral (who needed some sea time to keep his pay at a higher rate.) Sure enough, we picked up this guy outside of the entrance to the port and then turned around and headed back out to deep water.

For him to keep his sea duty certification, the Admiral had to be on board *as we dove* under the water and ran *submerged* for a required period of time. Needless to say, no one on board was happy with this clown since we were all looking forward to getting home. It took a couple of hours for us to reach deep enough water where we could safely submerge, and we dove when we got there. We ran submerged for a while when this guy told our Skipper that he wanted to dummy fire some of the torpedo tubes. WTF??

The Skipper told him no problem, we could fire the aft tubes and informed the aft torpedo room to ready the tubes. What happens when you dummy fire the tubes is that the tubes are flooded with water so that you can open the outer door, and when ready, a blast of highly compressed air is then shot into the tube, expelling the water. The Admiral didn't say a word as the aft tubes were fired.

Once the drill was completed and the tubes were drained, the Admiral turned to our Captain and said to him, "Now, let's fire the forward tubes." The SOB *knew* we had precious cargo in those tubes!

There was nothing we could do, so orders were given to flood the forward tubes, open the doors, and blast the water out of the tubes, one by one.

We could *hear* the tinkling of bottles as they were shot out of the tubes into the ocean! It was a good thing for that Admiral that he suffered no pressing medical problems, such as difficulty in breathing because that sucker was not going to get any mouth-to-mouth from anyone on board our boat! (I think we were close to committing mutiny!)

There were a lot of practical jokers on our boat, and no one was safe. The unqualified new guys were, without a doubt, an easy target, and so they bore the brunt of most of the jokes. Woe to the guy that let the joking get under his skin because once you complained, there was *no* letting up.

Some of the pranks were on the edge of crossing a line, and one example occurred while we were docked in Charleston. It was during the summer, and we were pulling maintenance on the exterior of the boat. I was a junior petty officer in charge of the "topside gang," which consisted of low-level seaman-grade sailors. The guys were wire-brushing the hull from the top of the deck over the side to the water line. To reach the sides and the top of the hull to the water, we used a modified raft. It was big enough to have three or four men in it, along with an air compressor and tools. It had ropes attached to the front and back of the raft, and guys would take turns being on the raft while two sailors were on deck and would position the raft by pulling it along the side as needed and then tying it off while the men worked.

The naval base was located on the Santee Cooper River that was a couple of miles from flowing into the Atlantic Ocean. The river had a strong tide flowing out and coming in, and on this afternoon, it was flowing out at a good clip. My guys somehow managed at one point to have three new guys on the raft working over the side. The two guys on top decided it would be a good day for a raft ride down the river, so they loosened the ropes to the raft and turned it loose! It took no time for the raft to head down river with my guys waving their arms and hollering their heads off.

The Coast Guard was notified, and they launched a rescue craft to retrieve the rafters. It wasn't hard to find them since boats and ships along the river were reporting the sighting of a raft with men on it waving shirts at everyone they passed. This incident made it all the way to the base commander's office, and our Skipper had to go see him in person. I don't know how he did it, but he managed to convince the base CO that the lines had simply come unhooked and it was just an unfortunate accident.

When Skipper got back to the boat, I was called to his office, and I wasn't nearly as successful as he had been in convincing the base CO that it had been an accident. When he finished chewing on my butt, it was clear to me that there would be no further raft rides. By week's end, everyone on base knew it had been Sennet sailors, and they had to admit that this prank was in the top three! Running close second to this raft prank was one I personally think should have been a contender for number 1. This prank involved a metal vise located in the forward torpedo room....

Our boat had pulled into Bermuda during the busy tourist season, and the Skipper had been approached about allowing visitors to tour the boat. It wasn't uncommon for submarines to host tours, and we had done it before. So he agreed, and we were told to make it ready for visitors. The boat would be available beginning at noon and remain open until four in the afternoon. I was part of the duty watch that day, so I had to remain on board along with the other sailors on duty.

The way the tour was organized was important to the success of the prank. Civilians would be brought on deck and then allowed to go below deck and walk through the interior of the boat from front to back. To go down below deck required climbing down a straight tube on a metal ladder that brought you into the forward torpedo room. When enough people came down the ladder and gathered in the room, the tour began.

The tour ended in the aft torpedo room, where a ladder led back up to the deck. Crewmen who were appointed as guides would take the group through the boat and provide them with information regarding each room. What was noteworthy was that you couldn't *see* much of the room until you were near the bottom and stepped off the ladder. The forward torpedo room was one of the longest compartments on the boat, and it had metal tables in front of the torpedo tube doors, and the tables had a large metal vise bolted to the top.

We had a new guy one day that had *just* reported for duty on the boat, and this was his first trip on the Sennet. He was a little on the arrogant side, and he seemed to know everything there was to know about everything. In other words, the perfect target!

It was about 15 minutes before 12:00, and a large group of tourists were already lined up on deck waiting for the tours to begin. Believe it or not, we always had a lot of women and kids that wanted to do the tour. Four of us were in the forward room, and we called the new guy to come up to assist us when we started the tour. He said he was on his way.

To set the trap, one of the guys put his thumbs in the vise, and we closed it just enough so that his thumbs were squeezed and held in the vise. When our target came into the room, the guy with his thumbs in the vise began yelling that it was all he could *stand* and that he couldn't take any more! We had forty dollars lying beside him on the table, and we were teasing him that he only had two and a half turns on the vise. By then, the target was there, and he wanted to know what was going on.

We told him that we had all put up ten dollars to see who could take the most turns on the vise, and at that moment, three and a quarter turns was winning. We let the guy out of the vise, and the two turns on the vise didn't seem like all that much. The mark then took out ten bucks, placed it on the table, and demanded *his* turn, all the while telling us that he would *easily* win the bet. By now, it was almost 12:00, and the tours were about to start. He put his thumbs in the vise, the vise was closed, and it was cinched down on his thumbs. He started yelling that he was at three and a half turns but that it was all he could take! His thumbs were locked in, and he demanded that we turn him loose.

We took the money off the table, left his ten-dollar bill lying there, undid his pants, and dropped them down to his ankles. This left him standing there in his shorts with his thumbs still in the vise! He was yelling and cursing as we walked out of the room, just as the tourists started coming down the ladder!

His yelling brought the duty officer to the compartment, and he had to work his way through a bunch of confused and unsure civilians so he could turn him loose. I imagine the civilians were wondering just what kind of sailors manned a submarine! Especially with that ten-dollar bill lying on the table in front of him! You know, he was never quite as arrogant from then on, and he remained awfully suspicious if he ever came up on several of us just standing around.

As much as we would tease and harass our shipmates, we stuck together when it came to outsiders. This became evident when we were in port in Ft. Lauderdale, Florida. Several of us decided we would go ashore and visit one of the bars off the beaten path. We felt that we had found the right place when we walked in and could barely see the bar because of poor lighting and a thick cloud of cigarette smoke in the air. We stepped up to the bar and ordered draft beer. All of us in the group were white except for our cook, who was black.

It was early afternoon, and the place was not really busy except for a few rednecks that looked like they spent quite a bit of time there. The guy behind the bar stopped us and told us that we could stay, but the "nigger" had to go! I was dumbfounded, and the other guys were just as surprised. The cook's name was Ward, and he turned to us and told us he would catch us later.

We told Ward he wasn't going anywhere, and then we told the bartender that he would serve us all or he would serve none of us. He calmly told us he wasn't allowed to serve "niggers" and that was that! We left and found another place that was much more accommodating. It was ironic that Ward, who had almost twenty years in the Navy, could serve his country but could be denied service in a public bar.

As we drank, we talked about it, and Ward told us that it wasn't the first time that he had been faced with that; he had learned that it did no good to argue with a *fool*. The more we drank, the more we became convinced that *we* needed to go back to that bar and set things right. Ward talked us out of it, and I learned another valuable lesson that the Rev. Martin King later referred to in one of his speeches. *The content of a man's character matters a hell of a lot more than the color of his skin!*

I knew I was drinking a lot, but all my friends were there with me. It hit me that my drinking was out of control when several of us would get a half-pint of whiskey and kill it first thing in the morning before reporting for duty when we were in port.

One morning I was in the barracks bathroom standing at the urinal when one of my close friends staggered in and began to use the urinal next to me. He started groaning as he peed and was gripping the pipe at the top of the urinal, obviously in pain. I asked him what was wrong, and he told me to look down at the bottom of the urinal.

I did and saw that he was peeing *blood*! I told him we needed to get him to a doctor, but he told me he had already seen one a few weeks earlier, and he had been told then that he needed to stop drinking. He didn't feel it was time yet and that he would quit later. Sadly, he ended up in the hospital and was eventually separated from our boat. I wish I could say that this incident caused me to stop drinking, but that didn't happen. Several weeks later, I slowed way down when I was introduced to a friend of a friend's girlfriend. My life was about to change forever!

Chapter 15

"dogs and sailors stay off the yard."

Any young, single sailor in a Navy town had the deck stacked against him when it came to meeting a single girl. Most girls my age still lived at home with their parents while they went to college, and they had their own circle of friends that they knew from school. In addition, a lot of young sailors did their best to live up (or down) to the general reputation associated with being sailors. I could personally identify with that.

I certainly did my best to uphold the saying "drunk as a sailor" and everything that went with that lifestyle. Some towns were more open about their dislike for sailors than others, and I guess the one that stands out in my mind was Norfolk, Virginia. We had to dry dock there for repairs one time and naturally pulled liberty into town. On one return trip to the base, one of my friends told us that he had seen a sign at a house that read, "Dogs and sailors stay off the yard!"

So when my friend Lennie asked me one day if I wanted to go on a double date to a park nearby, I was *more* than eager to go! It was a warm Saturday afternoon, and we picked up the girls right before lunch and headed for the park. They had prepared sandwiches, and we stopped and picked up sodas and chips. My date's name was Joyce. She was a beautiful young woman, and I didn't know what to do with myself.

We ended up playing on the adult swings and just generally had a good time. The afternoon flew by, and we dropped the girls off around six o'clock, and we went back to the barracks. On the way back, Lennie asked me what I thought about Joyce, and I told him that I liked her. He told me that he would talk to his girlfriend later and let me know how Joyce felt about *me*.

When I got back to the barracks, I thought about going back out, finding some of my friends, and doing a little drinking, but I decided to stay in that night instead. There was always a card game going on in the barracks, and I played cards for a while and then went to my room. Two men were assigned to a room, and my roommate was out that night, so I had the place to myself.

I cleaned up, hit my bunk, and started thinking about my date that day. The first thing that hit me was that I had not had even one alcoholic beverage all day! The second thing to hit me was that I had *really* enjoyed myself and hoped that Joyce had as well. For the first time in a long time, I felt that I had experienced what a normal day should be like when enjoying the company of a girl and just having fun.

Up to this point, I kind of danced around the lifestyle I was living as a sailor. Let me say right now that I am talking about *me* here. There were *lots* of sailors that didn't live the way I had chosen to spend my spare time.

The Charleston Navy base, like every other military base, had a front gate manned with security guards. This was the main entry point to the base and was also the way you left the base. Once you stepped out of the front gate, you were no longer on a military installation but entered the civilian world. Military towns may not like sailors, soldiers, etc., but they loved our money and did everything they could to get us to spend it at their establishments.

In Charleston, the street that led up to the main gate was called "The Strip." It had a regular street name, but I don't remember what it was because we all called it "The Strip." You only had to walk a few feet out of the gate, and you could sit down in a bar. There were dry cleaners, a laundromat, tattoo parlors, and various other businesses up and down the street.

When I first got to Charleston, I was already eighteen years old, so I went into one of the bars and ordered a draft beer. It was my first time to legally order a beer, and it felt pretty darn good! I really didn't know anybody on my boat yet, so I was by myself. The bartender was a pregnant woman who was noticeably well along and probably would have been much more comfortable sitting at home.

It was early afternoon, and there were a few other guys in the place. Three or four barstools down from me was a guy who had been there long enough to be drunk. He was giving the barmaid a hard time and kept asking for a refill of his beer. She refused and told him he already had enough and that he needed to leave.

Things got ugly, and he started to cuss her out. I was thinking I would have to intervene so that she didn't get hurt. Before I had a chance to stand up, she came around the bar and walked up to him, punched him in the face, and knocked him completely off the barstool to the floor! She then grabbed him by the collar of his shirt, dragged him out the front door, and left him on the sidewalk. So much for my saving this damsel in distress!

I looked around at the other guys, and they all seemed to have found something interesting to look at other than the front door. As I finished my beer, she came over and asked me if I was ready for a refill. There was no way I was going to say anything other than "Yes, mam!"

I want to share this incident so that you, the reader, will have a flavor for the atmosphere that I became a part of when I arrived in Charleston. Remember that while I was in basic training and later in submarine school, I didn't get a chance to spend too much time off the military base, so this whole environment was actually new to me.

Up until I met Joyce, my time off was spent partying with my friends. Sometimes a few of us would drive to Savanah, Georgia or to the tracks around Charleston and watch the dirt track races. The races were fun, but the fights that sometimes followed after one of the races were even *more* entertaining.

It goes without saying that we made sure that we had plenty of beer along when we hit the road. I don't know why I was *never* stopped by the police and arrested for DWI, but I never was. We also had a favorite bar located in North Charleston, which we claimed as our own. It wasn't on the strip, and it catered to local people as well as sailors. There were women, who were also regulars, and we all became good friends. But it wasn't exactly a place that I would have picked to find my future soulmate.

A few days after that first date, Lennie came up to me and told me that Joyce had enjoyed our outing as well as I had. Lennie asked me if I wanted to go to his girlfriend's house the following Saturday for a cook-out with some of their friends. That included Joyce, so I naturally said, "Yes."

Saturday came around, and when Lennie and I arrived at the mobile home park, there were already several couples there with some young kids running around playing. A barbeque pit was smoking. We had brought some beer, so we were welcomed and introduced around.

Joyce had walked up, and we had started talking when a little boy came over and called her, "Mommy!" Joyce introduced me to her son, John, and then told me that she also had a daughter named Cathy, who was a year younger than John. Well, that was a surprise, but we didn't get a chance to talk further because she had to go over and help the women start putting the food on the table. The hamburgers and hot dogs were ready, so we all fixed a plate and started eating.

John was sitting with the other kids, and Joyce came over, carrying Cathy, who was around fourteen months old. She was a beautiful little girl with wavy, dark brown hair. While we ate, I learned that John and

Cathy (Catherine) had both been born in 1965. John in February and Cathy in December, the day after Christmas.

Joyce was still married, but there were significant problems that they had been dealing with even before the kids were born. At this time, her husband was on a large ship on a Mediterranean run which involved docking at various ports in different countries. Lennie's girlfriend *knew* one particular sailor who was on the ship with Joyce's husband.

This particular guy had passed on some information that seemed to indicate that Joyce's husband was now acting more like a *single* guy than a married man. Marriage in the military is tough, especially when you figure in the long separations because of deployment…leaving all the responsibilities to that *one* person while the spouse is gone. Having already spent three years of my four-year enlistment, I had seen firsthand how hard it was for some of my married friends to maintain a relationship, and I had already decided that I didn't want that kind of life.

Not long after the barbeque, our boat left Charleston for a three-week run, and it gave me time to think about how I felt about Joyce and the whole situation. I really liked her, but I was unsure of how I felt about two children immediately becoming part of my life. To tell the truth, it was more than just a *little* scary to be around small kids and all the care that they required.

When we returned to Charleston, I still had mixed feelings, but I knew that I wanted to see Joyce again. When I called, she invited me over to her house but said that Cathy wasn't feeling well, so we would need to have supper there as opposed to going out. This was the first time that it would be just the *two* of us, along with her kids. Throughout the afternoon, I watched as she cared for her children, especially Cathy, and I could see that she was a good momma. We made small talk during the meal and generally enjoyed ourselves. Once again, it felt so good to just sit around, enjoying the company of a nice woman (and yes, her kids) without drinking and raising hell!

Once the kids were put down to go to sleep, we sat down and continued talking about our lives, and it was late when I left. I remember that while we talked, she would suddenly get up and tell me that Cathy was fussing; she would go check on her even though I hadn't heard a thing!

This was the first time that I witnessed the God-given ability that mothers possess when they have children. Their hearing is enhanced, along with the amazing ability to see out of the *back* of their heads!

When sailors are on an extended sea tour, they can send and receive letters, but it takes a while for the mail to catch up. Just as Joyce had heard about her husband and his activities from a friend of a friend, her husband had also received information that *she* was seeing someone. He had written her, and he asked her what was going on. She told me about the letter while we were at a local park, and I asked her what she planned to do. She told me that she wasn't going to lie to him. She planned to write back to him to tell him that when he got home, they would need to face some serious decisions. One thing I learned about Joyce was that she was always straightforward.

She then went on to tell me that, in *her* mind, her marriage was over, but that she would *never* give up her children! I knew that she was telling me in no uncertain terms that if *our* relationship went forward, it would *include* John and Cathy!

It was the spring of 1967, and Vietnam was really heating up. I was due to finish my enlistment on August the 13th, but rumors were flying that enlistments might be *extended* because of the war. I couldn't understand how I, as a torpedo man on a submarine, could contribute to a ground war in Vietnam, but by then, I had seen firsthand how our military brass could screw things up. I wasn't stressed about it, but the uncertainty of my future had me worried.

Joyce and I continued to see each other, and then one day, she told me that her husband was due to return. By now, we both had strong feelings for one another, and I knew that her marriage was in serious trouble. I was due to make a six-week run to Guantanamo Bay, so whatever took place between them would be while I was gone.

That was a long six weeks, and I was anxious to find out what had taken place between Joyce and her husband. Unfortunately, when we arrived, I was stuck with the weekend duty, so I had to stay on the boat. But my friend, Lennie, was off, and he went to see his girlfriend. He returned to the boat the next day, and he told me that his girlfriend had said that Joyce asked her husband to move back onto the base. Joyce had also asked Lennie to tell me that it would be better for me not to call. She said that she and her husband were talking and trying to figure out their future but that she would contact me later.

Several weeks went by, and one day I received a call while working on the boat that I had a visitor at the head of the pier. Civilians were not allowed to go onto the pier, so I walked down, and I could see that Joyce was waiting there. We were both nervous, and we didn't say anything as I walked with her to the parking lot to her car. She started by telling me that she was *sorry* that she had left me in the dark but that she had thought it was best that she focus on the state of her marriage.

She then went on to tell me that she felt that her marriage was over, but at her husband's request, she had agreed to take John and Cathy and move back to Philadelphia, which was her hometown. This would give her time to give further thought to what she wanted to do without me being around. I was surprised at how hard the news hit me, and I told her how I felt.

She admitted that it was hard for her too but still felt that she needed to take the time to determine the future for herself and her children. There was nothing left for me to say because she was right. She knew that I was getting close to leaving the military and that I was planning on going back to Texas.

Before she could leave Charleston, Joyce was going to have to sell the house trailer that she was living in; there was no way to know how much time that would take. We talked a few times on the phone in the following weeks, and one day it was time for me to report to a discharge company barracks, where I stayed until my discharge day. I had given Joyce my parents' home address, and she was still in the process of selling her trailer when I left Charleston in August of 1967 and returned to San Antonio.

Chapter 16

"I wrote back"

I arrived in San Antonio and took a few days off to relax as I settled back into my old room at my mom and dad's house. My brother, Ralph, had now joined the Navy. He was gone, so I had our old bedroom all to myself. My sister still lived at home, and she was working for USAA in San Antonio. I had no job prospects, but my father approached me about working for him at the bakery where he had started when he first immigrated here.

He was now the head mechanical engineer, and he had a job opening. I had nothing else going for me, so I agreed to take the job. I had concerns about working for him based on our relationship while I was growing up, but we were both determined to give it our best shot.

I guess that no matter the age, a son will always be, in the eyes of the father, someone that needs constant tutoring and guidance. It didn't matter that he and I could go to a bar and drink a beer together or that he could "bum" a cigarette off me; when it came to the job, I had to *prove* I could change a lightbulb without supervision! *Seriously!*

There were four of us working for him at the bakery, and one day he told one of the other guys and me to go to a different part of the bakery and change some burned-out light bulbs in the high ceiling. We left and got a ladder and new bulbs, and we headed out to change the bulbs. Since the ceiling bulbs had wire mesh covers, we first needed a screwdriver to remove the covers. So I went back to the shop to get the screwdriver, and when I got back, my father was there.

He asked me why I hadn't taken the screwdriver with me when we started out. I wanted to point out to him that the guy who was with me, who had been working there *a lot* longer than I had, had not thought of it either, but I said nothing.

This was a tall ceiling, and our step ladder was a twenty-footer. We set the ladder, and as I started to climb it, he stopped me and told me that the ladder wasn't in the right position. I got down and moved the ladder, and started to climb again when he asked me if I had the screwdriver with me. I had put it into my pants pocket so that I had both hands free to climb the ladder, so I told him that, yep, I had it covered.

I finally got to the top and started to unscrew the cover, and of course, I dropped one of the screws. The next thing I heard was him calling out to me that I needed to be more careful. (You remember me mentioning that I inherited some of his and his father's tempers?) I came down the ladder, handed him the screwdriver, and went back to the shop. Sometime later, he came in and told me that we were going to have to talk, and I agreed.

That evening after work, he and I went to a café, and we ordered a beer and sat down to talk. He started by telling me that I had made him *look bad* in front of the other guy, and in turn, I asked him if he had given any thought to how he had made *me feel* in front of the other guy .

Neither one of us said anything for a little while, then we both agreed that it wasn't going to work. He admitted that he wanted me to be like him but that he knew that I was different and that I would never make a career of working at a bakery. I told him how *proud* I was of him for what he had achieved working his way from janitor to being responsible for all the machinery in that bakery and several others, but he was *right:* I wouldn't spend the rest of my life working in a bakery. For the first time, he and I talked as equals, and I told him that I would start looking for another job.

A few days after my father and I had our talk, I heard on the radio that the San Antonio Police Department was advertising for police officer recruits. They were looking to fill a training class that would begin in February of 1968. They were also providing incentives for veterans who applied, so I decided to apply.

The initial screening test was in December of 1967 and was held in the basement of the downtown police department. It started at six o'clock in the evening, and I guess there were probably two hundred men that showed up. The basement was where the roll calls were held at the beginning of the shift, so there were tables and chairs for everyone. If I remember correctly, the exam was set for two hours, and we were told that we would be given a break while the exams were scored. Then, we would be brought back into the assembly room. I went through the exam and was finished with about twenty minutes to spare on the clock. We were allowed to leave to go to the cafeteria and wait until we were called back in.

Twenty minutes after the last guy had finished, we were called back in to hear the results. The man in charge announced that when our name was called, we could get up and leave, and we would be contacted within three days. He then started calling names, and the guys were leaving the room. He kept calling, and I was getting really nervous, wondering how I could have possibly flunked this basic test! More guys got up and left, and when he finished, there were about sixty of us left in the room. Man, I was devastated. The test had seemed so easy, and I just *knew* that I had done well.

When the door closed on the last guy, the man turned to us and said, "Congratulations, you have all passed the test!" All sixty of us let out a *huge* breath and began clapping. But probably, many of us would have gladly strangled that guy. He went on to tell us that those who *had not* passed would be receiving a letter thanking them for their interest within the next three days.

Everyone then settled back in their chairs, and the man at the podium (who I later learned was Sgt. Guy Buckelew of the Training Bureau) explained that we had cleared the first hurdle but that there remained many more ahead. We were told that over the next few weeks, we would be sent to doctors to check our physical condition, complete background checks that would include contacting our neighbors and employers, and taking a standard psychiatric exam. (Remember the woman who lived next door and witnessed some of my escapades? When they contacted *her*, she thought it was a practical joke!)

The last hurdle was an appearance before an *oral board* made up of a member of the training academy, two high-ranking police officers, and a representative from the city personnel office. Sgt. Buckelew concluded his presentation by telling us that if *half* of us made it through the process, they would consider it a success!

I was still working at the bakery for my father, but the word soon got around that I was trying out for the police department. It turned out that one of the guys in our shop had tried out for the department, and he had not made it. He told me that he was rejected because of an eyesight issue. Having just finished four years in the military, I really wasn't too worried about passing any physicals. I was more concerned about the *emotional* testing because of my *temper*. I had heard rumors that during the oral board, one of their aims was to see if they could get you to lose your temper. If that happened, it was almost a guarantee that you were finished.

It was the beginning of January when I received my first letter from Joyce, postmarked in Philadelphia. My mother usually brought in the mail, and when I got in that evening from work, she had this questioning look on her face when she handed me the letter. To her credit, she didn't ask me any questions, and I just said it was from a friend back in Charleston. (The "friend" had a nice handwriting that was evident from the front of the envelope).

I opened it when I got to my bedroom (another giveaway that I am sure my mother picked up on), and I found myself to be nervous as we all got out. After asking how I had been doing, she began telling me about what was going on with her. She and her husband had separated, and after selling their mobile home, she and the kids had moved back to Philadelphia and were living in an apartment. The Navy was still sending her a check for housing and maintenance, and this allowed her to be a full-time mom. She went on to tell me that she had asked for a divorce from her husband, but he was refusing to go along. She also said that she missed me and she would welcome a letter if I was inclined to write to her.

Roughly five months had passed since I had last seen and spoken with Joyce. I had gone to some dances with friends, but there was nothing even remotely serious going on with anyone else. I had certainly thought of her often, but since I didn't know her address, I had accepted the fact that there was nothing I could do unless I heard from *her*. But now, I had the letter…and I wrote back! Of course, I had to tell my mother and father about her and that she was in the middle of a divorce. I also told them about the kids. And they were *not* thrilled! Joyce and I started writing back and forth, and that had to suffice for the time being.

In the middle of January, I was notified that I had been accepted into the police academy and that I would begin their sixteen-week training regimen the first week of February. I was excited at being accepted, but my father was even *happier* because I think he had probably been under *more* of a strain than I had been in our working relationship.

Chapter 17

"...you're not finished until the paperwork is done."

The first day of our official start of training was Orientation. This included finding out where we could park and familiarizing ourselves with downtown San Antonio. In 1968, the Academy was in the basement of the Police Department in the middle of town.

The Orientation included us being introduced to the training staff and to each other. There were 34 of us that started, and I believe that about 85% of us were veterans, recently discharged. We had black, brown, and white males, no females. Policing was still generally a man's world in 1968, although there were several women who *were* on the force, but none of them worked in a "marked" police car (cars that had the police logo on the doors) responding to dispatched calls in uniform.

I should have mentioned that in addition to passing the basic entrance qualifying test, and the physical and background tests, you also had to be at least 5'7 inches tall and 21 years old. If you were not 21, you had to turn 21 by graduation day.

A guy named Billy was the youngest guy in our class, but he would turn 21 by the time of graduation. However, besides being the youngest, he wasn't a veteran, so he wasn't used to a lot of the *teasing* that went on around a bunch of guys. He was short and stocky, and several of us kept looking at him, teasing him that there was *no way* he was 5'7! One day when a few of us were sitting around, we asked Billy how he had managed to pass the height requirement. He finally admitted to us that he was just shy of 5'7.

So how did he pass the height requirement? On the day we were scheduled to take the physical, we were given time to arrive. Billy and his mother left home early, went to the gym, and he spent a long-time hanging upside down on one of those inverter tables! His mother drove so that Billy could lie down on the back seat until he had to walk in and get measured. They measured him twice and pronounced him 5'7! He wanted the job in the *worst way*. He turned out to be a very good police officer *and* a good sport.

As we settled into the sixteen-week training, I found myself starting to enjoy myself, and I found that I *was attracted* to the field of Policing. I initially applied for the job as a way of escaping the job of working with/for my father, but now, as the training progressed, I began to feel that this was something I could do for the rest of my life.

As in the Navy, I was part of a group dedicated to serving and fulfilling a common goal or cause. The physical training instructors here tried to simulate military boot camp, they would get in your face, scream and yell, and poke you in the chest, but they didn't even get close to military boot camp! Some of the non-veterans thought that verbal abuse was the *worst* thing they had ever experienced. They obviously hadn't grown up around My Old Man, nor had they ever had to do for themselves. It was fun to watch them totally lost and confused; the instructors *sensed* weakness, and they piled on the abuse! Hey, when *they* were the target, at least I was not!

The Physical Training included self-defense which meant boxing and some Judo. Hard as it is to believe, there were a few guys who had never been in a fight and had never been punched in the face! Boxing took care of that oversight, and it gave those guys a taste of physical contact in a non-friendly way. (In case you think that some of this may have been uncalled for, I'd like to point out that it was a lot *better* to find out that you were easily rattled or incapable of dealing with a physical confrontation at the training center than later fighting for your life on the street.)

Physical training was necessary and intense, but it was only a small part of our academy regimen. By far, most of our time was spent on learning and studying the laws of the state and ordinances of the city, which would be our duty to enforce. There were countless rules and regulations that had to be memorized, plus we had extensive training in writing reports.

At the outset of our report writing class, the instructor started his presentation by stating, "No matter what action you take as a police officer, your job is like going to the bathroom: you are not finished until the paperwork is done!" We laughed, but he wasn't joking. This proved to be true throughout my law enforcement career.

Our skill at being able to convey in writing what took place at the scene of any action that involved us was critical in defending whatever actions we took. There were no "body cams" or cell phones, so it came down to describing what happened in writing. If the case involved an arrest, the report you wrote was what the prosecutor and defense attorneys read first. Reading and writing were right up my alley, and I excelled in that part of the training, (Thank God, Math wasn't a major part of the curriculum!)

Of course, I was getting a lot of practice since Joyce and I were still writing, and she knew I was in the Academy. One day I received a letter from her telling me that she was thinking of driving down to San Antonio to see me. She was going to bring the kids and wanted to know what I thought. She had included her phone number and asked me to call her *collect* since I still lived at home and didn't have my own phone.

I called her and told her I would *love* to see her and the kids, and she could meet my parents. We agreed that she would call me when she got settled in a motel after she arrived. I told my parents about her visit, and they asked me if she was divorced. I was honest and told them that I didn't know. My mother told me that she wouldn't meet her if she was still married. My father was uncharacteristically quiet and never said one way or another. Joyce got into town on a Friday afternoon and called my house, leaving a message with my mother. I was given the message when I got home from the academy that evening.

My mother and I talked about her meeting Joyce, but she had not changed her mind. This didn't surprise me because once she said something, it was settled! I remember as a kid if we were out somewhere and I started acting up, she would give me that "look," and if I kept on misbehaving, she would simply say, "Later!" I don't care if it was even several *hours* "later" when we got home. I would be making small talk, hoping that the storm had passed, but nope, the whipping was administered! I always respected that about my mother; she was true to her word. I didn't always like it, but I always respected it.

I got the call Friday evening that she was settled in a motel not far from where I lived. I went over, and I had not realized how much I missed her until I saw her open the door. John and Cathy were on one of the beds watching TV, and we joined them and watched a cartoon movie.

They fell asleep, and Joyce and I started catching up on what had been happening in our lives. I asked her about the status of her marriage, and she told me that she had filed for divorce but that her husband was still not willing to sign the papers. She had made it clear to him that there would be no reconciliation, and he had responded that he wouldn't agree to a divorce.

She then asked me about my parents. I told her about the conversation that my mother and I had a few days prior to her arrival. I told Joyce that I wouldn't lie to my mother, and she told me that she understood and didn't want to mislead her either. We talked into the small hours of the morning and made a date to take the kids to a park later in the day.

I went home, and it was one of those rare days when I slept late. Since it was Saturday, my parents and sister where all home when I walked into the kitchen. Breakfast had come and gone, but coffee was still warm, and I had a cup and sat down at the kitchen table. As far as I knew, my sister didn't know of the talk that my mother and I had regarding Joyce, so Jeanine began to ask me for particulars. I filled her in and could tell that without being too obvious, both my parents were listening, so they heard when I honestly told her the status of the marriage.

When the topic of the kids came up, both of my parents started talking about how expensive it was raising one child, let alone *two* small kids. I agreed and told them honestly that it was scary to even think about the responsibility that children presented. My sister asked me where Joyce was staying, and I told her the name of the motel.

Joyce and I spent the rest of Saturday and all-day Sunday touring some of the sights in San Antonio, and we had a ball. Joyce was a good mother, and the kids were well-behaved. We returned to the motel Sunday evening and were watching TV when there was a knock on the door. Joyce opened the door, and to my surprise, I could hear my father introduce himself!

She stepped back, and he came in. He looked at the kids, and everyone was sort of speechless. We introduced him to John and Cathy, and that finally eased the tension. We stood around and made small talk for a few minutes, and he announced that he couldn't stay but just wanted to meet Joyce and the kids. I followed him out, and he told me that they seemed nice, and then he asked me if I would be home later. I told him that I had to be at work the next day so I wouldn't be *late* getting home. I was true to my word, and Joyce understood that I needed to get an early start, so we called it a night, and I headed home.

I guess it was around ten o'clock when I pulled up and went into the house, and both my mother and father were sitting at the kitchen table. My father asked me if I would sit down and talk with them, and I agreed since it was bound to happen sooner or later. (As I write this, it strikes me that the kitchen table in my parent's house was the center of some serious moments in my life. This was the same table where my father tried to "beat" Math into my head, confronted me when I came in one night from a date with lipstick smeared on my face and neck, and served some of the finest meals that I have ever eaten, and too many other things to mention!)

Apparently, my mother knew that my father had come over to the motel to meet Joyce and the kids. He started by telling me that he was impressed with Joyce and that the kids were cute and well-behaved. Then they started listing all the *pitfalls* that were in front of me if I moved forward with this relationship. We talked for a good while, and when they asked me where I saw this going, I honestly told them that I didn't know! I told them that she was going back to Philadelphia and that I planned on staying in San Antonio and becoming a police officer. It was hard to say good-by when it came time for Joyce to leave, but she needed to go back. Training at the academy was intense, and that helped to take my mind off Joyce, but we continued to write and talk constantly.

Every April, the City of San Antonio hosts a three-week affair called "Fiesta San Antonio." It consists of various parties, a large carnival, plus a night and a day parade. It's a big deal and brings in a tremendous amount of revenue each year. Hundreds of thousands of people come downtown to spend their money, with *a lot* of it spent on beer and food. It doesn't help that during Fiesta. The city suspends the ordinances against carrying and drinking alcoholic beverages in public. When you combine all this with music blaring from stages that were set up at various locations… you have yourself one heck of a three-week party! As a result, the police department becomes stressed to *the max* at providing a visible presence at all the various events with the goal of maintaining public safety. To maximize the use of uniform police officers, cadets in training are used to supplement sworn officers for patrol in the downtown areas. Anyone considering a career in law enforcement would be well served working a three-week stretch of "Fiesta," dealing with thousands of people in confined spaces with non-stop alcohol available. It serves as a real education!

As cadets, we were required to report for training each day and carry out assignments as usual. At the end of the regular workday, we were sent out on an overtime basis to Fiesta events where we were needed. Since both the day and night parades typically drew well over 100,000 people, these parade days were the days that *everyone was* used.

Since we were not sworn officers yet, we didn't carry a weapon, and we didn't have official power to arrest anyone, but we *could* carry handcuffs. I really enjoyed myself! I had done some stupid stuff in my life, but I was able to see people *outdo me* practically every day that I worked the various events. Of course, the sworn officers I worked with had a whole different attitude about having beer spilled on them. This included trying to keep drunken females from dropping their pants and relieving themselves on the street because the portable bathrooms had long waiting lines! Years later, after several "Fiestas," I, too, found the luster and excitement of dealing with large drunk crowds had disappeared.

Fiesta came and went, and as we entered May, I realized that we were about six weeks out of finishing with the Academy. We would be promoted to probationary status if we passed our Probationary Exam, and then we'd be sent out to ride with a sworn officer for a two-week training period. The time seemed to rush by as we were constantly exposed to new material, but now I knew that I had surely found a career and what I wanted to do with my life. Several of us had become close friends and would go out "honky-tonking," but we had to be careful about getting into trouble because we could be fired for absolutely any reason. Girls were part of the group, and I admit that I enjoyed being around them, but Joyce stayed in my thoughts constantly.

The closer graduation day approached, the more conflicted I became about my future. It was obvious that once I took the oath to serve, I felt I would be totally committed to living in San Antonio and establishing my life there. During one of our tearful phone conversations, the "I love you" words dropped out of our mouths, and just like that, everything changed! She was miserable because she wasn't making any headway with her husband, and *I* was miserable because there was nothing I could do to help the situation. We both realized that this long-distance relationship was for the birds. It was the end of June, and the Probationary Exam was a few days away when I walked into the Training Academy Captain's office and handed him my resignation.

He was dumbfounded, and he just looked at me and told me to get out of his office and back into the classroom. Well, *that* didn't work like I'd thought it would, so I went back to the classroom. During the break, I talked to my favorite instructor, Sgt. Guy Buckalew and told him the story. Once he found out I was sincere, he told me he would go and talk to the Captain, and we could go on from there.

At the end of the day, Sgt. Buckalew took me back into the Captain's office and explained that I was serious. They both tried their best to talk me out of it, but my mind was made up, so the process started to separate me from the Academy. I guess I handled it the right way because the city personnel director at the time, a man named Jerry Goodloe, was the last person I had to see as one of my final steps to complete the process. The last thing he told me was that if it didn't work out for me in Philadelphia and I wanted to come back, as long as it was within a reasonable time, he would try his best to make it happen. That became very important later on.

Just like that, I no longer had a job, and I had the pleasure of telling my folks of the change in plans for my life; I was headed for Pennsylvania! They took it about like you would expect, and they made sure I knew that I had completely lost my mind. I wasn't really sure that they were wrong.

Chapter 18

"...nobody up here dresses like that!"

At the time that I quit the Police Department, my brother had finished Navy boot camp in San Diego, California, and he was home on leave. He had signed up for submarine school, too, and would be flying to New London, Connecticut, to start school. I finished up what little business I had around San Antonio, and I started my plans to leave for Pennsylvania.

When I left the Navy in 1967, I had a 1961 Pontiac that had a big motor and was set up for street racing to some extent. It would top out and run as fast as you wanted or until you got scared. It would also automatically pull into every service station and demand fuel. As I planned my trip, I realized I needed a car that would be easier on my wallet. Looking around the used car lots, I came across a 2 door Ford Falcon sedan. It had a six-cylinder motor with an automatic transmission and had been owned by a person who cherished the car. I made the trade, drove away free and clear, and never had a single regret.

As it was time for me to leave, my brother and I decided that instead of flying to Connecticut, he could ride with me. It would give me company, and Ralph could kick in a little with gas money. The day we left was hard on my mother, but you would never have known it as we said good-by. No long-drawn-out drama, a "Just be careful and give us a call when you arrive." My father just shook our hands, and that was that.

As we started North, I remember feeling a little *scared* because, for the first time in my life, I had *no clue* what life had in store for me. I had maybe 300 dollars in cash, no job, no place to live, and I was not really sure what Joyce's marital status would be when I reached her. Even though I was scared, I was dead sure I was doing the right thing, and I felt we would work out our problems together. My brother probably never realized how *much* I appreciated him traveling with me, but it made the trip fun and took much pressure off me during the driving.

When we got to Philadelphia, I called Joyce, who gave me directions to her apartment. It turned out that her apartment was located on the outskirts of Wilmington, Delaware. When we drove up and stopped, the front door opened. Joyce came out, and I *knew* I had made the right decision! In spite of some tears, Joyce looked stunning, and I realized how much I had missed her. Introductions were made, and Ralph met John and Cathy as we unloaded what we needed out of the car. Joyce had supper ready, so we ate and started catching up. At some point, Joyce fixed up a couch and a chair, and Ralph and I slept in the small living room.

The next morning we had breakfast, and then Ralph made arrangements for his flight to New London so he could get to the submarine base and begin school. I think he stayed with us for two days, and then we took him to the airport, and he flew out.

For the first time in as long as I could remember, I didn't have some place to report for work, and I felt lost! I told Joyce I needed to find a place to stay, so we took a tour of the area. We ended up finding a furnished room above a bar in Chester, Pennsylvania. This place had several furnished rooms for rent, and when we walked up and entered "my" room, I found that the sole window was facing the front of the street. They were charging a *weekly* rate, and all-in-all, it wasn't bad. We unloaded my belongings, and as I looked around at everything, I realized I didn't have very much since *everything* fit in the drawers and the one closet.

Entry from the street was a door that opened to a set of stairs that led up to the rooms. The street door was next to another door that led into what turned out to be a neighborhood bar. There was a large lighted sign over the entrance to the bar, which made the place easy to find. This was now home!

Having a place to stay, I settled in and turned my attention to my next priority: finding a job. We returned to Joyce's apartment with a Philadelphia newspaper, and I began to look through the job postings.

There were lots of jobs listed, but many I could rule out right away. One that caught my attention was the announcement that the Philadelphia Police Department was looking to hire recruits. Hmmm…this I would have to look into.

After a few phone calls, I was directed to go to a police Philadelphia precinct building and talk with the man in charge. So I drove over to the nearest precinct and went in. Talk about culture shock! The place was filthy, people were sitting and hanging around everywhere, and the place echoed with noise.

A uniform officer behind a counter called me over to find out what I wanted. I told him, and he looked me up and down and told me to wait. A few minutes later, another guy in uniform walked up and looked me up and down. Then he told me to follow him to an office behind the counter. Once in the office, the door closed, and behind the desk, there was an overweight black guy in the uniform of a captain. He looked me up and down and then asked me where I was from. I told him Texas, and he said something along the lines of "That explains it," and he stared at me some more. He asked me what I wanted, and I told him I was interested in applying for the Police Department.

He looked at the other officer, then turned back to me, and asked, "How did you vote in the last election?" What? I told him I didn't vote. He then told me that wasn't good, and he went on to say that I was going to have to find *an alderman* and talk to him about a recommendation. When I asked him what an alderman was, they both cracked up and started laughing. I was beginning to think that I had stumbled into a Rod Sterling Twilight Zone show. When they stopped laughing, the captain told me that jobs in the city were filled with people who had received recommendations from their political representatives, AKA "Aldermen." (Once again, this boy realized he was no longer in Kansas…er, Texas.)

I returned to Chester, and after telling Joyce what had happened, she was able to fill me in on how politics played a part in almost everything that happened in Philadelphia. She went on to tell me that

Democrats ruled city and state politics and that they guarded their power base by controlling access to city jobs such as the police and fire fighters.

I decided to make some further calls and finally talked to someone in the city personnel office. When I explained what I wanted, I was told that I wasn't eligible to apply because I had to be a *resident* for at least six months. I also checked with the Pennsylvania State Police, and their residency requirements were a *year*. It seemed that law enforcement was not going to be a part of my future.

I went to several interviews at various places, but nothing clicked. One thing immediately became obvious to me: politics and unions controlled a large part of the workplace. Then one day, I saw an ad seeking applicants for an opening at a nearby Woolworth's. I walked in and picked up an application, and after filling it out, I interviewed with the Store Manager.

He told me that he would forward my application to the main office but that he felt I was perfect for the job. We had been sitting at the soda fountain counter, and I noticed he kept looking at me when he thought I couldn't see him. Finally, he asked me where I was from, and I told him I had recently moved to Philadelphia from Texas. He smiled and then said that explained a lot. This is the *second time* I have heard that from someone up there! When I asked him what he was talking about, he pointed at me and said, "Man, you are wearing boots, blue jeans, and a western-cut shirt; nobody up here dresses like that!" He had me there. What could I say but…"Go Cowboys!"

The job had the title of Assistant Manager, and it paid $425.00 per month. I got the job! I had been in Pennsylvania for a week and a half, and I admit that I had been feeling down without a job and watching my cash dwindling every day. Adding to my misery was *my room*.

You may have heard the saying, "You could take a jackass and swing it around on a rope with it kicking with all four feet, and it wouldn't do $25.00 worth of damage." That was my room! To further add to my misery, there was that large sign on the building advertising the bar. It was neon, and it lit and flashed all night long. My window looked out on it, and the curtains could not blot out the *light!* The kicker of all was that the bar was a favorite of a group of motorcycle riders. They parked along the front curb, and when the place closed, they fired up those motors in sync. I felt like I could sometimes levitate over the bed for a moment or two! Dang, that was one hell of a way to wake up out of a sound sleep.

I reported for my first day at the new job on a Saturday. I was introduced to most of the crew and then taken to the rear of the store and into the Warehouse area where they kept extra merchandise. Since I was an "Assistant Manager," I asked the Manager who else I would have working with me. He said I was it! (Odd.) He then began to explain what my duties would be. These included opening and closing the store on alternate days, and receiving merchandise at the loading dock (truck drivers simply put the stuff on the dock; drivers were union people, and they made sure not to exceed the limits of their duties), so it was my responsibility to move the boxes into the warehouse.

I also had charge of the birds, gerbils, lizards, and fish we sold, along with stocking the shelves with merchandize as warranted. Oh yea, I also had the privilege of sweeping and mopping four different aisles every evening when we closed! I later learned that Store Managers made their money by how well they controlled their overhead. My guy figured out that employees were part of the overhead, and he ran it pretty lean and short in numbers. But it was a job, and I was glad to have it, but I didn't see *retail* in my future. I also hated having to clean those gerbil cages! (Those little suckers would do anything to escape!)

Chapter 19

"You are one fast white boy!"

It wasn't long before I spent all my off time with Joyce and the kids. Her husband still refused to budge on her request for a divorce, and she was adamant that the marriage was over. I still had my room in Chester, but I admit that the thing was sitting empty most of the time. During this time, she and I really started opening up to one another about our lives and backgrounds. I knew that her mother and father were deceased. He had worked as an editor for the largest Philadelphia newspaper and had apparently been a successful businessman.

I learned that Joyce had a much older brother who was in the military, and they were not close due to the differences in their ages. She went on to tell me that she had an older sister who had been murdered in a shooting at a toll booth a few years earlier. Basically, when her parents died, she was just out of her teens and was on her own. She was financially taken care of and attending nursing school when she began dating the man that would become her first husband.

Apparently, he was from a working, blue-collar family background, and I believe they had known one another while they were growing up. I don't know how they came to marry, but after he joined the Navy, the kids were not long in arriving. With two young children to raise, Joyce's nursing education then came to an end. She said that the marriage was a mistake from the beginning because she basically felt that she agreed to marry to avoid being alone.

One day I was at work and had just sat down at the soda fountain, eating my lunch, and looking at a newspaper when I saw an ad for the Wilmington, Delaware Police Department. *They* were looking for police applicants! I called the number and decided to pick up the application to see if there was a path for me to pursue.

Once I reviewed the paperwork, I was relieved to see that they didn't have a residency requirement, so I filled out the application.

Unlike San Antonio, the initial test was administered when you arrived for your scheduled appointment time. When I finished the test, I was immediately told that I had *passed* and would be contacted with further instructions! It wasn't long before I began the process of working my way through their system, taking the required steps to see if I qualified to go through the police academy. I was accepted, but I had to explain why I had gone through the entire San Antonio Police Academy only to walk away two weeks before graduating. When they heard my explanation, they were satisfied that I had committed to living in the Wilmington area, and I was good to go.

Once again, I found myself in a regimented schedule: going to class, doing daily physical training, practicing firearms certification, and learning first aid. I was in my *element,* and on top of everything else, I had gotten a large pay raise! As I spent more and more time with Joyce and the kids, it became clear that I was wasting money on keeping my room. I moved in with Joyce, and despite her marital situation, we both felt we were making a statement that we were going to be together no matter what.

The Wilmington Academy was shorter by a month in duration, and I was in the best physical condition of my life. Graduation day arrived, and Joyce and the kids attended the ceremony. I called home, and told my parents that I was *officially* a police officer of the Wilmington, Delaware Police Department. I know it was bittersweet for them as they would have preferred that announcement to have been made in San Antonio.

Policing in the United States is generally committed to maintaining law and order, with the safety of the citizenry being the first and foremost objective. (At least that is how it was back then.) The means used to carry out that commitment can vary dramatically from one jurisdiction to another. San Antonio generally patrolled with *one-man* patrol cars assigned to "districts," and they made calls in that particular area. Wilmington used *two-man* cars that patrolled designated districts. I was assigned to a senior officer named Bill, who continued with my training, and we were "partners." Bill was married with young kids, and he and I became good friends. It wasn't long before we were also socializing when off-duty.

As I already mentioned, I wasn't a political person at that time of my life, and I wasn't much for watching the news. However, it didn't take me long to figure out that Wilmington was deeply divided according to race and politics. The Police Department was predominantly made up of white males, with the Irish and Italians well represented, and the rest of us were made up of people like me and some African Americans. I often separated myself because they thought being from Texas made me a foreigner!

My partner, Bill, was Irish. He was stocky in build, was about 5ft, 7-8 inches tall, and had reddish-blonde hair. I could always count on him to have my back. He was as fair and impartial as anyone I had ever been around, so we always treated everybody the same. This couldn't be said for some *other* guys working around us. I was amazed at the prejudice some of those guys harbored toward black-skinned people in general. It was also clear that a portion of the black population *hated* the police department. This made for a tough environment to perform as a police officer, but nobody had it tougher than *black* police officers!

Initially, I was puzzled by the hard feelings that were so readily displayed by both sides when my partner and I responded to calls. Bill finally began to fill me in on the reason(s) that we encountered so much hostility. When Martin Luther King was murdered on April 4, 1968, many cities across the country blew up in full-scale riots. Wilmington was one of the more *violent* cities included in that list. The governor of Delaware brought in the National Guard during those times, and The Guard remained in Wilmington for almost a year. (Wilmington *still has* the dubious distinction of being the city with the longest record of military occupation in the entire country!) The black population resented *soldiers* dressed in combat gear, driving their neighborhoods in jeeps with weapons, and often helping the Police Department enforce curfews.

Another reason for the animosity was the disparity in the quality of schools in different parts of town. Wilmington was unique in that the daytime population consisted of predominantly white professionals, with one of the largest employers being DuPont. At the end of the workday, *these* people all left for the suburbs where they lived and where their kids went to school.

The people who lived in the *inner city* of Wilmington were predominantly black, with a few of Asian descent. A lot of *these* people lived in large tenement housing blocks with multi-story apartment buildings that should have been condemned! Their children attended inner-city schools that were inferior to the suburban schools. Wilmington also had Irish and Italian neighborhoods, which were extremely proud of their heritage. Lastly, there was also an affluent section of well-to-do people who were well-insulated from the rest of the town. My partner and I had a district in the heart of the tenements.

Like most cities, the Wilmington Police Department split the workday into three eight-hour shifts: 7 AM to 3 PM (day shift,) 3 PM to 11 PM, and 11 PM to 7 AM (dog watch.) The day shifts were the easiest to work as most of the calls were routine, and the real troublemakers were still sleeping after having been up all night. The 3 to 11 shifts provided a bigger variety of calls as the day rolled into the evening, and people began to visit the bars.

The dog watch was when a lot of the *serious* stuff happened. The bars would begin shutting down, and people who may have been *overserved* hit the streets, heading for wherever they were headed. This was when the fights began, drunk drivers were on the road, family disturbances flared up, and a host of other problems were reported to the police Dispatcher, who then sent a police unit to respond to the situation for resolution.

Dog watch was a time for some real police work in addition to responding to those calls that were dispatched out to Units. Around two or three in the morning, things would quiet down, and we would concentrate on checking businesses for burglars or stopping suspicious people who were hanging out on the street. The military would pay $25.00 for arrested deserters, and we would receive "Wanted" bulletins identifying people known to live in our area, so we would go out looking for them.

One day Bill and I received an arrest warrant for a deserter whose momma lived in our district; he and I decided we would try to check out the address later in the evening to see if we could spot him. Sure enough, we stopped a block from the address and could see several males standing on the corner. Using binoculars, Bill started looking them over, and since Bill had known the deserter before he went into the military, he spotted him as part of the group.

Bill was driving, and we circled the block so we could come up from behind them, and with a little luck, we could be closer to them before they spotted us. It was a cool evening, and I had on a police-issued coat over my uniform, but I was going to jump out as we got close and snatch him before he had an opportunity to take off. We approached with our headlights off, and almost made it when one of the guys noticed our car. It took him a moment to realize who we were; when he finally saw the red light on top of our car, he sounded the alarm to his buddies.

I bailed out, and the foot chase was on! Since we were between him and his momma's apartment building, he took off, running the opposite way down the street. I was behind him a few feet, but we were staying about even. He was also wearing a coat, and he took it off and threw it over his head, hoping I would trip over it. I avoided it and managed to pick up a couple of feet on him. The next thing I knew, he kicked off his shoes and was now running barefoot! My partner was pacing us in the police car when we came up on a cross street. At the last second, the guy made a sharp turn, leaving Bill having to back up before he could rejoin the chase.

I guess I caught my second wind and found another gear because I managed to catch up to him and grab him by the back of his shirt. I knocked him off balance, and down he went. Bill had pulled up, jumped out of the car, and had him handcuffed before he could start again. Thank you, Lord!

We brought the deserter to the station where he would be held by the military police. As we were putting him in a holding cell, he turned to me and said, "You are one fast white boy!" I felt like telling him that after going through two police academy training regimens, I *should* be fast, but I just smiled instead. I knew if we had gone another block, "this white boy" would have been left on the sidewalk!

As I previously mentioned, we would also check businesses for possible burglars. One night I learned how dangerous policing could be. We were coming up to an appliance store when we noticed a black male step out from the recessed doorway. He spotted us, called over his shoulder, and two more males stepped out; all three took off down the street. I was riding as a passenger again (funny how that seemed to work out) and bailed out on foot pursuit.

The burglars turned the corner and then turned again into an alleyway behind the businesses. I lost sight of them, but as I turned into the alleyway, one of them stopped and started shooting at me with a pistol! I skidded to a stop and jumped back around the corner. Yes, sir, I was still "One fast white boy!" My partner heard the shots and stopped just short of the alleyway; he jumped out of the car, joining me as I peeked around the corner, but those guys were now nowhere to be seen. We searched the area but never found them. When we went back to the store, we discovered that they had almost succeeded in prying the front door open. I guess we arrived just in time to prevent them from getting in. At the time, I felt I was one lucky son-of-a-gun since I wasn't hit. Many years later, I realized that *luck* had nothing to do with it!

Chapter 20

"The fuse was lit…"

By now, Joyce and I and the kids had settled into her apartment. She was driving a VW "bug," and I still had my Ford Falcon, but we realized that neither car had sufficient room to accommodate all of us when we went somewhere as a family. We decided to begin looking for a bigger car, and since the VW had such fantastic gas mileage, I decided that we would trade in the Falcon. We ended up buying a station wagon, and I began driving the "Bug!"

The weather in Pennsylvania and Delaware brings occasional snow, and this South Texas boy wasn't used to driving in that type of weather. I soon discovered that the natives didn't know how to drive in that kind of weather either! I also realized that the "Bug" could handle the snow better than most of the other cars/trucks on the road, and when I got stuck, I simply got out and pushed it out of trouble!

With the start of winter, the streets were not nearly as busy as they were during the summer. People were forced to spend more time indoors. That included bars that furnished a heated place to congregate and provided *internal* warmth through the drinks they served. This combination resulted in a busy time for police calls in the form of fights, drunks, family disturbances, and various other calls.

The holiday season also meant police offices were getting together during their off time, throwing parties at their homes. Joyce and I were invited to my partner Bill's house, and for the first time, I was able to meet his family. It was also the first time that I was introduced to row homes. He lived in the Irish section of town, and all the houses had two stories with a basement. It was a beautiful home, but it shared a common wall with the house on either side. There was a tiny front yard and not much of a backyard. I was blown away as I was used to having a large front and backyard with ample space between the houses.

Neighbors visited by standing on their front porches and talking with their friends and those who walked by on the sidewalk. There were very few garages, and the cars were normally parked on the street in front of the house. The people were nice, and I felt welcome, but I wasn't sure how I felt about living in such a cramped neighborhood. Row home or not, we had a good time, and Joyce drove us home.

Most of the fellows that I worked and socialized with liked to drink, so I fit in all too well. It seemed that drinking and I was linked arm and arm. Later in life, that would become a serious problem, but at this time of my life, it fit the lifestyle that I found myself living in, and I had no reason to want to change.

January 1, 1969: a new year, but still no resolution to Joyce's divorce case. I was gaining experience as a police officer and liked my job, but racial tension was always present. The Black Panther group was well established, and they were always a reason for concern. They made no bones of their intention to hurt or kill police officers and were not shy about announcing their intentions. This communist-affiliated group, founded in California, was also involved in several deadly confrontations with the police in several parts of the country.

I had an opportunity to work an extra job now and then in uniform at a diner with another officer, and I often teamed up with a black officer named Stewart. As I mentioned earlier, a lot of blacks hated police officers, but they especially hated black police officers because they were looked at as betraying their race. Go figure!

Black officers were called Oreo cookies, or Oreos: black on the outside but white on the inside! One night Stewart and I were working at the diner when a group of five blacks came in the diner. Suddenly two of them began to fight near where he was standing. I was at one end of the place, and my partner was near the door and the cash register, which was where the fight started. I say "fight," but it was more yelling and grabbing and shoving than fighting.

As Stewart moved to break it up, the other three blacks jumped *him* from behind. I was already running to him and could see that one of them was trying to get his gun out of his holster. Luckily, I was able to jump in and get close to Stewart so we could cover each other. He and I managed to handcuff two of them, and the others took off before on-duty officers arrived to help.

We later learned that this had been a planned attack by the Black Panthers aimed primarily at a *black officer* intending to scare other blacks away from the police profession. I guess they hadn't seen me, so we were able to surprise them enough to get the upper hand.

As spring approached, intelligence began to filter into the department that the Panthers were planning to instigate social unrest in Wilmington. This was supposed to take place on the day of the anniversary of the shooting of Rev. King. You could feel the tension begin to grow within the black community and throughout the entire city. It hadn't been that long ago that the city had suffered through some awfully bad rioting, and everyone was on edge.

It was noticeable that something was going on because groups of young black males were bunching on the street corners and blocking sidewalks and entrances to businesses. When we responded to calls in our district, small groups of guys would block the path until we were almost in front of them and would then grudgingly move aside to let us pass. Behind our backs, the name-calling would begin along with threats to our safety. If we arrested anyone, attempts were often made to pull the person away from us. "Officer-in-trouble" calls were becoming more frequent as we found ourselves having to use physical *force* to make an arrest much more often than we had before.

The fuse was lit when three Black Panther leaders were arrested and placed in the City Jail housed inside the Police Department. I was off duty at the time and didn't know what led to the arrest, but this quickly escalated to protesters demanding that their leaders be released. The Department had 250 sworn officers in 1969, and everyone not already on duty was called in to prepare for *any* response that might be needed to stop the escalation of violence.

When I reached the station, there was a large crowd of protesters in front of the building, but our parking lot was in the rear and fenced off, so I was able to drive in and avoid the crowd out front. I was already in uniform and was given my riot gear which included a helmet, shield, and a long nightstick. Officers were already out in front of the building, lined up facing the crowd, which was growing larger. The entrance to the Jail, as well as the Magistrate Court, was at the rear of the building, so quite a few other officers and I were lined up across the entrance. This had started in the late afternoon, and as it grew dark, the crowd kept building and becoming more aggressive, demanding the immediate release of the prisoners.

It was obvious that a lot of the protesters were swept up in the energy of the mob. The real agitators (the cowards) wearing their Black Panther colors were just behind the front lines, urging-on the people in front. When it had become totally dark, the police and the agitators were lined up with only about four to five feet of distance between us. You could say *"spitting distance"* since a lot of that was going on! The rioters were also using balloons filled with liquid (urine or bleach, etc.,) lobbing them toward us over the crowd with occasional rock and bottle mixed in. We had orders to maintain our united front and not step out toward the crowd but hold our position. During our Police Academy training, we received extensive riot control training, so we were well prepared to respond as a unit.

The crowd had a mixture of black and white participants, and *we* had Undercover Officers who were mingling with the protesters to identify the so-called ringleaders (agitators) while they also looked for people armed with weapons. This information was passed onto the supervisors who were behind us in the front lines, and those agitators would be the targets of arrest once the order was given to disperse the crowd. I remember thinking: I never anticipated that I would be trying to keep people from breaking prisoners out of our jail!

I don't remember how long we stood in place (but it seemed like a long time) before a supervisor announced to the crowd through a bullhorn that the people were engaged in an *unlawful assembly* and ordered them to disperse. Of course, all this order did was increase the shouting, yelling, and tossing of various missiles our way!

I have to tell you that by then, all of us were ready to take some action (kick some a__!) because, speaking for myself, I was tired *of* the yelling and taunting…waiting for some idiot to produce a gun and start shooting! A supervisor pointed out two agitators that I and the men on each side of me would try to arrest, so I was locked in on these two guys.

The order to "disperse immediately" was repeated, only to be met with the same reaction from the crowd. The word for us to "move on command" was passed down the line, and we prepared to move forward. I guess our body language signaled to the idiots immediately in front of us that the situation was about to get more intense because as I looked at the three or four in front of me, I could see a little *fear* begin to creep onto their faces. They weren't completely stupid! Maybe it was due to my *grin*!

The order to "Execute" was announced through the bullhorn, and we began to step forward in unison, holding our line with shields *up* and batons *ready*. As we contacted those in the front of the crowd, we started shoving them back with our shields. Anyone who didn't move back was pulled through our line, grabbed by officers behind us, zip tied, and shoved to officers behind them to be taken to a holding area. Almost immediately, the crowd began to *panic* and was trying to get away from the front by forcing their way to the rear. The two agitators that had been identified as our particular targets were trapped by their own people, and as the crowd was trying to back up, the three of us zeroed in and reached them before they could get away! They were arrested with minor injuries and taken to the holding area. I don't remember how many were arrested that night, but it stopped any other attempts to free the "Panthers" we already had in custody.

I went into detail regarding this incident because I wanted to share my experience when confronted by people who allowed themselves to be swept up in a "cause." These folks bought into the *lie* that three blacks had been arrested *for no reason* and that they were being abused in jail. Facts no longer mattered. Most of them allowed agitators *to prod them* into participating in an unlawful action that led to their being arrested and in some cases, needing medical treatment for the injuries that they sustained. Police officers were also hurt and had to receive medical treatment. I learned from this experience that people will sometimes surprise you by behaving in unexpected ways that are not warranted by the facts. This revelation contributed toward shaping me into the police officer I would become, and it still guides me today.

Even though we were able to disperse the crowd that attempted to storm the Police Station that day, the community relations in Wilmington continued to worsen. Groups of men (young and old and mostly black) were always on the streets, and they continued harassing businesses and customers.

An Asian store in our district became a regular target for shoplifting and numerous assaults on the store owner. This was a family-run store that had been in the neighborhood for years, and they were well-liked by the people living there. But all of a sudden, they were receiving death threats, and we were making disturbance calls there on a regular basis. We also started getting false calls that were booby traps at the end of a blocked street... to block our police car while objects were thrown *down on us* from the upper stories of the apartment buildings.

It wasn't long before the fires began, and a curfew was imposed. The National Guard once again started covering us on calls, and they would keep an eye on the upper windows while we went in to address the call. They drove army jeeps and were dressed in full riot gear. This included having machine guns and bright spotlights so they could shine on the windows of the upper floors. (This might sound like overkill to some of you reading this now, but you would have a different perspective if you were sitting in a police car when a trash can full of all kinds of metal and rocks was thrown out of a third-story window, falling on the top of your car!) Talk about the world seeming to come to an end!

As things kept getting worse and worse, the city would remain open for the daytime Commuters, but the major streets and highways into and out of Wilmington were often shut down during the curfew, which started as it got dark. One of the jobs we were required to fill on a rotational basis was manning the closure barricades.

Along with State troopers and National Guardsmen, we would check to make sure that anyone wanting to enter Wilmington was a resident. This had become necessary because non-resident instigators were coming in, stirring up our local people. The first barricade on the side of the road into the city had a lighted sign that ordered approaching cars to turn off their headlights as they approached the second set of barricades. Since random shots were being fired at us from time to time, no one wanted to be lit up by a car's headlights and become a target.

One night a car approached with its headlights on full beam, ignoring the sign telling them to turn off their lights. As it came to a stop, we could see two people in the front seat; the driver's window was down. The driver was repeatedly ordered to turn off the lights, but instead of turning them off, he began to *argue* and demanded an explanation as to *why* he should turn them off, all the while looking at several guns pointed in his direction.

An officer walked up to his car with his night stick and busted out both headlights. He then demanded to see the identification of the occupants of the car. It turned out that they were not Wilmington residents, and they were told to *leave*. The driver wanted to know what we were going to do about his headlights. Several of us headed to *his side* of the car, and I guess the reason for their visit was forgotten. They now felt that any further arguments with us would probably be detrimental to their health, so they left!

This was *not* my vision of Policing, and it was probably not the vision of Policing that *most* of the residents of Wilmington had either. One time, while my partner and I were attempting to arrest another military AWOL, a fight broke out, and as we were trying to leave with our prisoner, a thrown bottle broke the side window of our Police Car, and I was cut on the neck with broken glass. A trip to the hospital to be treated for the minor wound ended up being written up in the paper. It seemed that the flames just *kept* getting stoked in one form or another.

Most of the troublemakers were young guys who seemed to have nothing better to do, and they were egged-on by the professional agitators. I felt sorry for the *older* people who were often caught in the *middle* and had to put up with their property being damaged. For the sake of honesty, I admit that the police *were* often part of the problem. Once we identified one of the regular characters who always seemed to be in the middle of a troubling situation, he received our undivided attention. In other words, if he was walking down the street doing nothing, he was going to be approached and hassled. Remember the saying, "The squeaky wheel gets the grease?" *So true*!

Fortunately, the apartments where Joyce, the kids, and I lived were far removed from the unrest. During my off time, we were able to go to the parks and lakes and enjoy ourselves. But it was becoming more apparent that I didn't feel at home in this northeast part of the country. When I spoke with my parents and asked them about what was going on in San Antonio, nothing was said about racial unrest, buildings on fire, or the police being the target of violence. I was becoming more *convinced* that I needed to make a change, but now, that change would include Joyce and John and Cathy, no argument.

Chapter 21

"We looked like the Clampetts coming to town."

As the summer went on, Joyce and I had several conversations about what we wanted to do about our future, and surprisingly, she was ready to move to Texas! I contacted Sgt. Buckalew at the San Antonio Police training academy, and he suggested that I call the Assistant City Manager in charge of Personnel. I did that, and he told me that he would look into the possibility of me coming back and what would be required of me. A few weeks went by before I heard from him again.

One day around the first of September, Joyce told me that someone had called from San Antonio and asked that I call them back. I was working the day shift then, so I called them back the following afternoon. I was told that the reason it had taken so long to get back to me was that numerous people had to be contacted within the Department to do *another* background check and obtain approval for me to return. Tentative approval had been obtained, but the Wilmington Police Department would now have to be contacted to verify my employment and work record there. SAPD needed my permission to contact Wilmington, so they sent me a form I signed permitting them to do so; I returned it as soon as possible.

Before the form arrived at Wilmington, I went to work for my regular shift and spoke with my sergeant about my intentions. I then made my way up to the chain-of-command until I met with the Chief of Police. Everyone was sorry to hear that I was thinking about moving back to San Antonio, and a few tried to change my mind. I was flattered that I had been accepted as part of the police brotherhood to the extent that no one wanted to see me leave, but by then, I had made up my mind that the Northeast wasn't a place I wanted to live. Once they realized that my mind was made up and everybody had been notified of my intentions, they accepted my decision to leave.

Another two weeks went by before another letter arrived with the San Antonio letterhead on it. In the letter, they explained that I appeared to be eligible to return to the Police Department, but they required that

I come in person for a physical exam and complete the final paperwork before it could become official. Joyce and I talked about it, and we decided that I would fly to San Antonio, keep my appointments, and then fly back to Delaware. The arrangements were made, and I was lucky in that my days off at Wilmington, combined with taking a couple of leave days, was enough to get things done. I called my parents and told them what was going on. It seemed that a bed was still available at the house so that is where I stayed while in San Antonio.

When I went to the City Personnel Office in San Antonio, I met with the man who was working on my paperwork to come back. He was the Assistant City Manager, Jerry Goodloe, and if it hadn't been for Jerry, I don't think it would have happened. I spoke with him several times, and the last time we spoke, right before I left to go back to Wilmington, he told me that he was going to try to place me into a cadet class that was approaching a graduation date that was only a couple of months away! This meant I wouldn't have to go through the academy training again; I could graduate in November of 1969! He told me that he would let me know as soon as possible but that I should immediately begin to make plans to move to San Antonio. Talk about pressure! I wasn't sure how Joyce was going to take the news, but I *knew* that this was something that I had to do.

I should have known better than to worry about Joyce. She was checking on packing boxes and a U-Haul van the very next day! She and her husband were no closer than ever to resolving their problems, and he cut off her Navy financial support. I guess he was hoping that this would force her to stop the divorce proceedings, but there was no going back as far as she was concerned.

As we started making plans to pack, I took stock of our stuff and realized that we had grown in ways I couldn't have foreseen when I first arrived in my Ford Falcon in the summer of 1968! When my brother and I drove up to her apartment and gone in for the first time, it was obvious that she had initially furnished the place to accommodate her and the kids. Now, numerous things gave evidence that it wasn't just her and her kids but that someone *else* also lived there, too. The Falcon was gone, replaced with a station wagon, but we still had the

Bug, more furniture, a boat, and two German Shepherds. Since the transition took place over time, it was subtle enough that I didn't even realize that we had become a family.

My German shepherd male dog, Thor, was one thing that I decided was a necessity for us when the violence in Wilmington had first started. With everything going on at work, I wanted to make sure that Joyce and the kids were safe. Even though it was quiet where we were living, there were still times when trouble might have presented itself simply by going to a park or the store, and Joyce wasn't comfortable carrying a gun.

My male Shepherd was K-9 trained, and he *loved* Joyce and the kids. I worked out with him every chance I got, so I knew what he could do if required of him. He bit two people over his lifetime when it appeared someone was posing a threat to Joyce and the kids. He only bit two people because everyone else had the good sense to respect his presence!

A few days after I got back from San Antonio, I got a call from Jerry Goodloe telling me that everything was cleared for my return, and I could rejoin the class scheduled to graduate in November! I couldn't believe my good fortune! The preparations for the move picked up speed. By then, the Wilmington PD brass all knew I was going back home, and they did everything they could to get me processed out as soon as they could.

This is a good place to stop and mention how much I appreciated my time with the Wilmington PD and everyone at the department where I worked and socialized during my time there. The experiences that I was exposed to became an invaluable part of my law enforcement career and stayed with me, even after retiring. My prayer is that my friends on the force that I came to like and respect, are all now enjoying retirement, as I am.

The day arrived for us to leave, and it was quite a show. Joyce drove the station wagon pulling the boat, carrying the kids and both dogs. I drove a rented U-Haul truck filled with our belongings, pulling the VW Bug. Destination San Antonio, Texas!

Chapter 22

"Well, congratulations, you passed!"

Before we left Delaware, I spoke with my veterinarian about driving the dogs all the way to Texas, and he recommended that I give them a sedative which would make their trip a lot more comfortable, so that's what I did. Right before we left, I gave them a little meat treat with the capsule in it, and in no time, they were both asleep.

We stopped about 4 – 5 hours later, and the dogs were just waking up. I would walk them and let them take care of business, and I gave them another treat and night, night! I don't think they remembered much about the trip, which was probably just as well as they were both in dog carriers. When we arrived in San Antonio, we found a motel and rented a room by the week.

I moved in with my parents and immediately began looking for a place to permanently rent for Joyce and the kids. We were lucky and found a small house on the Northeast side of San Antonio that allowed dogs. Everything seemed to be moving at 100 mph because I had to report to the police academy just *days* after arriving and going to work. I stayed with my parents often, and it was tough trying to be in two places at once. Fortunately, between Joyce's inheritance and my paycheck, we were able to keep up with the household bills without Joyce having to work so she could take care of the kids.

It didn't take long for me to adjust once again to the routine of the Academy classroom. Since the class that I joined had been together for almost 4 months, they were more than a little *curious* about this stranger that showed up. Once they heard the story, half of them thought I was crazy, and the other half was intrigued with my experiences as a Wilmington Police Officer.

This class was two weeks away from taking their final exam (known as the Probationary Police Officer Exam) which would officially certify that they had passed the Police Academy training, and they were now ready to be sworn in as officers. I had already taken it once before I left, but I was told that I had to take it again.

On the day of the exam, we all sat down and there was a lot of anxiety in the room, because if you didn't pass, you were let go! The test was passed out, and everyone got to work. It was a two-hour test and about 20 minutes into it the door to the classroom opened and in walked Jerry Goodloe along with one of the instructors. Goodloe began walking toward the rear of the room and walked up to where I was sitting. He stood there looking down at my papers and then *picked up* my papers and told me to follow him out of the room! Today you would say that I was totally freaked out! I didn't have a clue as to what was going on, but I was sure that something had gone wrong, and I was out of a job.

When we got out in the hall, we went into the Academy Captain's office and Goodloe looked at my partially completed test and said, "Well congratulations, you passed!" I was speechless! He then went on to tell me that he had just found out that since I had passed my earlier test, there was no need to take it again!

After their test was over, I walked back into the classroom, and people were looking at me like I had grown a second head. I relayed what I had been told and after a few questions, everyone congratulated me. Since everyone *else* had also passed the test, it was time for a party! I'm still not totally sure what really transpired that resulted in me not having to retake that exam, but there was no doubt that I was exactly where I needed to be!

There were two weeks of Academy training left after the Probationary Exam, but the time went by in a hurry. It was time to go to the uniform clothing store and be fitted for uniforms. We were issued our weapons and leather gear, and I took it in stride since I had been through this once before. The rest of the guys were excited, and I couldn't blame them in the least. It rubbed off on me some when the realization finally hit me that I was *home* and was getting ready to start my police officer career for the long haul.

Even though we would be dressed and equipped like every other officer on the force, we Rookies were still in a different category from all the other officers. We had to serve a 6-month probationary period, during which time we could be fired for *any reason*, because we were not yet covered under Civil Service.

This "probationary period" was a means to *weed-out* someone who might begin to give evidence of unsuitability to serve as a police officer despite having performed well in the Academy. All the training and screening in the world doesn't take the place of real-life experiences. Occasionally someone was let go when it became obvious that they were not going to be able to perform as advertised!

The other difference between "Rookies" and "seasoned" officers (besides the new clothes and leather gear) was that we were assigned to a field training officer (FTO) for a two-week ride along. This meant that we were watched as we handled the calls to see how we performed. If the FTO felt that you were not prepared to handle the job, you were given another chance with a *different* FTO. If the second FTO wrote a similar report, you were in real danger of being let go. At the very least, you could be reassigned to go back to the Academy for additional training. This was a good system when it was administered by competent personnel (FTOs), and for the most part, it was.

Most of the FTOs were very good officers with a lot of experience, and they genuinely wanted you to succeed. There were a couple of them who had convinced themselves that they had been officers since the dinosaurs walked the earth, and the Rookie was that brown spot between the toes of a Brontosaurus. Luckily, I didn't get assigned to one of them, but it was jaw clenching to just be around them at a call!

I guess I was fortunate in that unlike the rest of the class I graduated with, I was *not* considered a Rookie. Once the word got around that I had been on the Wilmington PD and had worked through the rioting and unrest there, I was given credit for my experience. But this didn't mean that I was spared some good natured hassling!

I think that hassling (some would call it hazing) is a natural part of being accepted into a group. I admit that this can be taken to the extreme, but, by and large, good natured hassling is productive. It gives people around you a chance to see what type of person you truly are, and it's also a way to get acceptance from the group.

Chapter 23

"…for our honeymoon I went to work…"

I was twenty-four years old when I started my two-week ride along with an FTO. I felt like I had crammed a lot of living into those twenty-four years. I also felt that I didn't get much of chance to be a kid! By the time I was 11 – 12 years old, I was around adults as *much*, if not more so, than I was with kids my age. This was the way my parents were raised, and it was natural for them to treat us in the same way as they had been treated.

I mention this because a lot of the guys out of my cadet class would get together and meet for a few beers after the completion of our shift. At just 24 years old, I was *still* older than a lot of the other guys, and I now had a family! I would be invited to go along, and every now and then I would. It was fun to see their excitement as they told stories of their first traffic stop or family disturbance call.

After I had been shot at, had steel trash cans thrown on top of our police car, fought with various people that wanted to hurt me while they were busy burning buildings…it was hard for me to get *excited* about someone running away from a traffic stop! Yet a traffic stop had as much potential to turn into a dangerous situation as almost *anything* that you could think of. So, since a lot of these guys were single and basically playing the field, and I was already deeply involved with Joyce and two young children, I didn't have much in common socially with "the Guys."

Joyce was still trying to legally resolve her split from her husband, and even though he knew she had moved to San Antonio, he was still refusing to agree to a divorce. She was still living in the rental house while I was staying with my parents for the most part. I couldn't help but wonder why her husband would not acknowledge that their marriage was over. In fairness to him, I only knew *one* side of the situation, so I had no way of seeing the complete picture. One thing I knew for *certain* was that even if something prevented Joyce and I from getting together, their marriage was over.

I was frustrated because there wasn't a lot I could do other than to support her in whatever action she felt she needed to take. She had initially filed in Pennsylvania, but she decided to see a San Antonio attorney and that proved to be the right decision. He provided legal advice that allowed her to file for a divorce, which she did, and sixty days later her marriage was terminated.

A copy of the divorce decree was sent to her husband, and as far as I can remember, that was the last communication that Joyce had with him. Ironically, we received a notice of divorce from her ex-husband, informing her that a final decree of divorce had been granted in Allentown, PA, on 12/6/1974. We concluded that he was marrying someone, and this document provided proof that she had been notified.

Joyce and I were married on April 23, 1970, and for our honeymoon, I went to work the next day because we had no one to watch the kids! To be honest I felt like I had *already* been married long before the official paperwork was certified. She and I, John, and Cathy, and our two German Shepherds were still living in that small rental house on the Northeast side of San Antonio, and we were happy; *crowded*, but happy!

It didn't take long to realize that we were going to need a *bigger* house so the hunt for a place of our own was launched. I knew that we wanted to stay on the North side of town, and with the Police Department's city residency rule (requiring police officers and fireman to live within the city limits,) we narrowed our search area quite a bit. Around the beginning of May we found a new subdivision outside Loop 410 beyond the airport.

The builder had just finished a 3-bedroom, two-bathroom house on a large lot in a cul-de-sac. The subdivision was known as San Pedro Hills. The rock house had a fireplace, and the backyard had lots of trees, and it was absolutely beautiful. Joyce and the kids were already furnishing the house and picking out their bedrooms, and I was telling myself that there was *no way* that we could afford this house!

We told the builder/salesman that we would talk it over and get back with him. When we left I looked at her, and I told her that there was no way we could afford to buy the house. She looked at me, and told me she *wanted* to buy it and she wanted to pay cash! Luckily there wasn't a lot of traffic on the road back then because I think I ran *off* the road and back *on again* before I could come to a stop on the shoulder! It may be hard to believe, but Joyce and I had not had a serious discussion about her personal finances, although I knew that she had inherited money and property when her parents died.

While we had been seeing each other in Charleston, she had mentioned that she had bought their mobile home, but that was about all I knew of her finances. I had always assumed that I would be the breadwinner, and she would stay home while the kids were young. I had envisioned us buying a "starter house," and eventually end up in a nice "forever home." That's the way my father and mother did it, so that was my vision. We decided to go home and talk more when we were safely off the road.

After we put the kids down for the night, we took up the conversation from earlier, and she informed me that she had savings she had inherited, and she had also kept the money from selling the mobile home. Even paying cash for the house still left her with a substantial savings which her father had invested. I was conflicted since this didn't mesh with my breadwinner role.

After another long conversation the following day, Joyce won me over when she pointed out that if we bought the house, we could afford for her to stay home with the kids until they started school. A day later we called the builder, and we told him we would like to meet with him back at the house to look it over one more time. He met us out there, and after looking around again, we told him we wanted the house. As he started the paperwork to apply for a loan, there came one of those rare moments in life when we told him there would *not* be mortgage! He looked at us and said, "You're paying cash?" and we said, "Yep!" He was having a hard time believing that, but he put the paperwork together anyway.

On June 1, 1970, we closed on the house, and it was probably the best decision we ever made. Years later the house sold for almost five times the amount we paid for it in 1970! I lived in that house for 18 years, and they were some of the best years of my life.

Chapter 24

"...I thought someone had run their car into the side of the house."

Since our new home was ready to move in to, we did just that without any delay. If you are familiar with San Antonio, this subdivision in 1970 was the beginning of a building boom that was beginning to move north of the airport. It was still surrounded by a lot of undeveloped ranch country, and we could hunt deer out of our backyard! That brings me to the first pressing problem that we encountered, the lack of a backyard fence!

Our two German Shepherds were basically outside dogs, so the fence had become an immediate concern. They had spent a lot of time living inside when we lived in the apartment in Pennsylvania, so they were already housebroken, but there was *no way* we could continue to let them live inside our new home, so fencing was contracted, and installation began. It didn't take me long for me to realize that paying cash for the house had been great, but the spending had just started!

We contracted for a chain link fence around our entire backyard, and as we had no adjoining neighbors, we had to foot the entire cost ourselves. The fence would run all the way around the back and come into the sides of the house with a gate on one side. The house contractor had sodded most of the front yard, but he had done nothing for the back.

My first project prior to beginning the fence work was to bring in topsoil and get it ready for seeding grass. As I was a patrolman who usually worked rotating shifts, I would spend my time off moving dirt with a wheelbarrow, a shovel, and a rake. I was able to complete the dirt work and let the fence people come in and do their job. I waited until the fence was up, and then I put out the grass seed.

Since it was now summer, I had to keep the dirt *wet* so that the Bermuda grass seed would sprout. This made for a muddy backyard, which meant the dogs had to be confined, which meant an additional fence had to be built to form a kennel. More money! With me diligently watering my dirt, I was rewarded with little grass stems beginning to sprout out of the mud. Yes!!

I had now rotated to working the "dog watch" shift, 10:30 at night to 6:30 AM. This meant I had to sleep during the day, and I hated it! The only way I could sleep was to go to bed as soon as I got home. We had put up blackout curtains in the bedroom, and Joyce would have John and Cathy ready to leave for school about the time I walked in. This would work if nothing woke me up early. Once I woke up I couldn't go back to sleep, and it didn't matter if I had gotten 3 hours or 10 hours, when I woke up, I was done!

One morning I had come home and gone to bed, and I had been asleep about an hour when a terrible crashing and loud banging woke me up. Animals running (?) I had *no idea* what was going on, but all I could think of was that somebody had run their car into the side of our house and that our animals had escaped. Our bedroom was at the back of the house, and the fence and side gate came into view not far from our bedroom window.

I threw on my pants and ran out the front door, expecting to see car tracks and a car crashed into the house. There was none of that, but my fence was completely knocked down, and the backyard was trampled and churned up with my little grass sprouts pulled out of the ground! Then I noticed big, round tracks in the mud that disappeared to around the back of the house. When I turned the corner, I was met by a big, yellow horse tied by a rope to a log! What the…!!!

I really thought I had to be dreaming. That brief thought ended because my dogs were barking and going crazy in their kennel. The horse was still stomping around scaring itself and fighting the rope with the log behind it. People were coming down the street running toward me.

When the people came into my yard, they went straight to the horse expressing their concern for its safety, totally *ignoring* the guy standing there barefoot and shirtless! By now, that guy *was really* beginning to get angry! As they started to untie the horse, I yelled,

"Stop!" Everybody stopped. My dogs, the horse, the idiots on my property... *all* stopped where they were. I have always had the talent of being able to yell really, really loud (just ask my wife and kids.)

It turned out that the people were owners of the horse along with a couple of their neighbors. They explained that they would gladly untie the horse and take him home. I explained that not only was I the owner of this property, but I was also a Police Officer, and *no one* was taking *anything* *anywhere* until I was presented their proper identifications. I told them to hold their horse, but not to untie him while I went in the house and got paper and pencil.

The brief time it took for me to put on a shirt and get something to write on was enough time for me to cool down and for them to realize the seriousness of the situation from *my* perspective! (Oh, by the way, the shirt I put on was my police uniform shirt, badge, name tag and all.) When I went back outside, they had taken the time to look around and see the damage to my property. The front of my fence was knocked down, and posts and the top rail were bent, and my new grass and dirt were torn up all over the yard!

They explained that they had tied their horse to a log so they could put a saddle on him, but something spooked him, and he took off with the rope still tied to the log. As he ran, the log bounced behind him, scaring him even *more* as it would bump his hind legs. He somehow managed to find *my* street, and he began running downhill. In his panic he just ran straight at my fence, jumped it, and the log caught the fence and did the damage. As he rounded the corner of the house he was confronted with my dogs that were going crazy, and at that point I think he just gave up, and he stood where I found him. He probably was hoping someone would shoot him, and put him out of his misery! For a moment or two the thought entered my mind.

It turned out the people were nice enough, and they were able to provide me with identification and assured me that their insurance would cover the damages. I said they were nice people, but I should have added that in my opinion, they had no business owning a horse!

Everyone left, and I knew that my sleeping was over for the rest of the day. Joyce came home later that morning and found me sitting at the kitchen table. She wanted to know what I was doing up. The damaged portion of the fence was opposite from the driveway, so she didn't see it when she came home and drove into the garage. I walked her outside and showed her the fence and yard. The look on her face was priceless. It took her a minute before she finally asked me what had happened. After explaining the whole thing, she just sat there and then she started laughing! I tried to tell her it wasn't funny, but then I started laughing, too, and that was that!

Chapter 25

"…shots fired…"

Right after graduating from the Police Academy, I was assigned to the Eastside of San Antonio to work through my six-month probationary term. The population on the Eastside was comprised of a large portion of black people. Since I had worked around black people, beginning with the restaurant during high school, and in Wilmington, I wasn't uncomfortable around them like some of the other officers.

It was surprising that a lot of white people were often intimidated when dealing with blacks because of the way they interacted between themselves and others. I am not being derogatory here, I'm just saying that cultures are often distinguished by the way they express their emotions and carry-on their conversations. Some of us like to get *close* when talking to someone, and others like to maintain social *distance*, some get excited and *loud,* and others get *quiet.* In my dealings with people, I found it to be important to be able to figure out what type of personality I encountered, because that would help me deal with that individual in the safest way possible.

I recognized that a lot of black males tended to be loud and animated. They would get close and often be joined by friends and family. And when females arrived on the scene, things could escalate rapidly. Hispanic males were often more *reserved*, but the females were extremely *excitable* and were capable of escalating a situation out of control in a hurry.

Caucasians tended to be more *low-key*, and by-standers were often reluctant to get involved. Having said all this, it goes without saying that there was no hard and fast rule that any one of any group would behave in a predictable way. The trick was to assess each encounter with an individual and try to determine how that person interacted with other people. More importantly, as far as I was concerned, was how a person responded to somebody with a badge. I found that *idiots* came in *all* skin colors, and it was best to judge people by their actions.

I liked working the eastside, but when my probationary period ended I was reassigned to the South side of town. The majority population here was a combination of working class and low-income whites and Hispanics. This move came about the time that Joyce and I had bought our new home. I was still working shift work where we rotated every two months from daylight to evening to dog watch.

I was on the dog watch shift on the 23 of December of 1970, and I received a call for an accident at the south end of my district on Interstate Highway 35 near the small town of Von Ormy. I had no sooner started that way when the call was updated to a shooting, and Officer Reggie Bays was dispatched to cover on the call with me.

As we got close to the location, Reggie and I started getting shot at by a guy with a rifle, standing by a stopped pick-up truck on the shoulder of the highway. Both our windshields were hit, and we blew by the guy and pulled over about two hundred yards beyond his truck. Of course we called in "shots fired," but we still had no idea what was going on.

Almost as soon as we pulled over, we heard additional shots, and a southbound pick-up veered, and pulled up in front of our police cars. A young guy jumped out of the truck on the passenger side covered in blood. We ran up to him, and he was motioning to the inside of the truck. We looked into the truck and another young fellow who had been riding in the middle was leaning back; blood was pouring from his throat. There was a bullet hole in the windshield, and he had been hit in the exact center of his throat.

The shooter was still firing in our direction, so we had to be careful how we moved around. The driver of the truck was still sitting behind the wheel, holding the boy in the middle. He was crying as he told us that this boy was his brother. The three of them were coming from Louisiana, headed to South Texas to go hunting. We told him to put pressure on the wound to try to stop the bleeding, and Reggie and I informed the dispatcher of what we had. We requested an ambulance

ASAP, and as the guy was still shooting at us, we cautioned everyone else who would be coming our way to use extreme caution.

Reggie and I decided that we had to stop the guy from ambushing any further traffic since we would have an ambulance and other police officers coming, along with unsuspecting civilians. So we got in our cars, and turned on our red roof lights, and u-turned to try to arrest the shooter. I guess when we turned on our roof lights he realized for the first time that he had shot at police cars. When we started his way, he jumped in his truck, u-turned and started heading north again toward San Antonio. Since he couldn't shoot back at us while he was driving, we started closing the gap, and the chase was on.

San Antonio in 1970 had only one major traffic loop known as Loop 410. Interstate Highway 35 ("IH 35") is a north/south highway that goes all the way south through San Antonio to the Mexican border at Laredo. As we chased the shooter northbound on IH35, he turned off the highway before he reached Loop 410, and he took a road that ran into a large farming area. The road was paved, and the farm fields were unfenced; one field was planted in carrots.

We were now on this guy's butt and had our sirens going *along* with the red lights. I guess he was starting to panic, and he drove his truck right into the carrot field, jumping these rows of growing carrots. Reggie and I stopped because we knew there was nowhere for him to go.

Sure enough, about 50 or 60 feet into the field, the truck bogged down and came to a stop. These were irrigated fields, so the ground/rows were muddy. He was facing away from us, and we saw him jump out of the truck with his rifle. He laid down by the front of the truck, and his driver's door was standing open. Reggie and I were out of our cars and both of us were kneeling behind the side of Reggie's car with the engine compartment between us and the shooter. He started shooting at us again, but all he could hit was the cars. He didn't realize that we were both behind one car, so he kept shooting at both cars.

If you are not into guns, you might not realize that a person armed with a rifle normally has a significant advantage over someone armed with a pistol when you are shooting at one another at a distance. Up to now, neither Reggie nor I had fired a single shot at this guy since all we had was our pistols.

My car was parked behind Reggie's, and we determined that we needed a shotgun. All the marked police cars were equipped with a 12-gauge pump shotgun, so we decided that Reggie would shoot a couple of times at the shooter to distract him while I ran back to my car and got the shotgun. We waited until the guy cranked off another round, and then Reggie returned fire.

I ran back and got my shotgun out of my car and crawled back to where Reggie was while the guy fired off another couple of shots. Our police cars were also equipped with a rotating spotlight, but since our police cars were not facing him directly, the only light we had was from his partially open door! Reggie and I agreed that he would reach into his car while still kneeling, and at my signal, he would turn on the spotlight and try to put it on the shooter, so that I could shoot with the shotgun.

Sounded like a plan, so we counted down, and as he turned on the light, I stood up and could see part of the shooter's lower leg and foot (he was still laying on the ground,) so I fired! Immediate yelling told me that I had put at least one and hopefully more holes in him! He cranked off another couple of shots, and since we still had our light on him, Reggie fired at him with his pistol.

The guy stood up and started to stumble to get back into his truck, and Reggie and I unloaded on him. He managed to get in, but he fell on his back with the gun laying across his belly. We waited; his voice faded away and his legs stopped moving. We both approached the cab of the truck from different sides, and when we got to him, he was gone...dead. This all occurred two days before Christmas.

Here is the condensed version of what happened: The initial call for an accident was called in by a pregnant woman who didn't know that the shooter had shot and hit her windshield, breaking it. She had

169

stopped at Von Ormy at the convenience store and called in to report the "accident."

As we approached where he was stopped on the highway, he began to shoot at us, and after we stopped down the road from him, he shot at the three hunters who were simply driving to their hunting lease, killing the boy in the middle. We shot and killed him in that carrot field. It was later learned that this guy had gotten out of prison six weeks earlier after doing time for armed robbery. He broke into someone's house, and among other things, he stole the rifle that was used during this incident.

Both Reggie and I went home to our families later that morning, and we both celebrated Christmas with them on Christmas morning. That boy from Louisiana was honored with a funeral, and I know it was a Christmas that his people will never forget. I have gone into a lot of detail about this incident because once people find out I was a police officer, they will often ask me if I have ever shot anyone. When I tell them *yes,* they will often follow-up that question by asking me if the person died. When they hear *yes* again, I have had someone say something along the lines of "How awful that must be to have to carry that "burden" of knowing you killed somebody."

A lot of police officers never pulled their weapon or fired a shot during their entire career. For some reason, maybe because I worked in violence-prone areas along with other reasons, I was involved in several shootings. Some died; some didn't. Those times when deadly force was required of me, it was the conduct of the *"bad guy"* (or woman) that precipitated a police response and the eventual use of deadly force!

I think it's also important to note here that there were several times (at least three incidents come to mind) where I was legally justified to use deadly force, but I didn't. The "burden" that Police Officers carry is the responsibility of knowing when you have to use deadly force to keep someone safe.

Rules and regulations can describe the authorization and justification for using deadly force, but ultimately it comes down to the circumstances present when the officer arrives at the location. Police Officers are human beings, not programmed robots, so emotions are present at every incident. The challenge is to *control* your emotions as much as possible! I swore to uphold the laws of the city, state, and government, and to protect life and property. But I think some people overlook the fact that an Officer's life is also worth protecting!

(I wrote this chapter in April of 2022. The past three years have been chaotic in America with civil unrest, Covid, and deep political, social, and racial division. The political Left demands that policing needs to be re-imagined. "Defund and/or eliminate the police" are the headlines in the mainstream media, and the talking points of our Left-leaning radical politicians. A few of the idiots even suggest that police officers don't have to shoot to kill, but should just wound the criminal! People spouting that BS have no idea what they are talking about. It is called "deadly force" for a reason!)

Chapter 26

"...snip what needed to be snipped."

Life was good for the Jacobs, and early in 1971, Joyce started talking to me about us having a child. I was conflicted to be honest because I felt that John and Cathy were already *my kids*, and I wasn't sure if we could afford another one. We finally decided that she would stop taking birth control pills and see if nature would take its course.

Sure enough, she got pregnant, and on June the 14th of 1972, in the waiting room of the San Antonio Methodist hospital, I was told that I was the Daddy of a baby girl! Everyone was doing fine (except me,) and I would be allowed to see them both once they were moved to a room. While I waited, all kinds of feelings were going through me! I was proud, nervous, happy, and curious as to what she would look like, and I didn't know whether to laugh or cry! Then I got *anxious* as to how I would affect her life, and how she would affect ours!

When I walked in that room and saw Joyce holding the baby, I was completely overwhelmed. The nurse was there, and she took the baby, and gave her to me. She began wriggling around, and I started to cry! I had been shot at, been in car chases, fights, and riots, but I had never been so completely overwhelmed by the feelings I had when I held my daughter for the first time.

The nurse and Joyce both laughed because I was holding her like she would break if I didn't do it just right. All her body parts were accounted for, and the nurse assured me that her head would round out instead of resembling a cone, and the wrinkles along with the red complexion would fade in no time. I was skeptical but, since this was my first close contact with a newborn baby, I had to take their word for it, and Joyce didn't seem concerned, so I calmed down.

I think Joyce and the baby were in the hospital three days and we had to come up with a name for the birth certificate. Back then you didn't know what sex the baby would be until it was born, so we had to work on a name. We had played the "if it's a boy" or "if it's a girl" game and everyone had suggestions, but we finally settled on Suzanne Marie.

I took John and Cathy to the hospital to see their new baby sister, and they were both excited about the new member to the family. When we got everyone home, they had their first opportunity to hold Suzanne, and I think they did better than my first attempt! By then her color was much improved, and she wasn't a crying baby, so everyone was content. Of course it wasn't long before my mother and father showed up, and the baby was being passed along. I was glad to see that my father was no better at holding her than I had been, but my mother took her as if she had lots of experience! (Go figure!)

Earlier, when Joyce and I got together, two little kids were part of the package, and we had been functioning as a family, but now, having a newborn was a whole different ballgame! It was like having a box, wrapped in bright paper, sitting under the Christmas tree with no name on it; you were constantly wondering about it! Even though I was the oldest of three, when my sister and brother were brought home, I didn't have a lot to do with them. But Suzanne Marie got my attention as soon as I got home, no matter what else was going on around the house.

She would make noises and wave her arms around and let you know when it was time to eat. She would also let you know when it was time to change her diaper, and sometimes she didn't have to say a thing because my sense of smell worked very well. John and Cathy were already potty trained, our dogs were potty trained, but this tiny bundle could get me retching with one whiff! Fortunately Joyce recovered quickly, and since Suzanne was my mother and father's first grandchild, my mother was only too happy to come over and help! I was at work most of the time so I was able to *avoid* a great deal of the dirty jobs involved with caring for a newborn.

Joyce was a natural mother and having practically raised John and Cathy on her own (as many military spouses were forced to do,) she was in charge. My mother learned that lesson as Suzanne became accustomed to sleeping in her crib.

One weekend my mother and father came over to the house just after Joyce had put Suzanne down for her nap. Suzanne by then knew voices, and I guess she heard my mother's voice, and she started fussing and began to cry. Of course my mother got up and headed for the bedroom, but Joyce stopped her and asked her not to go in. Mom was saying something along the lines that something was wrong, but Joyce told her that it was just Suzanne wanting attention.

Mom sat back down, and a few minutes later the crying stopped. About fifteen minutes after that, Joyce let mom check up on her, and Suzanne was sound asleep. Along with my mother, I learned right then, don't mess with Momma Bear! I also knew that, because Joyce wouldn't let anyone spoil Suzanne by running to her at every whimper or cry, we were blessed with a baby that cried very little, and most of the time if she cried, there was a good reason.

Joyce loved all kids, and she would have been happy to have as many as I wanted. I loved kids, too, but I was content with the three that we had. The question came up, "Wouldn't it be nice to have another boy?" but the thought entered my head that he might be just like me, and that scared me to death! So a few months after Suzanne was born and Joyce was back on birth control pills, I committed that I didn't want any more children. Joyce and I talked about our options, and we finally agreed that I would have the simple sterilization operation.

I spoke with a Urologist, and we agreed that I was a good candidate for the procedure, and he set a date. I asked him how long I would have to stay in the hospital, and he told me I could come into the day surgery center, and he would make two very small incisions, snip what needed to be snipped, and I would be on my way. That "snipping" talk prompted me to ask him what sort of anesthesia he would be using, and he laughed and said he would just give me a shot in my testicles! Whoa!!

Having taken a shot to the testicles on a couple of prior occasions, this wasn't what I wanted to hear. He must have been a mind reader because he could see that he had lost me, and in spite of all his efforts to tell me that he had done this hundreds of times, he realized that I wasn't going to be a good candidate for a local anesthetic after all! He set me up for the twilight sleep procedure, and that is what we did. I took some teasing, but I never regretted that decision even though it meant a little longer stay in the hospital as opposed to his office.

Chapter 27

"…carrying a Polaroid picture."

My brother is four years younger than me, and he had signed up for the Navy in 1967 for a four-year enlistment. As I mentioned previously, Ralph also ended up serving on a submarine, and he was stationed at Key West, Florida until he was honorably discharged in 1971.

While he was in the Navy, his boat made a run to Europe and he was able to make a visit to Belgium. I was envious because he was able to see our grandparents, numerous uncles and aunts, and several cousins. By the time I made my single visit back to Belgium, a lot of those folks were no longer living.

When Ralph was discharged, he came back to San Antonio and moved back in with Mom and Dad. Our father also got him a job at the bakery, but he didn't stay much longer than I had. He worked at a store for a while, and eventually went to work at a metal fabricating shop. I don't remember how long he worked there, but when he told us that he wanted to find something else, everybody was glad to hear it. That was a dangerous place to work. It didn't take but one careless moment to lose a finger or hand around those machines.

When he started looking around for another job, he and I talked one day, and he asked me how law enforcement was working out for me. When I described the work and the benefits (which were nothing *then* compared to what we later achieved,) it was miles better than the metal shop. It didn't take long for him to decide that he would apply. My brother was always better at school, and he has a different personality from mine. Whereas I had our father's temperament (immediately blow-up, yell, curse, and then calm down), he had our mother's. He was more reflective, quiet, and thoughtful, and was patient, but he wouldn't forget a transgression against him.

I had no doubt that he would be a good police officer, and he was! After he graduated from the Academy and began to work out in the street, he would run across some of the guys I worked with, and once they found out he and I were brothers, they would give him a hard time saying there was no way he and I were related! (I never figured out if that was good or bad).

Unlike some brothers, I was lucky that he and I almost always got along. Part of the reason that he, our sister, and I have remained *close* is that, as immigrants, we had some of that "us-versus-them" mentality as we started to assimilate into the culture of our new country. Trying to fit in at school had a lot do with that along with having no close friends at the beginning.

When I went through the Academy, there was a pretty girl working in the office as the secretary to the Academy staff. A lot of the single guys would try to take her out, but they never got very far. "Carolyn" was studying for her nursing degree, and she was serious about her career path.

When my brother started at the Academy, they hit it off and began dating. He and Carolyn were married in 1974, and since they were on a tight budget, we had the reception at our house. Ralph and Carolyn were teetotalers, so I felt that I would have to take up the slack! I did that *and then* some, and I was three days getting over the hangover! I mention this because at this time, I was still drinking a lot. I had been working on the Southside of San Antonio for a while, and I had gotten to know and become friends with a few of the business owners in that district.

One guy, "Don," owned a used car lot and liked to drink, and he liked to hunt so we had a lot in common. I would go by his car lot while working to visit him and write up my reports. I ended up taking a slot on his hunting lease, and we became personal friends. If I was on that part of town on my day off, I would stop by the lot, and Don and I would sometimes have lunch and visit.

Sometimes he would have some other friends over after he closed for the day and host a dice game. I was always invited, and I would go if I was off from work. Don would have some beer and whiskey, and it was always a good time. When the game started, it seemed that the time flew by and when it was time to stop, it was usually late. It seemed like I had always drunk more than I should have. I would have to drive clear across town to go home, and there were times I didn't remember how I got home!

I realized how bad it had gotten when I woke up one morning and I felt awful, I mean I felt *awful* from head to toe! I remembered nothing about driving home, absolutely nothing! Joyce was home, and the kids were at school, and I showered, took aspirin, and went into the kitchen where Joyce was sitting with a cup of coffee. She fixed me one, and didn't say anything for a while, but I could tell what was coming.

Finally she asked me if I remembered coming home, and I had to admit that I didn't remember anything after leaving the car lot. She nodded, and then she told me that she wanted to show me something. She got up and went into the living room and came back carrying a Polaroid picture. She put the picture down on the table in front of me. The picture was of me with my shirt off, my pants down around my ankles... passed out, laying around the toilet in our bathroom! She then told me what had happened when I got home.

She had awakened when she heard me come in, and I took off my shirt as I stumbled into the bedroom. I threw up in the toilet bowl, pulled my pants down and sat down on the toilet, and then passed out, falling on the floor. She managed to get my clothes off, and apparently I crawled into our shower where she turned the water on and left me laying under it for a while.

After a while she dried me off, and I stood up and was able to get into bed and went to sleep. But I remembered *none* of that! Then, she dropped the bomb...she asked me what our kids would think if they had walked in instead of her and found me like I was in the picture? This was sometime around the end of 1974, and in the forty-eight intervening years since, I have never been drunk like that again!

Chapter 28

"…suicide by cop."

I believe that television formed the public's perception of what it's like to be a police officer more than anything else. Most people would spend an hour or half hour watching a crime show, and all they would see was an action-packed, condensed version of what policing was generally not like at all! Oh, there was plenty of action at times, but most often it was very routine, consisting of responding to various calls for thefts, damage to property, accidents, and assisting the public with complaints of loud music or other minor civil disturbances.

As a Police Officer, what you couldn't do was let yourself become complacent with the ordinary and not be prepared to react to something out of the ordinary. A perfect example was that initial call for an accident on IH 35 which turned into a shooting that I described in an earlier chapter. Something like that will take your "pucker factor" to the top of the scale, immediately!

When I am asked what one of my scariest moments was during my policing career, I give them this example: It was 12:30 AM on a Sunday morning, and a lot of the Saturday night drinkers were driving back home, drunk. It was a busy night with all of us handling calls for fights and accidents, and I got dispatched to a house for a drunken disturbance.

Since everybody was already tied up on other calls, I was on my own. As I was on the way, the dispatcher called again, and he told me that a couple of more people had called in on the same issue, so I knew that the drunks were going at it hot and heavy. Just before I turned down the street, the dispatcher called *again,* telling me that a shot had been fired at the location! When I pulled up I notified the dispatcher that I was there, and as I got out of the car all the lights went out at the house. The neighbors on either side had all their lights off, too, (they didn't want to be involved) so it was dark! But I knew somebody was up because they had turned off the lights, and a shot had been fired; someone could be seriously hurt. The job requires that I go up on the dark porch and knock on the door! Would you be ready to do that?

When I knocked and announced that I was police officer, a teenage girl came to the door and informed me that her father had passed out, and that she and her mother were OK. Whew!! He had shot once up in the air from his back porch for reasons only a drunk would understand. Since he was no longer a danger, I had her bring me the gun, and I took it with me and placed it into our property room where he could try to get it back after he sobered up. All was well when I came down from the adrenaline rush. What makes these calls scary is that there is no way to know in advance what the circumstances are before you arrive.

Here is a different outcome to a similar call. My brother, Ralph, responded to a location for a man creating a disturbance at his home. When Ralph knocked on the door, a man opened it, and started talking to him through the screen door. The porch was dark, so it was hard for Ralph to clearly see the man, but he felt something was wrong. He could see a woman and someone else in a room behind the man, and they both had scared looks on their faces. As the man continued to talk, he suddenly brought up a pistol and pointed it at my brother. Ralph pulled his gun and shot the man through the screen door, killing him.

It turned out that the man's gun was empty, and he had wanted to commit what has now come to be known as "Suicide by Cop." The people in the house tried to warn my brother just before the guy pulled his gun, but it was too late. It wouldn't have made any difference since Ralph wouldn't have been able to rely on the gun being unloaded. This stressful part of police work is that often there is no way of knowing what you will encounter when you arrive on a call.

With these kinds of stressful situations, there had to be some way to ease the tension of the job. Police Officers are innovative, and pranks are a part of breaking not only the tension, but a lot of the times, the monotony of the job. I mentioned the "dog watch" shift (11:00 PM – 7:00 AM) and depending on the day of the week, the shift could be really busy, or it could get really slow. By three or four o'clock in the morning, guys were wanting coffee, and we only had one or two coffee shops that were open all night. So it wasn't unusual to have two or three patrol cars meet at one of the shops.

The problem was that we weren't allowed to have more than *two* cars at a time at any one location. (The police chief didn't want a citizen to drive by and see several police cars at a restaurant and get the idea that no one was fighting crime!)

Back then our radios were hardwired under the dash of the car, and they couldn't be taken out. This meant that if you were going to go in somewhere and be out of your car, you had to notify the dispatcher so that he/she didn't assign you to a call. If *two* cars were already checked out, and a *third* guy wanted to go in, then a *fourth* guy would have to relay any calls to the guy inside. The first two guys would park in front, and anybody else would park around the back, out of sight. It wasn't very often that we had slow nights, so everybody enjoyed the "down time" when it came along. The last thing you wanted to hear on a slow night was radio chatter regarding minor, mundane issues.

We had a new guy once who had been recently assigned to our patrol section whose name was Ray. Being new, he was constantly on the radio checking on this business, or that car. It didn't matter if it was a "slow night" or not… he was on the radio. Police officers are like most people in that they have to get to know you before you become part of the group. So he wasn't invited to coffee or made aware of places we would gather to write our reports away from the eyes of the public.

Since Ray wasn't familiar with "slow night" protocol, in our patrol section he became a target for some extra attention. "KPs" was one of our favorite coffee shops, and it was located on SW Military Drive. One night Ray wanted a cup of coffee and when he drove up to KPs, he found that there were already two officers checked out with their cars parked out front, so Ray pulled around to the back where three other guys were parked.

181

He asked if someone would listen for his call number while he went in for a cup, and we said sure, but he failed to lock his car. Department procedures demanded that you lock your car when you weren't in it because every car now had a shotgun mounted in front of the dash, and you had other personal stuff on the passenger seat, including flashlights and so on. Ray was soon to find out that there was another good reason to keep your car locked.

Ray had been inside for about twenty to twenty-five minutes when he came back out and got into his car and left. About 15 mutes later, several of us were still at the rear of KPs when Ray hollered on his radio that he needed cover at West Southcross and Pleasanton Road! By the sound of his voice you could tell this was *urgent*. The dispatcher started sending units to his location and asked him what he had, but he didn't respond.

As four police cars arrived at his location, we found Ray standing about 15 feet from his running car, which was stopped partially on the curb. He had his gun out and pointed at the wide-open driver's door. We rushed to his side and asked him what was going on, and he told us that as he was coming up to the intersection, something grabbed his neck from the back seat. He had managed to shake it off, throw the car into park, call for help, and jump out. He was certain that whoever it was, it was *still* in the car.

Ray called out to the car that they needed to show themselves, and he wanted to see *hands!* Nothing happened. He repeated his demand. By then three other civilians had driven up, and since the intersection was blocked, they had also gotten out of their cars, and they were watching the events unfold.

Just as Ray was going to repeat his order to come out, we saw this small furry ball climb over the back of the driver's seat, climb down the seat, and hop to the ground. The baby raccoon stopped for a second, looked at all the commotion, and ran off down W. Southcross. The dispatcher was calling for an update, and we all felt that Ray should be the one to fill him in, so we all got back into our own cars and told the dispatcher that we were back in service. Ray told him he would call him by phone and explain the situation rather than tying up valuable airtime.

After that incident, there were several days when Ray refused to talk to us as he seemed convinced that one of us had planted that critter in his car at the back of KPs. Our feelings were hurt that he would believe that we could have done something so vile! Apparently the guilty party struck again when a dead rattlesnake that looked surprisingly alive was found coiled up on the driver's side floorboard of a policeman who was known to be deathly afraid of snakes. We never identified that culprit, but we damned sure locked our cars, especially at KPs! I am eternally grateful that there were never any shots fired during these escapades, but I am also saddened that some guys could hold a grudge way beyond what I felt was healthy.

It wasn't just guys I worked with that would provide comic relief. You can't beat the ordinary citizens (or *not so* ordinary in the case of our criminal element) for bringing a little humor into your life, even through hard times. Out of many incidents, there is one in particular that stands out in my mind that involved a classic romantic relationship gone bad.

In my district, I had several trailer parks. Some were very run down, and a couple were nice, where everyone kept up their property. It was in one of the very nice parks that I was dispatched to contact a young woman when I arrived. She told me that she and her boyfriend had recently broken up, but he was coming by late at night, knocking on her window and door, trying to get her to let him in. She had a small child by a previous marriage, and she was scared that he might become violent.

We had just started our "Dog Watch" shift when I made the first call so I told her that I would drive by now and then for the rest of the evening and hopefully he would see the car and get scared off. A week or so went by when I got the next call at the house. He had come by again, knocked on the windows, rattled the door, and called out to her, declaring his undying love and devotion for her, and adding that if he couldn't have her, no one else would either. (This woman had a good job, but the stress of this situation was affecting her employment because she wasn't able to rest for fear of what this guy would do next.)

After three calls in the first two weeks, I had yet to catch a glimpse of this knucklehead! The woman's trailer was close to the entrance of the park and on one of the calls, I had been just down the street when I was dispatched there. I arrived only two or three minutes later, and yet he was already gone. As in a lot of the parks, the residents didn't have a garage, so they parked their cars in front of the trailer. She had her car parked just outside of her front door, and I checked the car, but it was locked and secure. The guy had disappeared without a trace. Needless to say, I was getting more than a little aggravated!

The boyfriend's threats were also becoming more violent, and I was really concerned that he would eventually break in and harm her and her child. One night around 12:30 in the morning, I got another call, and just like every time before, when I arrived he was gone. I stayed a while and drove through the park, but he was nowhere to be found.

When I left I decided that I would stop and write my report just outside the park entrance. I had not been there 5 minutes when the dispatcher called me and told me the guy was back! I left my headlights off and drove back into the park and pulled up in front of her trailer and turned my lights on. Nobody! The guy was gone again! No way!! Another officer covered me on the call, and he had driven through the park from another entrance, and he hadn't seen anybody either. By now, she had come out of her house, and she was really scared. I couldn't blame her one bit: we were dealing with a ghost!

I was trying to calm her and come up with some sort of game plan when we heard a faint voice. As we looked around, we heard it again…"Help!" What the heck? Then again, but this time it was strained, "Please, help me…." I heard some scuffling noise from around her car, and I finally realized it was coming from *underneath* the car. When I looked under the car with my flashlight, I found my ghost!

I told him to get his butt out of there, but he could barely talk and told me he was stuck. Then, I noticed that the car seemed to have gotten lower and that he was having difficulty breathing. As I saw this, my cover officer told me he could hear *air* escaping. He walked around the car and found that air was escaping from the tires. The idiot had punctured the tires with an ice pick when I left the first time, but when he saw me drive up the second time, he crawled under the car just as he had done those previous times when he had gotten away. In other words, this guy had always been under the car every time I made a call, probably laughing his butt off!

Well, he wasn't laughing now because there was no way we could stop the car from sinking lower as the air continued to leak out of the tires! Since we didn't carry jacks in our police cars, I had the dispatcher notify the Fire Department so they could send out a rescue unit. By the time they arrived, he wasn't saying anything because he was trying really hard to keep some air in his lungs. I had been updating the dispatcher on what was going on, and since it was a slow night, some of the other guys had shown up. We looked around for something that we could use to block the car from sinking lower, but nobody found anything.

We could hear the fire department sirens, and I think a few of the guys were talking about a small pool to see if they were going to get to him in time. I admit I was conflicted about where I stood on this guy being saved. When he punctured all four of her tires this time, there was no doubt in my mind that he would hurt her if he got the chance. I had experienced numerous similar circumstances in the past where a spurned lover would come back to terrorize his ex-girlfriend/wife and other family members.

When the Fire Department showed up, they checked out the situation, and I told them what was going on. When they heard the facts, it didn't seem like they got into any hurry, but they got one of their inflatable balls and slid it under the car. This was able to lift the car so we could get him out from underneath it. Fortunately for him (or unfortunately?), he survived, and we sent him to the hospital, where he recovered. The woman moved out, and I never heard from her again, and I never dealt with the *"Ghost"* again, so I guess it all worked out!

During my years as a Police Officer, a lot of the interactions I had with people were like this one: a combination of serious, scary behavior mixed with humor resulting from the stupidity of one or more of the people involved. I know for a fact that sometimes justice is administered in ways that have nothing to do with a courtroom. (I don't know if you, the Reader, found any humor in this story; maybe you just had to be there!) One of my friends asked me if I didn't want to kick myself in the butt for not thinking about that guy's hiding place sooner. Huh!

Chapter 29

"...she started yelling, "Rape! Help me..."

Both in Wilmington and San Antonio, as a new officer, you were assigned to work the street in uniform. The thought remains that if you couldn't perform the basic duties of police work, you were probably not cut out for a career in law enforcement. TV glamorizes the detectives, but responding to the needs of the *citizens* when they called for help was the bedrock of being a police officer.

Police Departments are modeled after the military as far as chain-of-command is concerned. The Rank structure begins with a Patrolman, then progresses to Detective, Sergeant, Lieutenant, Captain and then the Chief and his assistants. San Antonio required a new hire to put in at least 2 years as a Patrolman before you could try to take the Detective exam. This held true for advancement for all the other ranks, too: You had to put in 2 years in each rank before advancing to the next one. I had been in uniform about 5 years when I decided to try out for the Detective's exam.

In 1975 San Antonio along with other large cities was expanding the department because the city populations were growing. As the department was hiring, the chances for promotion were also expanding. Prior to this time promotions were few and far between, with maybe only a handful of people advancing in rank. When I took my first Detective exam, it was projected that probably 50 or 60 people would be promoted off the list which lasted for a year. I wasn't a great test taker, but those odds were attractive enough for me to sign up and study for the test. The test material was made available 2 months prior to the test day. Believe me when I tell you, that the competition was *fierce* since people who had tried before were committed to getting a much better score "this time!"

I received the study material, and I thought I had done a good job of preparing. When test day arrived, I was ready. There were probably 200 people taking the test. But I didn't even get close! I just thought I had studied. My score was in the mid-eighties, and when they began reading out the scores, probably at least *50* people had scored in the *nineties*! I was so far down on the list that I didn't stand a chance on filling a Detective position that year!

The following year I again tried and fell short! I beat myself up, and I swore that the next year I would make it. In the meantime, the department had formed a plain clothes "Task Force" that was comprised of patrolmen. I was accepted when I applied, and I really enjoyed this facet of policing.

Typically when working in uniform, you are showing up after the incident has occurred, and you're basically documenting that it took place. The Task Force was formed to anticipate various crimes (vehicle thefts at malls, burglaries of houses and businesses, robberies, and even assaults committed in public places,) with the aim to stop the commission of the crime as it starts to happen or make an arrest during the act.

This was the stuff that TV viewers of police shows enjoy watching! Of course the TV shows don't have time to show the boring stuff that is involved, such as the efforts made in finding the bad guys, doing the surveillance of watching them, and waiting for them to finally act. But when the action finally started, it was Cowboys and Indians. Oh man, I loved it because you were rewarded with instant gratification when you watched the criminal begin to commit the crime, and then you swooped in and captured the SOB!

Of course since we didn't wear a uniform and drove plain unmarked cars, most everyone would let their hair grow long and stop shaving. For some reason a lot of the guys felt that only policemen shaved every day, so to look like something other than a policeman, *i.e., a criminal*, we had to grow a beard!

By now, women were joining the police department and working in the field. We would sometimes "borrow" a female officer from Patrol, and have her working with us in plain clothes on the Task Force. They were invaluable, especially when working some of our stakeouts because few people noticed a "couple" walking around or sitting in a car as opposed to two guys.

Plain clothes undercover work isn't for everyone. This isn't meant to minimize or elevate one form of police work over another; they each have their own specific value. Just using the term "plain clothes" means that I'm talking about units such as Homicide, Burglary, Theft, Robbery, etc., (where you generally wear slacks, sport coat, and tie and have your badge or credentials openly displayed so that the citizen knows you are a police officer.) These units follow up on a particular crime after it is reported and identify the perpetrators and arrest them when possible.

In plain clothes <u>undercover</u> work you don't want people to know you're a police officer. This means that you can blend in with the civilians, but it also means that you don't have the protection and deference that the uniform or badge normally provides. I say normally provides, because there were (and still are) a lot of people out there that could care less that you are a police officer! So you can imagine that since there are people who will resist arrest by a uniform officer, it becomes even more of a problem when you're wearing plain clothes and a beard and tell them they are under arrest!

For that reason, we tried whenever possible to have a uniform unit standing by when we were going to make an arrest, but it wasn't always possible. To be fair, I could understand civilians being skeptical when two or more bearded, sometimes scruffy looking guys, walked up, and said they were police officers. I remember one incident where my appearance created a bad problem.

As a patrolman married with three kids and all that comes with that, money was tight. I wanted to provide not just daily basic needs, but also wanted my family to enjoy recreation related activities. Since we had a boat we would often go to Canyon Lake outside of San Antonio and ski and picnic at the lake. I also liked to hunt and fish, so I had a deer lease in South Texas. These were all things that we as a family liked to do. To be able to afford these extras I, as so many other policemen, worked extra jobs.

There was no shortage of extra jobs, and many of them involved security type work where you were present in uniform and acted as a deterrent to criminal activity. Since I was working undercover, I couldn't wear a uniform unless I cleaned up. This meant I would have to shave, cut my hair, and generally dump my undercover look. Fortunately there were some large retail stores who had problems with shoplifters, and they wanted police officers to catch and arrest the thieves. Uniform officers couldn't do this because the crooks would just go to another store that didn't have this security, but a guy in plain clothes wouldn't be recognized by the crook.

A friend of mine had landed a contract to provide off-duty officers to work plain clothes security for a chain of grocery stores, and he wanted me to be part of the team. We would work different stores all over town, so you didn't have to work the same store too often and have someone recognize you.

One day I was working the store at S. Presa and Pereida Streets. I watched a young woman put several cosmetic items in a handbag and start walking to the front of the store. It was summertime, so she was wearing shorts and a loose top, and as she started to leave the store, I was right behind her. (Back then to complete the act of shoplifting, the thief had to walk *out* of the store without paying for the item. This was to prevent the person from saying that they were going to pay for it if you stopped them too soon in the store.)

As she walked out the door, I said, "Police Officer, you're under arrest," and I grabbed her arm. She looked back at me, and the fight was on! I was a large guy in good shape, and she was petite and was probably 5'5" tall. It was like trying to wrestle with an octopus! (Have you ever tried to cram a cat into a carrier when she didn't want to go? It was like that!)

I didn't want to hurt her, so while she was trying to pull away from me, I grabbed her around the waist from behind and lifted her off the ground. She was trying to throw the bag that contained the cosmetics away from us, and she was kicking and screaming the whole time. This place was busy with people coming and going, so it didn't take but a minute for a crowd to gather around us. As she continued to fight, we fell down with me still on top of her! I had my arm over her bag and around her waist while I was trying get my handcuffs out so I could cuff her.

About then, a beer delivery guy with a dolly… loaded with cases of beer… came up. She saw him and started yelling, "Rape! "Help me!" and I looked at him and I could see the concern on his face as he saw this big, bearded guy on top of this poor little woman with her clothes about halfway off. She was crying and getting asphalt burns everywhere, and the delivery man left his beer and started coming to the rescue! I am yelling, "Police Officer!" and thankfully about then, the store manager finally came out, and he began to verify to the crowd that I was indeed a Police Officer. I got her cuffed, and stood her up and arranged her clothes to where they covered some of what needed covering. And all this for $45 dollars' worth of cosmetics!

The crowd and the deliveryman were still giving me dirty looks because she was still carrying on her act, and I had to wrestle her back to the rear of the store so I could call the "Wagon" to transport her to Jail. I wondered, after everything settled down, if that delivery guy really thought I was trying to rape this girl in broad daylight, on the ground, at the front of a busy store? Turned out she was no stranger to Jail as she had prior arrests, but I added "Resisting Arrest" and "Assaulting a Police Officer" to the theft charges so she would stay a while longer than normal. That was one time when I really missed my uniform!

Another change from working in uniform was that we worked with a partner, and eventually I was fortunate to partner up with a guy I had known since my younger days at St. Mary Magdalene Catholic School. Before coming to Task Force, he had spent his patrol time working the Eastside of San Antonio, and he knew a lot of the crooks on that side of town. He was a very good policeman, and he was also a trickster that you had to watch every minute of the day.

Harold could clear a room by his sheer presence. This had nothing to do with his size (he was short and stocky,) it was what his body could manufacture at will! He could eliminate gas on demand! No kidding! I had never seen anything like it! And to top it all off,

191

he was proud of his ability and would willingly demonstrate it for the unbeliever when he thought the time was right.

On numerous occasions he shut down our briefings on the day's assignments since we all had to leave the room, waiting for the air to clear. If we were driving together, it wasn't unusual to have to pull the car to the side of the road and get out, leaving the doors open to let the car air out. I mentioned that Harold was a very good policeman, and as a result, he arrested a lot of people. Even the crooks remembered Harold's "gift" because he would sometimes leave them in the closed car if they gave him a hard time until he would transport them to jail!

With a guy like this as my partner life was rarely boring, and we had fun while still carrying out our police mission which was to apprehend law breakers and reduce crime. I'm not about to go into all the various ways that we used to try to catch the crooks, and I can't say that we caught them all, but what I can say is that we sometimes used some unorthodox methods to affect criminal activity within some parts of our communities.

Harold knew the criminals on the Eastside of San Antonio and that gave us an edge when we would spend time there, proactively driving around, looking for wanted persons. It was commonly known in those days that an Icehouse on W. Commerce Street was a very active dope connection.

This public location served beer and wine, it had an ongoing dice game in the back, and it trafficked in narcotics right on the front curb. On a Friday or Saturday the place would be jumping with people coming and going, including prostitutes soliciting on the sidewalk. This place had a front patio that was covered with a metal roof with tables and chairs scattered around. We would cruise by to see who was hanging around from time to time.

It was no secret what was going on there, but it was hard for our Narcotics Detectives to get close to the location because the crooks had their lookouts at various places up and down the street. Task Force was made up of two shifts, and the shifts rotated between daytime and evening. Since this place didn't get going strong until it got dark, Harold and I didn't mess with the place until we were on the evening shift. Then, if we had no particular assignment, we would try to think up ways to give them some special attention.

Now Harold and I are both white, but this place was in the predominantly African American part of San Antonio, so we had the same problem that our Narcotics Unit had. No way were these white boys going to get anywhere near this location and grab a dope dealer with some dope on him. Part of what made Harold a good policeman was his tenacity and commitment to making the lives of crooks miserable. He was frustrated that we couldn't find a way to get some of these dealers off the street.

It was almost impossible to see what was going on because this place was in the middle of the block. The business closed around 5:00 PM, so there was no place to set up surveillance. But there was a large cemetery diagonally across the street from this place, and it had a lot of big trees and other cover, not to mention some very large gravestones.

One day we found that we could park our car at the other end of the cemetery, walk across without being seen, and be able to watch the front of the place. This gave us a clear view of the dope dealers and prostitutes as they conducted business. We weren't really interested in the prostitution, but when we saw somebody stop their car in front of the place and buy dope, we would radio a description of the car to another unit who was parked a block or more away. This unit had a marked police car with them, so when the bad guy left with his dope, we let them know, and the police car would do a traffic stop and hopefully make an arrest.

This worked sometimes, but it wasn't long before the word got out and the number of lookouts was increased, and they started driving around looking for a parked police car. If they spotted one, they would shut down or they would have the buyer do the drugs there at the location instead of driving off. Once again, we had to come up with a better way to mess with them, and we decided that if we couldn't outright stop them, then we should at least make them uncomfortable.

In no time, Harold came up with a plan that would incorporate some equipment that had been around for a long, long time, but it wasn't used much anymore. It turned out that Harold had a couple of "wrist rocket" launchers also known as slingshots! (I must have missed the lesson in the Academy that described the slingshot as being a necessary part of a police officer's gear!) I carried my gun, nightstick, flashlight, and badge, but no slingshot. Thankfully my partner had that component of police gear that was going to be vital in completing the mission!

From the time that I first used a sling shot, I knew that for it to work as designed, you had to have the proper ammo. I'm talking about smooth, oblong stones that were just the right weight. We were fortunate because not far from the target location were some railroad tracks that had an abundance of the right stones. The only thing left to do was to find the right launch site.

I think it was a Saturday night and business was booming when we snuck into the cemetery and got into position. We launched our first projectile, and it landed in the middle of the metal roof over the porch. Some of the patrons reacted to the noise, but shrugged it off and went back to enjoying themselves. The second projectile was launched, and it, too, hit the metal roof and drew a little more attention. It was immediately followed by two more projectiles, one of them hitting the roof, but the other one hitting one of the dealers standing out on the curb.

We heard a, "Yow! What the f____! And more people drifted out to the curb to see what was going on. Reloading was extremely fast, and we had two projectiles on the way in the blink of an eye. Since we now had the elevation figured out, we started dropping those babies in the middle of the group who were staring up into the sky. We heard more yelling and cursing and we could see panic beginning to set in along with some obvious signs of fear. I think some of these people had at one time read the Bible… and probably spent some time in the Book of Revelation... where it mentions large hailstones raining down on men!

They knew that whatever it was, it was coming down from up above and they had never experienced anything like it before! But being the idiots that they were, they kept standing out there looking up, instead of getting under cover. Naturally, we continued to accommodate them while our "rocket" supply held out. They finally started running under the patio, but the place had lost its glow as they started leaving. Several of them were still cursing and complaining that something stung them as they could feel large knots, and it was hurting like hell!

We could see that a couple of them were looking toward the cemetery, but a lot of people are not fond of going into cemeteries at night, and I guess these people felt that way. At any rate, we decided that we had accomplished our goal, and it was probably time to go, so we snuck on out of there and left.

We didn't stop drug trafficking at that location, but I like to think it wasn't as comfortable for patrons there as it once was, and based on information from our Snitches, it was the talk of the Eastside for a week or two. I have to admit that I couldn't believe that we were getting paid to have this much fun.

For some reason, when I checked with the people who issued our police equipment about getting my authorized "Wrist Rocket," they looked at me like I was from Mars! Not really! We had to furnish our own.

Chapter 30

"...the handwritten letter was on a dresser..."

Once I got that first taste for undercover work, I was hooked, and I looked forward to reporting for duty every day. I was lucky to work with some really good people and our Sergeants were right there with us on the streets. The downside to enjoying what I was doing was that it was hard to get motivated to study for the promotion exam. I knew that if I was promoted, it would mean having to go back to Patrol in uniform for a minimum of two years.

As a uniform Detective/Investigator ("DI") it was your job to respond to crime scenes and process them to assist the plain clothes detectives. This meant looking for fingerprints, taking pictures, collecting evidence... just like on TV... but there was no proactive police work involved, and that was something I knew that I would miss.

But I also knew that I wanted to advance in rank in the Department, and I could use the little bit of extra money that the promotion would bring. I say a little bit of money because this promotion wasn't that much of a pay raise. The big raise came when you made Sergeant, but you couldn't try for Sergeant until you made Detective, so I made up my mind to go for it.

After the last test, I had talked to some of the guys who had been promoted and done well on the exam. When they told me how much time they had put into studying, I knew immediately that what I thought was studying was just casual review of the materials! These guys had a regiment of studying *every* day for *at least* 8 hours! Some would lock themselves in a room every day, and totally ignore their families for that two-month time!

I had no idea if I could do that! I decided that I would give it my best shot, and I talked to the family because it would be a sacrifice for them as well. They didn't realize what they were agreeing to, but happily committed to doing their part. Their part was to leave me *alone*! That turned out to be not as easy as everyone thought. During the day, it wasn't bad because they were in school, but the evenings and weekends were a different story. It wasn't just them; I wanted to be part of what was going outside my room, too.

We hung in there, and I improved my score significantly over the previous tests. I was still by no means in the top ten, but my number on the final list was now up in the mid-twenties. This meant that I would be promoted to DI sometime during the life of the promotion list. Yes!! A few months after the list was posted, several of us were notified that we were scheduled to attend a Detective Investigator training class to prepare us for our promotion and new job. My time in the Task Force was now at an end. I had mixed emotions in that I would miss working with Harold and our adventures of catching criminals in the act, but I was looking forward to doing something new.

August 13, 1977 was my promotion day to Detective Investigator. Promotions were always a big deal as the families were invited to attend, and the Chief-of-Police presided over the ceremony himself. The Press was also invited. They would document the ceremony, air it on TV, and write it up in the newspapers.

After the Chief gave his remarks along with the City's representatives, they began to call our names, and they had us to step forward to receive our new Detective badge. What made this special was that the Chief asked each one of us who we wanted to pin our new badge on our shirt. Some wanted him to do it, but there were a couple of us that asked our wives to pin it on, and that sealed the deal. I realized that this was the first time that Joyce and the kids had ever been inside the Police Department.

As a new uniform DI, you are assigned to a Patrol section, and you rotated with the section. So this meant going back to the 2-month shifts beginning with daylight to evening, and then good old "Dogwatch." It didn't take long for me to remember how much I hated working Dogwatch!

I mentioned that as a uniform DI, the job description changed. You weren't expected to make the routine calls the Patrolmen were assigned, but if it was a slow night from the standpoint of DI related calls, (burglaries, thefts, major fatality accidents, etc.,) and the Patrolmen were very busy, it wasn't unusual for the DI to cover officers making their calls. Dogwatch could be really slow, or it could have you running all night long. I would take busy over slow any time since the night seemed to fly by when you were going from one call to another.

Over the years as a Police Officer, I responded to thousands of calls. Every Police Officer that works any significant time in uniform can make the same claim. And probably all Police Officers, if you asked them, could tell you the details of the call that will remain with them forever. I have many memorable ones, but there are two that come to mind now and again, and they both dealt with death.

Unlike the shootings which I was personally involved in, with these two cases I was sent to the scene, and I ended up simply being the recorder of the circumstances that I found when I got there. They were both Daylight shift calls, and when I arrived both locations were peaceful, and yet they both involved violence inflicted with a firearm. Death was the result, yet they were so very different regarding the reason for the violence, the ages of the victims, and the conclusion of the cases.

The first one occurred when I, as a uniform Patrolman working the Daylight shift was dispatched to a secluded part of my district on the southside of San Antonio. It was around 8:00 AM on a Sunday morning, and someone had called the Dispatcher, stating that they had seem something *suspicious* laying in the front yard at a certain address.

On Sunday mornings when we were on the Daylight shift, several of us would kick in some money, buy some barbacoa (Mexican-style barbecue) and tortillas, meet at a location, and eat breakfast while standing around our Patrol cars, preparing for the day. When the call came out, I told the dispatcher I wouldn't need cover, but would let her know what I needed, if anything, when I arrived.

As I said, this area wasn't densely populated, and when I got to the location, there wasn't a lot to see because there were trees shielding the yard and the house. There was a chain link fence enclosing a very large front yard with a gate. I got out and went through the gate, glancing around the yard; I went up to the front porch and knocked on the door.

Do you ever have that feeling when you go up to a house that no one is home? *That* was the feeling I was getting when I knocked, but there was something else I was sensing. The door had a glass panel with a curtain which I could see through, and when I didn't get an answer after knocking even louder, I looked through the glass and saw someone laying on the couch. But there was something funny about this person. I knocked even louder, and called, "Police!" but the person didn't move. When after several more knocks there was still no movement, I knew that something was wrong, and I forced the door open.

I yelled "Police!" again and went over to the couch. I saw an older man lying there on his back with a small young little girl on his chest. They were both fully dressed; both had been shot in the head and were dead.

It appeared they had been dead for a while, but not too long. Now I was worried if the killer was still in the house! I was in the small living room, and there was an open door to what turned out to be the kitchen. As I went to the doorway, I found an older lady, fully dressed, also shot dead on the kitchen floor. The house wasn't all that large, and I made my way through two bedrooms and a bathroom, and I found no one else there.

I called the Dispatcher and notified her of what I had, and she "started cover" (She began calling available Officers and Homicide Detectives to come to the scene.) Detectives don't like you walking around the crime scene, so after I cleared the house, I went back out on the front porch to wait for my cover and the follow-up units. A while later another body was found on the property. This was a young boy who had also been shot and was also deceased.

I now had four people murdered; Two of them were small innocent kids ages 7 and 4! When Homicide Detectives arrived and started piecing together what had happened, it appeared that someone had been able to surprise the homeowners and to carry out the killings.

The older couple were the grandparents of the young kids who they were raising. The killer had come in the back door and killed the grandmother in the kitchen, then run into the living room. There, the grandfather and his granddaughter were watching TV with her on his chest, and he shot them both in the head. It was believed that one of the victims cried out and alerted the little boy who had been in his bedroom. He climbed out the window, and he started running away, across the front yard. Apparently the killer saw him running and shot him in the back and killed him, too.

Several weeks later the killer was identified and arrested in California, and he was brought back to Texas. This turned out to be a "reprisal killing" because the father of the kids had ripped off a dope dealer! The killer was given the death penalty, and he was eventually executed! (I always hoped the so-called father of the children lived a long time …!)

What I think about sometimes is the terror and fear that the little boy must have felt as he was running from the house. His sister and grandparents mercifully didn't have much time, if any, to have those feelings. It takes a special kind of sick *hate* to kill defenseless people, especially children!

The other case that remains in my thoughts is one which I was dispatched to as a Uniform Detective. It happened when an Officer had been sent to perform a wellness check. A relative of an old couple had called the Police Department, asking for someone to go by the location to make sure they were OK.

The Patrol Officer received no answer when he had knocked on the door, but he had previously received permission from the caller and his Supervisor to enter the home. When he went in, he found the old couple in bed, dead, with each one having suffered one gunshot wound. He called the dispatcher who notified Homicide, and they sent me to the location to take pictures and process the scene as Homicide needed. (Then, we didn't have the elaborate crime scene technicians that are used today, so a Uniform Detective worked with the Detectives at the scene to process any evidence.)

It wasn't long after arriving that it became obvious to all of us that this was a murder/suicide. I had made several suicide calls through the years, but the reason *this* one stayed with me was the *staging* of the scene and the *note*! The couple was lying side by side, and the lady had on some nice night clothes. Her husband was nicely dressed, too, and a shotgun was lying between them. The handwritten letter was on a dresser in the bedroom.

I can't remember everything in the letter, but the gist of it was that this couple had been married 60+ years, and she had gotten to the point that she needed constant care. He was her sole care provider, and he had recently found out that she had contracted a fast-growing cancer. His wife would be in pain until she passed, so they would have to keep her medicated as much as possible.

It turned out that he was also dealing with some serious disease of his own; he didn't know how long he would be able to care for her. He couldn't bear the thought of being separated or have anyone else take care of her. We found ample evidence of the truth of their medical condition, and it was further confirmed later by one of their children. Death was present in both of these cases, but *love* separated this one from the previous one.

Chapter 31

"…but Daddy, she has really pretty brown eyes."

I have always liked being outdoors, and I loved hunting and fishing. During my time on Task Force, my brother and I and two other guys I worked with started hunting in Colorado. We went every fall for several years, and it was a time to get away from all the stress of the job and enjoy the mountains. It was hard hunting as we hiked and walked and would sit perched on the side of the mountain, spotting for animals. It was generally cold in the mornings, would warm up during the day, and then get really cold as the sun went down.

Because of school and the harsh conditions of the way we hunted, my family couldn't go along to Colorado for those hunting trips. To make up for them not going with me hunting, we spent a lot of the summer going water skiing in our boat and camping out. This was fun but I also wanted to introduce them to hunting and spending time outdoors, watching the wildlife. So when I got on a deer lease in South Texas, I started taking them along with me when I could.

My deer lease was located about 85 miles south of San Antonio on the way to Laredo, a town on the Mexican border. We sometimes left San Antonio with the temperature at 80 degrees, arriving at the lease wearing T-shirts and jeans. It wasn't unusual to wake up the next morning to find the wind fiercely blowing and the temperature in the mid to high 30s! In Texas, we refer to that as a "Northern" that had blown in during the night. Some of the best times I had with my family were on that deer lease.

I think it was the first time we all were there when we had our first "memory maker!" I had loaded up the three kids in the truck, and we took off looking for firewood for the campfire. We had found some mesquite logs and had thrown them in the bed of the truck. As I drove up and down the *senderos* (straight dirt roads that had been man-made by bulldozers pushing through the brush thickets,) the kids continued to ride in the back, looking for more. Suddenly they pounded on the top of the cab of the truck, signaling for me to stop. When I did, they pointed to two very large rattlesnakes just a few feet off the roadway. The snakes were intertwining around each other in what I have been told is a mating ritual. Don't know if that's true, but it was fascinating to watch, and they were paying us no mind.

I got my shotgun and waited until they were cheek-to-cheek, so to speak, and I killed them both with one shot. I had blown both of their heads off! I waited until they stopped moving, and by then the kids were right beside me, mesmerized by the snakes. They were both between 4 & 5 feet long and *big,* and of course, they wanted to take them back to camp to show their momma.

The snakes were harmless with no head, so I threw them in the bed of the truck among the firewood, and the kids climbed back in, hopped up on top of the wood, and we took off towards our camp. I had gone about 100 yards when suddenly I heard yelling and screaming coming from the back, and all three kids jumped out of the truck before it even came to a full stop! I got out and ran back to where they were, and all they could do was point to the truck, telling me that they were positive that the snakes were still alive!

I walked over to the side and looked in, and sure enough, the snakes were crawling around the wood! John told me they had been standing right behind the cab when Cathy felt something up against her leg! When she looked down she saw one of the snakes had crawled over to where they were standing. I tried to tell them it was just their nervous system causing them to move around, but that wasn't going to sell. It was pretty crowded in the cab of the truck going back to camp.

When we got back the race was on to tell their mom the story. She thought we were making it up until I pulled the snakes out of the bed and threw them on the ground. Joyce was starting to freak out, but once I assured her that they were headless, she settled down. As we continued to watch the snakes, sure enough, they started to move around. They tracked us as we walked around them, just as if they still had their heads on! It was dang creepy, Man!

Joyce wasn't a hunter so she would sit in a deer blind with a couple of the kids just watching the animals. I took turns taking each of them with me to let them kill their first deer. I took John first, and he made a good shot on a young buck, and we hung it up, and I took out my knife and "cleaned it" (of its guts and hide.) Cathy was next, and she had no hesitation about taking a young doe. Unlike John, she insisted that I let her help with cleaning the animal, and she did a good job of it. It was no surprise to me that later in life she became an EMT!

Eventually, it became Suzanne's turn. We were sitting in one of the deer blinds and, as I had done with John and Cathy, I didn't want to rush anything, so we sat and looked at various animals that were darting around. I would ask her what she thought of this one or that one but she kept turning them down for one reason or another until finally a good fat doe walked in.

We watched her for a while, and I told her that this would be a good one to harvest. She was looking through the scope and finally she looked up at me and said, "But Daddy, she has real pretty brown eyes!" I smiled and agreed she was a pretty animal and took the gun out of her hands, put it against the wall, and told her we could just watch the deer for a while. When the doe left, we got out of the blind and returned to camp and enjoyed breakfast. It had been a good hunt even though Suzanne never killed a deer! (By the way Suzanne did *not* become an EMT.)

My brother shared my love for the outdoors, and he also loved to hunt and fish. He and I began to talk about the possibility of buying a small ranch and eventually maybe building houses on the property. I guess my short time spent working with those farmers in Devine had a stronger impact on me than I realized at the time. We started looking for ranch property North of San Antonio but quickly came to realize that land values were way out of our league. Since we were both familiar with the Devine area, we began to look to the South of town.

We finally found a 94 Acre tract about 45 miles South of San Antonio near a small post office town called Yancey. The price per acre was significantly cheaper than the prices in the Hill Country, it had cleared land, and some very good wildlife potential, so we decided to buy it. Since he and I were both veterans we used a government loan program designed for Texas Veterans, and we were able to buy it!

We were now "ranch owners" (well, us and the *bank)* and, as with the house in San Pedro Hills, it was one of the best buys we ever made. Ralph eventually built a house and raised his family on the ranch. I took an entirely different path, but some years later I, too, built a house there, and lived next to Ralph's property for many years.

Chapter 32

"...he took his hat off and was waving it over his head yelling, "Heeyaa!"...

There were times that we hunted in Colorado when the weather remained warmer than usual, but seldom did we have the drastic temperature swings you could encounter in South Texas. Of course we hunted in snow in Colorado, and we were prepared for that and looked forward to it, but there was this one year....

That year two of our regular guys couldn't go, so Ralph and I took my son, John, and a policeman friend of ours named, Joe, with us. Neither one of them had ever hunted in Colorado, nor had they ever hunted in snowy conditions. During the months leading up to the trip, Joe pestered us every chance he had with questions about what it was like to hunt and camp in the snow, and he was like a little kid waiting for Christmas.

The time finally came to leave, and we loaded up and headed for the mountains. We were already short the two regular guys and at the last minute one other fellow that was supposed to go had to cancel. He was going to bring his truck with a cab-over camper that we were going to use for sleeping and cooking.

Richard felt bad having to cancel, and he insisted that we take his truck anyway. Since we had made plans for the truck and camper to be our base of operations, we accepted his offer. We always pulled my 4-wheel drive Jeep behind a truck and used that to hunt and carry out any game we killed. Richard's truck wasn't 4 -wheel drive, but we felt that it would be good enough to get us to our camping area in the forest. We took off and arrived two days later; we started setting up camp. We had always made it a point to get there a couple of days before the season opened, so that we could get acclimated to the altitude and do some scouting. The weather was beautiful, and we were walking around, wearing just long sleeve shirts, enjoying the sunshine.

Joe was devastated, and he kept asking us if we thought the weather would stay this way, and we told him that it would sure be nice if it did! He didn't want to hear that, so he was down in the dumps. I tried to tell him that walking in the snow with a lot of cold weather gear on (at the altitude we were hunting) wasn't a walk in the park. He didn't want to hear that either!

The next morning, it was another picture-perfect day, and we went about putting the finishing touches on the camp and checked our hunting gear because the next morning was opening day! The four of us got into my Jeep and drove around locating areas where each of us would sit the following morning, but as the afternoon progressed, the sky started to cloud up, and there was more of a chill in the air.

We stayed up after supper, and the excitement began to build as we talked about getting a look at a monster buck the following morning! Joe was griping that it would be so much better if we had snow on the ground! We all turned in and went to sleep.

Our alarm went off at 5:00 AM; It was opening day of the Colorado mule deer season! Everybody rolled out of their sleeping bags, and it was time to answer the call of nature. Someone opened the door of the camper to step outside, and a cold blast of air came in, and we heard him say, "Oh s___t! We asked, "What's up?, and he said, "Get Joe out here!" Well, Joe was still in his tidy whities, but he stepped up to the door, and when he looked out, he was greeted with a blanket of white!! It had snowed all night long!

He began jumping around and started getting his clothes on. Once dressed, out the door he went. It was still snowing when we all went out to enjoy the beautiful winter scene. But there wasn't any reason to get in a hurry since we weren't going to be able to see where we were going because of the poor visibility. So we took our time with breakfast and coffee, and every now and then, someone would look outside and report that it was still snowing!

After we finished eating, we went out to see if there was some way we could hunt, but it was impossible since the snow just kept coming down. Joe was having a ball walking around in it, making snowballs, and even laying down, doing a snow angel! We all finally resigned ourselves to the fact there would be no hunting on opening day, so we messed around camp. This was a small camper, so we had to be mindful of how we occupied space. It had a propane stove, and we were able to heat soup which worked out OK for the first day.

Day two, it was still snowing, and it was getting deep, and the trees and brush were covered with a white blanket, and Joe was taking pictures for all he was worth! It was the hunt of his dreams (except we weren't hunting.)

Day three. Still snowing, and the secondary road we had taken that branched off of the well-maintained forest road to the top of the mountain (where we were camping) had disappeared. This was a logging road, and not very wide, and there were stumps left behind on the sides of the road. So you had to be very careful that you didn't run off the side and onto a stump.

Joe had run through most of his film, he was no longer making snowballs, snow men, or snow angels! It was becoming hard to walk through the stuff since in places, it was almost up to our knees, and Joe wasn't the most physically fit guy in our bunch. He wasn't oohing and laughing, as a matter of fact he had gotten quiet, and when he did look outside, he got this worried look on his face. You could tell the pressure was building.

I guess it was that evening, after eating our soup and sandwiches (again,) that Joe finally let it out. He announced he was tired of this "fricking snow," and then he questioned if we thought it would ever end! There were some things I thought I might say, but I decided that it wouldn't make things any better, so I told him the truth: it wasn't unusual for the weather to change in a moment's notice. And it did; the snow ended that night!

The next morning, the sun was out, and it was beautiful, but the snow was up to a tall giraffe's butt! After breakfast, my brother, Joe, and my son were determined to look around, so they got their gear and walked off to scout for deer. I decided that I would look around and see if I could find the roadway to the better maintained forest road.

I walked for about thirty minutes when I realized that we were in trouble. The snow was so deep that I couldn't keep a straight track on the road. It was going to require all four of us to find our way out, so I went back to camp and started checking out my Jeep because it was going to be the only way we were getting off the mountain. It had snow tires and snow chains and a winch, and I was pretty sure we would need them all before it was over.

The guys drifted back into camp around lunch time, and I shared with them my concerns about getting to the forest road. Since the truck wasn't a 4-wheel drive, I was afraid that we might not be able to get it out if the weather warmed and the ground turned to *mud*, or if it started snowing again. When I mentioned snowing, Joe got a funny, worried look on his face, and he and everyone else agreed that it would be in our best interest to find a better, lower camp area.

After lunch, we started getting the truck and camper ready and found out that the truck wasn't going to be able to overcome the deep snow, it was stuck! Oh boy! We stood around and started discussing what we were going to do when someone mentioned that we might have to leave it until the following spring. That was the last thing I needed to hear since I was responsible for the rig. This truck minus the camper was also used by Richard for his family's transportation!

The camper was a unit that slid into the bed of the truck and extended over the cab and beyond the tailgate. When the camper wasn't in use, you slid the camper out of the truck, set it on jacks, and drove the truck out from under it. I was going to do everything I could to bring it back home.

The first thing we had to do was to find a way to get to the main forest road in the Jeep. To do that we had to blaze a trail from our camping spot to the road. I was going to be driving the Jeep so the other three started walking ahead with a shovel and sticks to probe the snow, looking for stumps. I had put the snow chains on my tires, and had the 4-wheel drive engaged and we started out.

Thankfully it was a beautiful day, but it was also a little after noon. The days are short up there during that time of the year, and we didn't want to be caught at dark still trying to find the road. The guys were struggling out in front of me, marking the road, and I could go about 20 feet or so when the snow would ball up, and I would have to stop. I would back up, go forward and ram the snow, and crash through it before I could go on any further.

I don't know how we made it, but we did, and we did it with daylight remaining. We had already decided that if we got to the forest road, we were going to go into the nearest large town which was Cortez. My hope was that we would find someone who could bring a tractor up to our camp and pull the truck and camper out to the main road.

If you're familiar with Jeeps, you know they aren't very big, and the four of us crammed it up with no room to spare. I remember thinking what a ride it would be if we had to leave the pick-up and drive all the way home in my Jeep, with all of our gear! Sardines in a can came to mind.

We got into Cortez late afternoon, and as we drove in, we spotted a camper dealership. I pulled in and found Mike (the owner) and told him our problem. When we finished telling him the location of our camp, he told us he knew exactly where we were camped. He then gave us some news we didn't want to hear.

Apparently another huge snowstorm was headed our way, and it was expected to impact us in about two days! He then added that there were numerous other hunters stranded at our location who were in the same boat as we were. Not only that, but he said that the ranchers were being advised to get their cattle down to the lower country as quick as they could. This coming storm was expected to bring *several* **feet** of snow on what was already there! To make our day, he finished by telling us that the forecast was that if you didn't get out in the next two days, you were probably looking at several weeks, if not months, before anything would be able to come down out of the forest.

The only thing that I could see missing in this show was an avalanche. I told Mike that it looked like we were out of luck. That's when he said a remarkable thing; he asked me if I wanted to get our rig out?!! (Do bears poop in the woods?) I started asking him questions, and he told me that he would arrange everything, and then he suggested that we find a place to spend the night and then to be back first thing in the morning. We found a motel with two rooms and after getting a good meal, everyone took their first hot shower of several days, and we spent the night in a real bed!

The next morning had us up early, and we were greeted with beautiful sunshine and clear skies. We stopped at a café and had a nice breakfast and headed for the camper dealership. I was hoping that Mike hadn't changed his mind or that some unforeseen circumstances were going to force him to change his plans.

When we arrived, he was there and had his tractor with a snowplow already loaded up on a trailer attached to a pickup truck, ready to go! He told us he was waiting for a friend of his to show up with his 4-wheel drive truck, and we would then be on our way. The friend arrived and after introductions, everybody got into their vehicles, and we started back to the forest. We first had to stop at a service station to fuel up. As we were finishing, I saw Mike and the other guy come out with two cases of beer! I began to sense that they were viewing this as an adventure, and I wasn't wrong!

Our caravan started up the mountain, and as we navigated the various switchbacks, I knew that if we didn't get our rig out now, there would be no way to do it after another snow. There were no guardrails and some of those drop-offs were pretty darned scary even on dry ground! We finally arrived at our logging road turn off, and we found an open area where we unloaded the tractor from the trailer. Crazy as it may sound; I couldn't help but get excited!

We put the tire chains on Mike's truck and my Jeep, and we followed my Jeep tracks back to our camp site. As he followed along with his tractor, Mike was plowing the snow from the road so we would have a better view of the roadway when we brought the truck

211

out. Even though the sun was shining, the temperature at our campsite was in the mid-twenties. None of us were really cold, and even our tractor driver, sitting on his open-air tractor, was wearing just a long-sleeved shirt!

By the time we finished packing all our gear and getting the camper secured on the truck, it was getting close to noon, so we decided to eat some lunch before we started out. Everyone decided that a beer would be good with lunch, so that's what we did. Lunch was over; it was time to get going, so we developed a plan and started out…well we tried to start out, but we found that the cumbersome truck wouldn't move a foot from where it was parked!

Before we could do anything else, we had to use a chain to pull the truck free of where it was frozen in place. Once that was done, we were finally lined out, facing the right direction. My brother got in the truck and kept driving it in our ruts behind the guy on his tractor. Me in my Jeep and the other fellow in his 4-wheel drive pickup were in front of everybody.

Our job was to make sure that there were no obstructions in our path, and when the tractor would start losing traction, we would put a chain from the front of the tractor to the pickup, and that allowed us to keep moving. As soon as we were free of the icy spot, we unhooked the chain from the front so that the tractor could make better time. Joe and my son John were walking alongside the truck on each side, and they would warn us if the truck started sliding off the road. I wish someone would have had the foresight to break out a camera (a video camera would have been even better) to record the event.

It was now early afternoon, and for the first time, I noticed that every time we had to stop to hook up chains from the pick-up to the tractor, our new buddy, Mike, and his friend were grabbing a fresh beer from the ice chest in the truck. The beer wasn't in the ice chest to keep it *cold*, but to keep it from *freezing outside* the chest.

As the day was progressing, the temperature started dropping, and since this was an open cab tractor, Mike was drinking the beer faster than normal to keep from wasting it when it turned to ice.

Sounds logical, right? There were quite a few icy spots, so we were chaining and unchaining pretty often. It wasn't long before we could *see* the effects of the beer on our tractor driver in full display. He had put on a thin jacket and a hat, and it must have been cold sitting out in the open, but he seemed fine as he started singing one song after another.

I wasn't really concerned until I looked back, and I saw the front of the tractor lift *off* the ground a foot or two! Mike stood up, took his hat off, and was waving it over his head hollering "*yeehaw*" as if he was on a *horse*! Apparently, the tractor had hit a slick spot, and Mike was giving it the gas to raise the front of the tractor. The guy in the pick-up wasn't a lot better because he would come to an open area and turn donuts in the snow! (I never told Richard (the camper/truck owner) everything that took place in getting us out of there that day. You know, some things are better just kept on a need-to-know basis.

When we were coming to the forest road and to the place where we had left the trailer for his tractor, I felt like I wanted to get out and kiss the snow! By then, the guys had cut way back on the beer drinking. Not because they wanted to, but because the temperature was now in the teens, and they could only drink about half the can before it was frozen *solid*! The Good Lord was taking care of us all along. Thank you, Lord!

Somehow, we got all the equipment loaded up, and we headed down off the mountain and into town. We arrived back at the camper dealership, and everyone was relieved and exhausted at the same time, and a couple were pretty damned drunk!

When his equipment was put away, we sat down with Mike and asked him what we were going to owe him for all he had done. (His friend had to leave, but before he did, he thanked us for the opportunity we had provided for him to go along and have so much fun!) By now, we were all having a beer, and Mike thought about it for a while, and then told me that he thought two-hundred dollars would probably be fair. I told him that two-hundred dollars was more

213

than fair, and the four of us got together and started counting out our money.

While everyone was counting, I said that we would spend another night at a motel so we could head out in the morning after having had a good night's sleep. That sounded good to everyone, but we had not budgeted for an extra two nights at a motel plus the extra meals.

Well when the counting was done, we didn't have enough money to pay the man his two-hundred dollars! Oh boy! Here was this guy who had closed his business for the day, gotten a friend of his to bring his 4-wheel drive truck to help, furnished a tractor, and worked his butt off to get us off the mountain. He could have charged us triple what he quoted us, and it would have still been more than fair. And now we didn't have the money to pay him!

I wanted to crawl under the ground with embarrassment, but I explained our predicament. He listened; when I finished, he said, "What's the problem?" I think I said something real intelligent like, "huh?" And he said, "Here is my card with my name and address. When you get home, just send me the money!" He went on to say that he and his friend had such a blast, and they were glad to have been given the opportunity to help out.

We hunted for several more years in Colorado. We were fortunate to kill some beautiful animals, and we always enjoyed the companionship of friends along the way. On this trip that I chose to share with you (the reader,) we never fired a shot, and we never spent a full day actually hunting! It was the only time I was able to take my son there; He never went back. Joe got to see the snow, and like a lot of things, figured out that you can have too much of almost anything. And, yet, it was one of the most *memorable* trips I had ever had in Colorado.

It was memorable because the hunting trips were never all about the hunting but were about the companionship of friends. In this case, I got a lesson on the good qualities shown by people, even when they are total strangers. Their willingness to drop what they were doing and supply resources only they could provide was an eyeopener. They didn't know us from Adam, and yet they never hesitated to jump in and do what was needed.

As a Police Officer, it's easy to fall into the trap of expecting the bad to manifest itself in people you meet or deal with every day. There is plenty of that to go around, just watch the news. I have to remind myself often that there are a lot more good people around us than we think… we just need to expect their arrival more often than we do. Later, we sent Mike his money plus a little extra, and although we never saw him again, he is not forgotten!

Chapter 33

"…one of my guys came up and told me that Doug was shot in the chest."

I had done my two years as a DI and was starting to get restless. To be honest, I missed plain clothes work, and especially undercover work. Since the Task Force was restricted to patrolmen, there was no going back there, so I started giving thought to one of the other plain clothes units. (As I previously mentioned, like every other major Police Department, we had Homicide, Robbery, Burglary, Theft/Auto Theft, and several other Units including Narcotics!

The Narcotics Unit was as close to Task Force as there was at the time. A lot of the cases required undercover work and they didn't wear a uniform. I decided to talk to the lieutenant in charge of Narcotics and see about joining the unit. The first chance I got to talk to him didn't go well. Before an in-person interview was granted, I had to submit a written form up the chain-of-command. This alerted every one of my desires to transfer, and it gave the people I was working for an opportunity to provide their input on my current performance.

I received good performance reviews from my superiors in uniform, but there was someone who had gone to the Narcotics' Lieutenant, and they told him I had a temper! Imagine that! I couldn't deny it, as all he had to do was go to my personnel file (known as the 201 file,) and there he would find numerous complaints regarding the use of force. It didn't matter if the complaint was later unfounded, it was still in the file. (For the sake of full disclosure here, I didn't put up with needless BS!) When the circumstances convinced me that an arrest was necessary, I didn't waste any time in letting an individual know what my intentions were. Once I told them they were under arrest, they were told to turn around and put their hands behind their back so I could handcuff them.

Any attempt to resist was met with immediate action on my part which could consist of forcing their arms back, or (depending on their level of resistance,) throwing them to the ground. Every case was different, and I tried not to use any more force than was necessary in order to complete an arrest. (The thumb on my right hand is still out of socket with a torn ligament because I had to wrestle with a strong guy, trying to handcuff him.)

I also felt (and still do) that it wasn't my job to engage in a touchy-feely conversation if I had to arrest someone. That was what their lawyer was for! Those that are old enough, might remember "Dragnet" with Officer Joe Friday and his "just the facts ma'am" TV series. Well, that was kind of my attitude when dealing with an arrest situation.

Let me add here that in 1969 thru the early 1970s, Police Officers were issued a badge, pistol, handcuffs, and a night stick. We didn't have the junk that most police agencies issue their officers today. Back then, we didn't have portable radios that you could use to call for help, if needed (that would have been nice). Instead you were expected to handle the situation as best as you could with what you had available, and that included your physical abilities.

Having said all that, the fact remained that the Narcotics Lt. was *leery* of bringing me into the unit. It took several weeks of talking to him, but I finally convinced him to give me a chance. For me, this was once again an opportunity to be pro-active in dealing with crime, and I was looking forward to the freedom that not having to wear a uniform would bring.

San Antonio, like any other large city, had all the usual narcotics being trafficked on the streets. In addition, the city is just 125 miles from the Mexican border, and that meant that we had large amounts of marijuana coming through the city as the traffickers moved the stuff up North. Compared to the current year of 2023, in the 1970s and 1980s, marijuana was considered a controlled substance, and it was illegal. We were fighting the war on drugs!

The Narcotics unit was comprised of teams of partners who would develop information (that we had obtained from working the streets) to the point that we could apply for a search warrant. To get a search warrant, we had to type-up a document called an "affidavit" and take it to the Judge. The affidavit contained the details that led us to believe that a person was dealing drugs. If the judge felt that we had enough Probable Cause, he or she would sign the warrant, and we would then "serve" the warrant by arresting the crooks that were named in the documents if we found narcotics.

People dealing and using drugs were/are understandably paranoid, so most of them had weapons. They weren't just paranoid about the *police*; they were just as often paranoid about their *rivals*. A lot of them also used their product, and when dealing with the users of Methamphetamines, commonly known as "Meth Heads," the paranoia reached new levels! This also affected the way a warrant was "served."

Part of our preliminary investigation was finding out all we could about the mindset of the crook. Was he or she prone to violence? What type of weapons were kept on the premises? What was the level of paranoia? And so on. Of course, we needed to know the type of narcotics that we were going after. If it was cocaine, heroin, or speed (Meth,) the entry to the location had to be quick or the drugs could be flushed down the toilet. If it was marijuana or large amounts of pills, it wasn't always necessary to get in as quickly. All these factors were considered when deciding how we would gain entry.

It's widely accepted that "family disturbance" calls are some of the most dangerous calls an officer can respond to. Several times while trying to arrest a drunk husband, I had to fight the wife (who had called us to come and arrest him,) because she changed her mind when we got there. But *"serving"* an arrest or search warrant ranks right up there with those disturbance calls!

I can share two examples of the danger involved during the execution of a search warrant. On the first one, I wasn't present when Det. Barney Salazar, as a member of a joint task force, was at the front door of the crook's house. He was shouting, "Police! Open the door!" when the crook shot his gun. The bullet went through the door, hitting Barney in the head, killing him.

In this next case, I was a Sergeant on the Repeat Offenders Unit and Doug Phillips, one of the Detectives assigned to me, obtained information on a guy dealing in Methamphetamines. We got our warrant and decided to execute (serve) the warrant very early in the morning. Part of the information Doug had gathered was that the crook was *extremely* paranoid and armed. We decided that the chances were good that he would be asleep at that time of the morning. We hoped this would give us the time needed to force open the front door and serve the no-knock warrant.

(A side note on serving our warrants: It was our policy that the detective who obtained the warrant was usually the first person through the door. On these "no-knock" warrants, we generally shouted "Police!" as we kicked in the door. We always tried to have a uniform officer with us to show everyone that we were indeed the police as we were in plain clothes.)

Around 6 o'clock in the morning, Doug kicked in the door, and I was the second man right behind him. The rest of the guys were behind me, and everyone kept yelling "Police!" Doug and I were probably 5 steps into the dimly lit living room when a guy sitting next to another guy on a couch raised up a shotgun and shot at us!

Doug and I had our guns out, and Doug fired one shot, and he kept running through the living room past the couch. The guy that had shot at us dropped his gun, and he slid to the floor. I saw the second guy drop his shotgun as I turned to shoot him. I held my fire, and one of the other men came up and handcuffed him and took possession of the weapons. I was checking on the guy that Doug shot, and I could tell he was dead when one of my other guys came up to me and told me that Doug was shot in the chest!

It was part of our procedure that when we served our warrants we wore our bullet proof vests with a steel plate covering the middle of the chest area, and over that we had fluorescent yellow windbreakers with the word "Police" on the front and back in big letters.

They took me to the backyard where I found him standing, bent over with his hands on his knees. These guys and gals that worked for me after I made Sergeant were not just detectives, they were my friends! I was sick to my stomach! But he was standing up! I got to him and asked where he was hit, and he straightened up and pointed to his chest. Right in the center was a round hole in the wind breaker. When we opened the jacket I couldn't believe my eyes!

Dead center of the steel plate was a dimple the size of my thumb. It was probably about a half an inch deep and had stopped the 12-gauge shotgun round that the crook had fired from about 7 feet away. Being that close, the BBs contained in the shell had not had time to expand and remained concentrated on impact. It was a miracle! The ambulance arrived and took Doug to the hospital where he was checked out and released. You should have seen the bruise on his chest a few days later, but Doug was still alive!

His vest was used as a training tool at the Academy for a long time so that new officers could see the need to wear their body armor. The time it took for us to kick in the door, to run into the room that none of us were familiar with, to the crook shooting Doug, and Doug shooting him, took all of maybe *5 seconds*!

A lot of today's news media want to treat law enforcement actions as if there is a replay or slow-motion button that you can hit while the action is going on! It doesn't happen that way, and it's normally not a 30-to-60-minute show.

I am not making any excuses for bad decisions, just saying that sometimes when you are in the heat of the moment, things are moving extremely fast. By the way, the other fellow sitting on the couch wasn't shot because he was fast and smart enough to drop his weapon; I wouldn't have missed at that range!

Barney, in the first story, was in my cadet class, and he was a super nice guy; he left behind a wife and kids. Doug is a super nice guy, too, with a wife and kids; he got to go home. It's a dangerous profession, but I loved it, and that became a problem where my family was concerned.

Chapter 34

"…I was higher than a kite."

The follow-up plain clothes detective units like Burglary, Theft, Robbery, etc., pretty much worked 8:00 AM to 4:30 PM daily, and they didn't rotate shifts. The plain clothes units like Narcotics, Vice, Task Force and some others rotated from daylight to night shifts. Since the intent of the units was to be proactive, you had to be out there when the crooks were busy.

This all meant that a large part of the time I was working in the evenings when my kids were home from school. My "at home time" was shortened even more because I still continued to work extra jobs. When I would think about my time away from my family, I would justify it by telling myself that it was the way that we could afford the vehicles, boats, hunting lease, and so on, and best of all, my wife didn't have to work! Lastly, I could further justify my actions by pointing out that a lot of my friends were doing the same thing.

What I wouldn't admit at the time was that I didn't want a regular day job because I loved the adrenaline rush of chasing and catching the bad guys! The situation that I described in the last chapter involving Doug's shootout with the crook was scary as hell, and yet, when it was over, and we survived, I was higher than a kite! I guess it was probably like a drug; the high would come back down, so you began to miss it after a while.

When I worked Narcotics, most (make that 95%) of the information we received was through informants. They were, and still are, a vital part of proactive policing. Informants (also known as 'Snitches') were generally crooks themselves. Let's face it, the church deacon is usually not going to know a lot of the inside details of the distribution of cocaine at a certain location. He is spending time at home with his family where I should have spent more of my time.

On the other hand, a good informant (Snitch) is spending time with the people handling the drugs which gives him or her the inside information that we needed to break the case. Most of these peoples' home life rotated around drugs, so they couldn't appreciate the Detectives' home life.

Informants do what they do for several different reasons, none of which include the wellbeing of the community. They are often facing a pending criminal case against themselves and providing information was a way of doing away with their case or at least mitigating the charges. Some of them had a personal grudge against the other crook and would provide information as payback. Often times the information was provided because we would pay if it panned out. This is a common practice with all agencies including the Feds. The better the information; the better the payout.

As a result, it wasn't unusual to get a phone call from one of my informants in the middle of the night with urgent information. Depending on the nature of the information, I would sometimes have to leave and meet them to come up with some sort of plan of action.

There were times I wouldn't be home again until the following day. I can't imagine how stressful that was for my wife when I got dressed and headed out to some location to meet with someone that could easily be setting me up!

I mentioned that we worked with a partner, but not every partner was as dedicated to the job as the other partner. Dedicated is probably not the best way to describe what I am trying to say. It might be better to say that some guys didn't place the job at the head of the list of things important to them. I had such a partner for a while, and it resulted in me going out by myself from time to time. Not a good thing to do!

I didn't realize it was happening, but I was moving my family further and further down from the top of my priority list. Narcotics was a plain clothes unit, but we also ran a deeper undercover operation (called a "Sting") where a detective would assume the role of a crook and begin to associate with other crooks.

The idea was *to* become part of this population of narcotics users and suppliers and begin buying dope and identifying the players. As they were identified and documented, we would put the cases together, and eventually a grand jury would be empaneled, and indictments would follow. When all the indictments were issued, we would have a "round-up" and mass arrest day. This type of undercover operation always provided excellent news coverage and made for good PR for the department.

I think it was my second year in Narcotics when my partner and I had two informants who were extremely active in the narcotics trade. It was decided that we would do an undercover "buy" operation, and I would be the undercover doper. I was the logical choice since you could take this particular partner, strip him naked, even paint him orange, and everyone would *still* know he was the Police!

The way that the Sting worked is that the informant and I would get together, and he would take me to a location where drugs were being sold. We would go in, he would introduce me, and I would buy the drug that was being trafficked. My partner would be nearby, and when I left the location, I would meet him, turn over the dope, and it would be handled as evidence. The person selling to me would have to be identified, and I would be given a picture of that person to confirm that he was the right person.

The Sting lasted 2 or 3 months, and I believe I ended with 54 defendants indicted by the grand jury! During this time, I didn't go near the police station to avoid a crook seeing me and exposing me as a Police Officer. Most of the people I bought from were not a problem. But a few of the Speed Freaks were super paranoid, and I was always extra careful to check my surroundings. This made me paranoid, so during the rare times that I was out with my family, I was constantly looking at the people around me.

Sure enough I was out with my family at a Jim's Restaurant (one of San Antonio's popular eating places) one evening when several people walked in the door, and I recognized one of them as a guy I had bought Speed from just a few days before. This was a problem because my under-cover role was that I was a truck driver who lived in Houston. My story was that I needed the speed to make those long hauls without getting sleepy.

It would have been hard to explain my wife and three kids. Luckily, they went to the other side of the restaurant, and after explaining to my wife what was going on, I had her and the kids go out first, and I left alone a short time later.

Fortunately, I never brought any dangerous problems home to my family. That's not saying that I wasn't bringing home some problems that were work related. As I mentioned, my priorities had now shifted, and, sad to say, my family was no longer where it should have been, number 1 in my life!

Chapter 35

"destructive in effect..."

I have been dreading writing this chapter. I didn't know it would be Chapter 35 when I would start describing this stage of my life. But it's here, and I can't put it off any longer. I don't know how many chapters it might take, but if I am going to be honest (as honest as I can be), I have to write it, too.

When I began writing this book, I was talking to a friend who is also a writer. He initially thought that my book would be a book describing just my police experiences. When I told him it would be an autobiography, he wasted no time telling me he wouldn't want to write this kind of book. He was thinking about his own personal Chapter 35, I guess, and I can't blame him for feeling that way.

As I started this chapter I was reminded that our whole lives are based on relationships. From the moment we are born, we depend on our relationship with our mother and father for food, clothing, protection, shelter, and nurturing. The Bible says God created us to be in a relationship with Him. He "knew" us before we were even in our mother's womb!

So this chapter continues to not only describe my relationships with my wife and kids but other people that cross my path. I am certain that everyone has a Chapter 35 in their life and, like it or not, it's part of who we are, and unique to each of us. I wish I could change some of it, but wishing doesn't make it so. If there is anything good about a personal Chapter 35, we can learn and grow and maybe mentor others to help them avoid making the same mistakes.

Things intrude into our lives that we cannot foresee or prepare for so we deal with them as they make themselves apparent. An example of what I'm talking about happened one night after everyone had slept. John, being the only boy, had his own room, while Cathy and Suzanne shared the other bedroom. Sometime during the night, John came into our bedroom and woke us up. He told us that there was "something" in his room. I was still not totally awake, and I asked him what it was, and he said it was a snake with legs!??

Don't ask me how I knew, but immediately I thought of a centipede! We got up, went into his room, and couldn't see it. We had turned on the lights by now, so both girls were also up and in the hall. I asked John how big it was, and he held his hands out like he was measuring a fish! Of course, I thought this was an exaggeration. I continued to look around his bed and finally looked under it, and I could see this critter begin to crawl out from underneath the bed and head toward the closet. Good grief! It was even longer than John had indicated, with a red head, black body, and yellow legs. It looked to be about a foot long!

It scurried under the door and into John's closet. Now what the heck was I going to do? I went to get a small push broom from the kitchen while everyone else stayed by the door and made sure it didn't come out. When I got back, I opened the closet door, and I was met by the typical boy's closet...meaning that there was stuff everywhere on the floor.

Everyone was in John's bedroom, and they were close behind me when I opened the door. As I started moving the stuff on the floor around, Joyce and John crowded around me even more, wanting to see. I moved one thing more, and out came the critter moving toward us rapidly! (Sounds like the tarantula episode involving my father, huh?) Before I could react, somebody screamed and hit my back, and I guess I became My Old Man because I cursed in English and in Flemish and darned near knocked everyone down as I jumped back!

Dammit! Why does stuff like that scare us so *bad?* I recovered and managed to trap the critter under the broom, brought it out, and subdued it. We found a jar, and I put the little dragon in alcohol, and John took it to school for show and tell. We identified it as the *Red-Headed Giant Texas Centipede.* This one was close to 11 inches long, and I have been told that they will sometimes exceed 12 inches! I've learned that their sting is extremely painful but generally not deadly.

I wish I could say the same thing about some other things that can creep into our lives.

I'm not sure why, but some people are fascinated with Police Officers. It wasn't unusual to have folks come up and want to talk to me about my experiences. I have to admit that I was flattered when an attractive woman would come up to me at a party and want to talk. There was nothing wrong with just talking, but at one point, this would lead to mutual flirting and then sometimes progress to infidelity. Because of the hours I was working, it wasn't difficult to be away from home, and I found myself on the path leading to personal destruction.

In a previous chapter, I described the adrenaline rush associated with the dangerous situations that I often found myself involved in at work; I guess I associated the affair to be somewhat like that. I also mentioned that the high of the adrenaline rush eventually wore off, but this was a high that could occur more often and didn't seem as deadly. Boy was I wrong about that! If you are interested, pick up a dictionary and find the word "deadly," and you will be amazed at all the synonyms you will find related to "deadly" and "dead." I am not going to list them all, but the one that caught my eye about "deadly" was "destructive in effect." That nailed it.

Nothing stays hidden; Joyce found out what was going on. Unfortunately, Cathy overheard a conversation, so our kids knew something was wrong, but we were trying to carry on despite the tension in the house. The affair came to an end, and my wife decided that she wanted to work on our marriage. The question she posed to me was, "What did I do wrong?" I guess I could have mentioned something, but the honest answer was "Nothing," and that was what I told her.

When we were trying to restore our marriage, let me say she was trying; I was just going through the motions of trying. The problem was that I didn't change my circumstances at work. I was still working the extra jobs, still working undercover, and away from home more than I needed to be. And I didn't want to change any of these things.

I was sorry for the pain I was causing but not sorry enough to change. There followed a time during which it seemed that I couldn't avoid meeting women who wanted to flirt, and I played along.

One afternoon my undercover partner and I were sent to a business location on the far eastside of San Antonio to talk with the owner about possible narcotics trafficking in the vicinity of his business. When we arrived, we were met by his secretary (I will call her "Beth"), who began to fill us in on what was going on while we waited for the owner to finish his call. When he joined us, he wasted no time in telling us that his secretary had all the information we would need. She was there throughout the day, and he typically spent most of his time on the road.

One of the reasons for their concern was that they had a substantial inventory in a small warehouse in the rear of the property. This, combined with his secretary's welfare since she often worked late by herself, had prompted him to call us. From then on, he sat back while the secretary gave us the details.

Beth had recently noticed an unusual amount of traffic stopping at a house diagonally across the street from their business. It would happen during the day as well as in the evening. We agreed that it would be worthwhile to try to stake out the location to see what was happening. As we were discussing the problems of finding a good place to sit and watch, the owner volunteered his building. She confirmed that there was a front room that we could use to set up a scope with a perfect view of the location. We were working evenings, so we decided to bring in the equipment we would need the following afternoon. The next day we unloaded our stuff, and you could tell that they could barely wait to see real police work in action! You know, "Just like on TV."

I wasn't sure what they were expecting, but l I think watching two guys taking turns looking through a spotting scope and taking license numbers was probably a bit disappointing for them. We explained that initially, we were hoping to identify people who might already be in the criminal system to get an idea of what type of drugs we were dealing with.

This wasn't the only case we were working on, so there were days that either my partner or I would go out there alone. It became obvious that there were indeed narcotics being trafficked at that location. My partner at the time wasn't a very friendly guy, and as a matter of fact, he could be downright rude! So it didn't surprise me one afternoon when I was out there by myself that Beth asked if my partner had something against women!

I cracked up! I explained that she shouldn't take it personally but that he treated all women as the enemy. He had gone through a tough divorce a few years back, and it seemed that he wasn't getting over it any time soon. This led to her telling me that several years prior, her husband had been shot and killed during some type of road rage incident.

She had grown children and one younger teenage daughter. The conversation between Beth and me became more personal as time went on. She wanted to know about my family, and I told her about my wife and kids. I remember she asked me if my working hours made it tough on the family, and I told her it did. I eventually told her about how I once cheated on Joyce, but we were still together. She asked me if I loved my wife, and I couldn't give her an honest answer.

One evening I was at their business by myself again, and there wasn't a lot happening, but Beth was working late. When she finished, she entered the room where I was watching and pulled up a chair beside me. We were able to determine that they were selling marijuana, and I managed to follow some of them away from the location. I eventually stopped them after they committed a traffic violation. The dope was recovered, and after a little more work on the case, we busted the place and put it out of business.

Beth and I continued to see each other from time to time, but we both knew that it was wrong. One day she called me, wanting me to come by the business so we could talk. I went by there after work, and when we sat down, she grabbed my hands and told me that she really cared for me but that I needed to try to work out my marriage!

This was odd because my brief relationship with her had convinced me that my marriage was over. Not because I had been seeing her, but because I knew I no longer loved my wife! Beth and I stopped seeing each other, and a few days later, I told Joyce that I was moving out and wanted a divorce.

Chapter 36

"...have you ever read the Bible?"

After several agonizing weeks, Joyce and I sat down with the kids and told them I was moving out. I wouldn't wish that conversation on my worst enemy. There were tears and, I am sure, anger, but what can kids do? Suzanne was still in high school, and John and Cathy had graduated, but they were still living at home. Considering how the atmosphere had been around the house, it wasn't a big surprise to them, but that doesn't lessen the pain.

A woman who was an apartment manager had reported some narcotics dealing to the Police Department several months prior. So I contacted her when I felt certain that I was going to move out. It turned out that she was looking for a Police Officer to move into the complex to provide onsite security. In return for providing security, the apartment would be rent free. What a deal! Well it was a deal until you got called out at 2 or 3 o'clock in the morning to go and tell renters to turn down their music!

I took the job and started moving my stuff in. It was pathetic since I had next to nothing, but I had promised Joyce that I wanted nothing from the house except my clothes and personal items. This left me having to get a table, a couple of chairs, and a bed. I bought everything second hand, and it looked like it since nothing matched.

When Joyce and I first started going through those hard times, she decided that she wanted to go to work. Suzanne wasn't a little kid any longer, so we felt that it wasn't critical that Joyce stay at home. She had found a good job and seemed to enjoy it. It so happened that my apartment complex was probably 5 minutes from where she worked, so she began to drop by and check up on me. She wasn't spying on me, but it became awkward because I think that it fostered a false hope for her that we might be able to get back together.

I didn't immediately start divorce proceedings because several people told me it would be best to wait and see how I felt after living away from the house and my family. My mother and father were not happy since they had grown to love Joyce, and of course, they were worried about how the kids would do.

Speaking of the kids…they would come over to my apartment and sometimes stay overnight. It was like a camp out, and we had fun. Eventually, the conversation would turn to why I wasn't home, and when would I be coming home. I think Joyce was telling them that for the time being, it was better that I was not home while we sorted "stuff" out. Kids want honest, open conversation (why do we lose that ability when we get older?), so when they asked me when I was coming home, and I had told them that it was complicated, they had a difficult time with that response.

One evening I was at my apartment and there was a knock on the door. When I answered it, I was greeted by Beth! She was absolutely the *l*ast person in the world I was expecting to see! I invited her in, and after getting something to drink, we sat down. The first thing I asked her was how in the heck she had found out where I was living! She told me that she wanted to see how I was doing, but she had not wanted to call me at home in case Joyce answered. So she called my partner at work, and he filled her in on what was going on with me and gave her my address.

I admit that my mind was beginning to go back to our prior relationship, and I was wondering if this was an attempt to resume that again now that I wasn't living at home. She put my mind at ease, and she began to tell me that she had met a wonderful guy at the church she had started attending when our relationship ended. It appeared it was love at first sight for them both, and even though they hadn't known each other for very long, they both felt this was very serious.

OK, I was happy for her, but what was she doing here? So I asked her, and she said she was worried about me, and felt compelled to come and see me. She went on to say that she felt guilty about what had happened between us, and she still wanted to encourage me to do everything I could to save my marriage. I told her to not feel guilty, that since I *was* the one who had violated Joyce's trust, it was on me; I felt like no one else was really responsible for me being here and not at home.

She then shared how she had grown up in a church but had drifted away when she left home. It wasn't until we ended our affair that she was drawn back to a small church near her house; that was where she met her (now) fiancé. She then asked me if I had a church or a preacher that I could go to for counseling. I told her again that I was happy for her, but that *my* relationship with God wasn't exactly like He and I were on a first name basis.

We talked for probably another hour, and she asked if she could pray for me, and she told me that she and her fiancé had been praying for both Joyce and me. I said sure, but I felt weird and uneasy, and I was glad when she ended the prayer. As she left, we hugged, and she assured me that she was available if I needed to talk at any time.

After she left I went back and sat down and started going over our conversation. I realized that she was totally sincere when she told me that she had come over out of her concern for not just me, but for Joyce also. That started me down the road of looking back on my life and where I was at that very moment… and I realized that I had hit rock bottom!

Thank God I was working, so I had to get up, get dressed, and go. Some time went by, and I reached the decision that I didn't want to reconcile my marriage. I told Joyce of my decision, and I told her that I was going to talk to an attorney. She reluctantly accepted that and hired her own attorney. Fortunately when it was all said and done, we managed to remain civil, and our 18-year marriage came to an end in December of 1988.

It's hard to keep a secret around the police department, and it wasn't long before my coworkers knew what was going on, and sad to say, no one was very surprised. More than half of them had been divorced at least once. One of the guys had been divorced so many times that when he announced he was getting married, his best friend told him he wouldn't be able to attend the wedding, but that he would catch him at the next one!

One day I got a call from Beth at work, asking me if I could meet her for lunch at the Jim's at Blanco & Loop 410. She was already seated in a booth when I arrived, and after we ordered, I asked her what she wanted to see me about. She then told me that she had heard about my divorce, and she wanted to see how I was doing. She hoped that she had not been instrumental in my final decision, and I assured her that wasn't the case.

As we got our food, she told me she had gotten married! She told me about her new husband, and I could tell she was crazy about him, and I wished them well. She went on to tell me that she wanted me to find someone just like she had, and that was part of the reason she wanted to meet with me.

I was already more than a little surprised at how fast she had gotten married, and now I was totally confused, thinking she wanted to fix me up with a friend. Before I could say anything, she asked if I would just listen for a few minutes. She then started telling me that she had been raised in a Christian household and had gone to church while growing up. When she finished high school she went to work, and she started living the party life. She met her first husband in a bar, and that was where they spent their leisure time when they weren't working. The kids arrived, but that didn't change the way they spent their time. I don't know how long they had been married when he was shot and killed.

She then took me back to when she and I first met, and how nice a guy I was to her, and that she had really enjoyed being with me. But she admitted that even though all those things were true, she had always known that what we were doing was wrong. It was totally against her Christian upbringing which eventually led to her going back to church for the first time in years.

It seemed to her that as soon as she stepped through those church doors, she *knew* that her life had been changed! She met the man that would become her husband the *second* Sunday she attended, and that was when she made the decision to end our relationship. About then, I admit that I was thinking that this was interesting, but why did she feel

I needed to know all this? That's when the conversation became about *me*. She asked me if I remembered her telling me that she and her husband were praying for both Joyce and me, and I said, "Yes." "Well," she said, "we are going to continue to pray that God will work a miracle in your life!"

Here, I reminded Beth that God and I were not exactly on speaking terms, but that I appreciated her sentiments. She asked me if I had ever read the Bible, and I told her that was a silly question since I was Catholic, and I had attended Catholic schools until the eighth grade. She said, "Yes, but have you ever read the Bible?" Well, I had to admit that I had never even opened a Bible since Catholics had their own version of their so-called Bible. This is where she reached inside a handbag that she had brought with her, and she pulled out a brown, leather book. It was a Bible! I guess the expression on my face was priceless because I remember her saying that she wanted to explain before I said anything else.

She put it on the table between us, and I could tell that it wasn't a new book since you could see it showed some wear and use. Before I could say anything else, she pulled out a small, ruled sheet of paper, and it was addressed to me. The paper outlined what the Bible is, and how it came to be with some suggestions on how to begin reading it. She went over some of the "books" that make up the Bible, and then asked me to take it and spend some time looking at the passages she had recommended.

I took it, and I opened it to a dedication page in the front; I immediately saw that it was the Bible that Beth's new husband had given *to her!* There was *no way* that I could take this Bible, but there was also *no way* that she was taking it back. Beth added that both she and her husband wanted me to have it!

I took the Bible, but I won't try to explain what my feelings were when I left that Jim's Restaurant. I had no idea then that this woman and her gift and prayers for me were going to be the start of *a* new life for me. I am eternally grateful to Beth and her husband.

Chapter 37

"…don't be the last guy holding the hog!"

I mentioned earlier that I had a deer lease where I would also take my family camping and hunting. Then, I started leasing in 1983 from two men around the Pearsall/Charlotte area. I primarily dealt with one of them whose first name was Johnny. It was a year-to-year lease, so we would negotiate terms of the lease every year. It was on this ranch where the kids and I spotted the rattlesnakes by the side of the ranch road, and after I killed them, they "came back to life."

There were other times during the year that I would meet with Johnny. It happened that as we got to know one another that I was invited to join him, and some of his rancher friends for some hog hunting trips on various ranches.

The men had "Hog dogs," and the dogs would be used to find the wild hogs in the brush, chasing them until they could surround the hogs. This was called "baying" the hog. The hunters were familiar with the different sounds of each dog's bark, and the bark changed from a baritone to a soprano at this "catch." Even in the pitch-dark of the night, the hunters could tell when their dogs had caught their prey! With the hogs encircled, the hunters would race up and either *catch or kill* the hogs. If the hog was killed, it was usually cleaned, and taken back to town for further processing. (Unless the hog was a male/boar whose musk stunk to "High Heaven!")

So this form of hunting served several purposes. If the hog was young, the meat was usually outstanding, and it provided excellent fare for Bar-B-Ques. This group of hunters would also offer the young, gutted hogs to people in the community for their use, free of charge. Those families would, in turn, give the hunters several dozen of the tamales that they had made from the meat. It was a game where everybody wins (except the hog.)

Another benefit of harvesting these animals was/is that it cut down on the wild hog population. This was important because wild hogs in Texas (and much of the country) are regarded as a nuisance because of the damage their rooting in the dirt does to the farm or ranch country when crops and pastures are burrowed-up and ruined.

The way they hunted hogs was serious business! You couldn't appreciate this until you were one of the men who would have to crawl into a thick, brushy, thorny thicket to go to the hog and kill it. Not to mention carrying your pistol and flashlight all the while! This being south Texas, everything has thorns that stick you and critters that will bite, strike, or sting you! And to top it all off, when you got to the dogs and the hogs, it was total chaos as the dogs were circling and jumping in to fight the hogs who were squealing every time a dog's bite would rip their skin or tear at their ears. A real tragedy could occur if one of the boars would rip the dogs' skin open when they would sling their razor-sharp tusks at them! If a hog was going to be shot, you had better be darn sure that you didn't shoot one of the dogs!

Of course with ranchers/hog hunters, like any other group of guys, someone could always be counted on to come up with an idea to bring humor to an often-dangerous situation. And, of course, the object of the humor would naturally fall to the new guy. I was that object one night when the dogs had bayed a medium size boar hog. This hog had about 1-inch-long tusks and had put up a good fight, but it was winded from the fight and the chase. When we came up on them, one of the fellas told me to grab the hog's hind legs, and lift his legs off the ground which would render him helpless. Mission accomplished and sure enough the hog was helpless. It was like maneuvering a wheelbarrow since the hog is not able to turn his neck like most animals can!

It was then decided by the guy in charge that we would castrate the hog, and let him go. This was done often with a young boar to render him unable to reproduce, but he would still continue to grow, and his tusks would grow with him. The tusks were the trophy mount and symbol that the hunters prized when killing a large boar. A game-room goal and satisfaction, for sure!

The "Hog-tying", so to speak, took a little time, and it even gave the boar a chance to begin reviving his strength. The dogs had been called off, and they were taken to their "dog box" in the bed of one of the trucks, so they were not bothering the hog. When the castration procedure began, he was more than a little agitated. As a matter of fact, you could say that he was getting downright pissed! I was still holding onto the hind legs of my boar when everyone walked off toward the trucks leaving me with the boar! When they reached the trucks, one of them called back to me and told me to "Turn him loose when I was ready!" Huh?

I didn't for one minute think that I could convince this pissed off boar that *I* wasn't the one who had taken his testicles! This was going to be interesting since there wasn't a tree to climb, and *I* knew that he could run faster than I could. Nothing left to do but turn him loose and hope for the best. When I let go, he whirled around and ran right to me, and I kicked him in the head, and he veered around and took off! The guys in the trucks got a good laugh, and I learned a valuable lesson: Don't be the last guy holding the hog!

When a hunt was organized, it usually meant getting out to the designated ranch early, like before daylight! This meant that if I were driving down from my house in San Antonio to Charlotte, I would be leaving around 4:00 o'clock in the morning. Johnny offered me the chance to come down the night before and spend the night so I wouldn't have to leave so early.

Initially I felt like I was imposing since they had two young boys, and one of them was forced to move from his bed to another room. His wife, Jeanette, was insistent that it was no problem, so I felt better about my intrusion. Since I had been leasing from Johnny and his partner for several years, and as I came to spend more time with the family, I could tell that there was tension between husband and wife. Joyce and I were still married at that time, but by then, I knew all about tension.

When I first began leasing their hunting ranch, I had spoken several times on the phone with Jeanette (when I was trying to talk to

Johnny) before I met her in person. She had a soft, country voice, and since I knew she was the wife of a rancher, I formed a picture of what I thought she would look like. It turned out that she *was* nothing like my mental image.

Johnny was a heavy person, but she was not. He dressed like a working rancher/farmer; she dressed in class. They had a beautiful home, and I later learned that she had furnished and decorated by herself. She was also the person that maintained the yard and landscaping. Her appearance drew my attention because it wasn't just based on the fact that she was *(is)* a beautiful woman, but that everything about her (clothes, hair, and demeanor) combined to present this striking woman. I was impressed, to say the least. I was also surprised at the picture they made together because they didn't strike me as a couple.

Once in a while, I would have to go down to meet with Johnny, and he would have me go to their house to wait for him there. Charlotte was/is a very small community, and their farm and ranches were about 20 miles out of town. When I would arrive, Jeanette would invite me in, and we three would talk about my police work and our families.

She told me that her father had worked for Humble-Exxon Oil, and she and her sister had grown up living in one of the Exxon "Camp Houses" a couple of miles outside of Charlotte. When Humble shut down their Camp (of two rows of 10 houses per row,) the Company offered to let her parents purchase the house that they resided in. They did, and it was moved into Charlotte. I never met her father, Eulan, as he had died some years earlier, but her mother, Audrey Wells Cox, still lived in that same house until about 2010. (Her mom later told Jeanette that they paid $4,000 dollars for their shingled, pier and beam home which Humble had purchased and built as kits from Sears and Roebuck! To this day, some 65 years later, at least 12 of those homes are still being lived-in within the city limits of Charlotte.)

I guess Jeanette needed someone to talk to that didn't live in her home town for when I mentioned that my marriage was in trouble, she confided in me that she and Johnny were also on shaky ground. We spent quite a bit of time admitting that we were responsible for our choices, and with kids involved, we wouldn't be the only ones affected with whatever decisions were made. I also found out that she was raised *a* Christian, and she was struggling with God's command about marriage and divorce.

During this time at work, I decided that I wanted to try out for the Sergeant's promotional exam. This would mean that once again I would be going back to uniform on a patrol shift, but I felt that I needed to make a change. I talked it over with Joyce, and the two-month study ritual began again. I made it and was promoted on February 23, 1985! This was a significant pay raise for me, and I changed my duties as a Police Officer from active street work to supervising others engaged in active street work. After 17 years (counting my time in Wilmington) of working the "streets," I was once again showing up (most of the time) *after* the action was over.

It was an adjustment and one I wasn't overly fond of, but it came with the promotion. I held the rank of Sergeant longer than any other position during my policing career. I was promoted to Lieutenant in March of 1997, so I was a sergeant for 12 years. As a sergeant, I once again had the "privilege" of working rotating shifts which included good old Dog Watch! Even though I no longer responded to the usual dispatched calls, I would now spend a lot of my time out in the field. I liked showing up at various scenes, and if needed, I would cover the officer if his/her assigned cover officer took a while getting to the scene. Another part of the duties of the Sergeant was Job Performance Evaluations, and I felt that the best way to determine job performance was to be there as they performed their job! Some of the officers were not comfortable with having the Sergeant show up, but they soon realized that I liked being out in the field, so they got used to it.

As was required again, I had to do 2 years on patrol in uniform before I could transfer somewhere else. The thought of possibly going to another covert (undercover) unit kept me watching the calendar until my two years were up. Remember, I hated Dog Watch but loved undercover assignments.

Chapter 38

"You know, you speak Flemish like my grandparents!"

In 1986 my mother wanted to go to Belgium to see her family. My father was unable to go so, Joyce and I decided that we would take Suzanne and go with her. In all honesty, I guess we both felt that this might be an opportunity to get our marriage back on track. By then, John and Cathy were in their twenties, and it wasn't possible for them to go either. So the arrangements were made, and we left for what would turn out to be my only visit back to my homeland.

We flew into Brussels, and when the pilot announced that we were over Belgium, the plane started making its slow descent; I started looking out the window. Since the weather was clear, I could see the countryside and was struck by how small everything looked! By small, I mean that when we rented a car, we could drive for 2 or 3 hours and cover three countries!

We stayed with one of my uncles, and my mother stayed with her sister. The two weeks sped by, and then it was time to leave. I regret that we didn't take more time to stay because there was so much to do and so many people to see! It was funny that I could still speak *some* Flemish, but it didn't seem to sound the same as the natives. Some of the confusion was cleared up when I went to the local bank one day to exchange some dollars for Belgium franks. The young, female teller was helping me, and I was trying to carry my end of the conversation by showing off my language skills. As we finished and I was ready to leave, she said to me, "You know, you speak Flemish like my grandparents!" Talk about deflating the ego!

When we came back home, it was back to work and dealing with the same problems concerning my relationship with Joyce and our marriage. One evening, I had occasion to call Johnny at Charlotte, and Jeanette answered the phone. She told me that he was out hog hunting, and she asked me how my trip to Belgium had been. As I shared some of the details of the trip, I found myself really enjoying our conversation.

When we were finishing and getting ready to end the call, Jeanette said that she had missed talking to me. I admitted that I had been thinking the same thing. She then surprised me by telling me that she was ending her marriage to Johnny. She was going to have a talk with him when he came in that same night. There was not much to say, other than, "Are you sure?" but she didn't hesitate when she said "Yes." Neither of us said anything else, and we ended the call. Not long after returning from Belgium, I moved out and was again living in an apartment when my marriage was officially terminated in December of 1988.

One way I have always dealt with stress is to get busy doing something. Once I had my 2 years as a Sergeant completed, I began to look for another assignment away from patrol. As luck would have it, another plainclothes unit had been formed! It was called the Repeat Offenders Program, known as *ROPE*. When I was eligible to move, this unit was already in existence, and one of the sergeants was going to be promoted to a Lieutenant position elsewhere, so he would be leaving ROPE.

I put in for it, and I was chosen to fill his Sergeant spot! Once again, I found myself in a plain clothes unit, engaged in proactive police work. ROPE was designed to perform like the old Task Force, but instead of patrolmen/women, this unit was now staffed with Detective Investigators (DI.) One of the things that made this unit different was that it was run directly out of the office of the Chief of Police with the Executive Officer (XO) overseeing it. The XO and I were good friends, however, that became a problem later down the line.

One Lieutenant and four sergeants had direct supervisory duties here with two sergeants on each shift and each sergeant overseeing a crew of DIs consisting of men and women. The mission was to target *specific crimes* that were currently impacting a segment of the community. This could be anything from a serial rapist to car burglaries in parking lots. This gave us a lot of leeway, but there was also a lot of pressure to perform when a "crime wave" hit the news.

Narcotics addiction is a driver for much of the crime that takes place today, and it wasn't any different than in 1988.

Since SAPD already had a Narcotics Unit there was always a (healthy?) competition between the units. ROPE, by necessity, consisted of both men and women, with a good ethnic mix. This diversity is what made the unit so effective and made coming to work fun (most of the time!)

Back in Chapter 33, I described a narcotics warrant that one of my men obtained when I was working in ROPE. When we ran the warrant, it resulted in the bad guy shooting Doug, and Doug shooting and killing the bad guy. You might recall that I said then, that these were not just people working for me but that they were my friends. You can easily bond with a group of people when you are packed in the back of a van wearing your body armor on the way to serving a potentially dangerous warrant!

I also need to give credit here to the *females* that made up part of our crew; they were as tough as any of the guys!

There were many good cases made by ROPE, and the resulting press coverage was good for the Department. I could probably write another book on the escapades our unit engaged in, but I will just say that it was one of my most rewarding assignments. Things changed, however, when the Lieutenant that was in charge of the unit decided that it was time for him to retire. We were getting a new Lieutenant who I didn't know very well.

Lt. Tom Polonis was a nice guy from what I had heard of him, so I sat back and waited to see what the future held. Law enforcement should try to steer clear of politics, and that is especially true when it comes to internal politics. Since the unit worked directly out of the Chief's office and under the XO, whenever we made a good "bust" and the media was to be notified, the XO would respond to the location of the arrest. Since we made a lot of good arrests, he was on TV often!

All this TV exposure earned the XO the nickname of "Captain Video," and it placed a lot of pressure on the unit to perform when a crime or crimes were making the news. It also created friction between us and other plain clothes units because ROPE was in the news a lot. Lt. Polonis wasn't the celebrity type, and he preferred a more laid-back approach to our policing without all the notoriety. This difference in personalities contributed to the chilly relationship that existed between him and the XO.

This should not have affected me, but Polonis knew that the XO and I were friends. I guess he felt that I would be the in-house snitch for the XO. (Have you noticed that once politics rears its ugly head, *reason* seems to *leave the room?*") It wasn't long before I was told that the Lieutenant wanted to see me in his office.

We sat down, and he told me that he wanted to make some changes that would include replacing me with someone he was more comfortable with. He was the boss, so there wasn't a lot for me to say. The next day I was notified to report to the Chief's office to see the XO. On arriving there, I was brought into his office where he proceeded to tell me *exactly* how he felt about the Lieutenant.

He was upset that the Lieutenant had bypassed the chain of command *(him!)* and had gone directly to the Chief with his request to make some personnel changes. The Chief had come to the XO to find out what was going on and told him to take care of it. The XO then proceeded to tell me that *I* wasn't going anywhere, and if anyone was leaving, it might very well be the Lieutenant!

I admit that I have a temper, but the XO could really get wound up, and he was on a roll. He finally settled down a few minutes later, and I had been thinking while he was venting. I told him it wouldn't work if the Lieutenant was forced to keep me on, and it wasn't going to be worth the fight that would result if I stayed. He was still mad, but I could tell he knew I was right. So a few days later I was preparing to report to a uniform patrol shift when I got another call at home to come in and see the XO.

When I got there, he told me that he had just received a request from the US Marshall's Office for a *supervisor* and several San Antonio Police *Officers* to participate in a joint fugitive apprehension task force called "Operation Southern Star." It was slated to begin in August of 1990 and run through October of the same year.

I knew *a* lot of the people that were going to be assigned, and he asked me if I was interested, and I agreed. I think it was his way of making up for the unfair treatment I had gotten when released from ROPE. This special assignment was the last time I actively worked in a plain clothes unit chasing bad guys.

While I was on this assignment, an opening for a supervisor in the Traffic Bureau became available. The sergeant overseeing the DWI unit was leaving and needed a replacement. Since the DWI unit worked only evenings and did NOT work dogwatch, do I need to tell you where I went?!

Chapter 39

"All I had to do was admit I was a sinner…"

As I transferred to ROPE, Jeanette was working her way through a divorce from Johnny. She knew where I was working, and we started talking almost daily, and it wasn't long before we saw each other. She was still at home in Charlotte and had given in to the pressure of family and friends and agreed to go to counseling with Johnny.

It didn't take much time for the counselor to tell Johnny they were wasting their time and money, as he could tell that Jeanette had already made up her mind. Not long after that, Johnny found out that she and I were seeing each other. Within a few days, Jeanette called me and asked me if I would meet her and Johnny for a talk. I agreed, and it was probably one of the toughest conversations I've ever had. I considered him a friend, but by then, I knew I was in love with Jeanette.

We three talked about the divorce, how it would affect their entire family, and how what was happening was totally against God's will for our lives! There were tears from all of us, but it didn't change my feelings for Jeanette, nor her feelings for me. We parted with Jeanette and Johnny going one way and me the other. Jeanette told me later that on their way back to the house, Johnny asked her if she was in love with me, and she told him, "Yes."

Well, it didn't take long for the word to get out around Charlotte, and Jeanette found out who her real friends were. Some surprised her, others disappointed her, and it got worse when their divorce was set to go to trial. Her attorney had advised her to continue to live in their house if she wanted to keep her boys, whom she dearly loved. She was miserable with Johnny also remaining in the home. There was nothing much I could do other than to support her feelings as she prepared to go to court. The case was settled, and surprisingly to me, it was agreed by all that they would share Joint Custody of their two sons, and that the boys would live with their father at their home in Charlotte.

Jeanette explained that her older son Doug was crazy about horses, and he had his own horse at the house that he rode daily. Both boys played Little League baseball twice a week and continued to be very involved in their boys' group at Church. Plus, all of the boys' close relatives lived around them in Charlotte, including both grandmothers. Jeanette had recently rented a small apartment in San Antonio and had gotten a job to support her, but she came to realize that it would be cruel to move them to San Antonio, turning them into "Latch-Key kids." When both boys told her they didn't want to live in a big city, she knew her broken heart loved them more than she loved herself. So for all these reasons, she agreed to let Johnny have the house so that the boys could remain in their home, neighborhood, and community (even though the house had been a gift from her father to her when they had married.)

I was living in an apartment not far from where Jeanette had her apartment, and we decided that this was the way it should be for the time being. She wanted to have her sons come to visit as often as possible, and she felt it was wrong for us to be living together while we were not married.

We rectified that situation when we got married on June 10, 1989. My mother and father, my siblings, and Suzanne were in attendance, and Jeanette's mother and her two sons were there for her. Jeanette's sister, Jo, was adamantly opposed to Jeanette getting a divorce, so she and her husband refused to attend the wedding. It took a while, but eventually, Jo warmed up to me, and over time, all of the hard feelings were put aside.

Once we married, we rented a small house in the Northside of San Antonio and settled in, trying to regain some normalcy in our lives. Part of the changes that took place was that Jeanette talked me into going to Church! She had been raised in a Methodist church growing up, but when her sons became toddlers, she began to attend the Baptist Church in Charlotte where they had a better Sunday school program. So we began visiting the Medical Center Baptist Church that was just down the street from where we lived.

This was something completely different for me here, based on my previous experiences when I attended Catholic Church services. I could tell what was going on now because everyone spoke English (no Latin.) There was a wooden cross on the front wall of the Sanctuary, but it did not have Jesus on it, and there were no altar boys in attendance. I liked it, and I began to look forward to Sundays!

Besides the church service, I was told that they had a Sunday School class that began an hour before the start of the church service itself. Jeanette suggested that we begin attending Sunday School, and we did. Everyone had a Bible, including Jeanette, and I remembered Beth giving me her Bible at the meeting at Jim's restaurant, so I took that one with me. It still contained the personal letter she had included, and *I started reading the Bible.*

Jeanette and I began having some serious discussions about faith and my relationship with God. She referred to herself as a Believer in Jesus Christ and told me she was saved from her sins because He had died on the cross for everyone, including *me*!

It took a while for all that to sink in, but I was fortunate to be in a Sunday School class that had some first-rate Bible teachers and one older, retired Baptist preacher named C.B. Baker. C.B. became a mentor to me and a very close friend that I learned to trust and rely on for as long as he lived. He died when he was in his mid-eighties, but he still influences my life in many ways.

Thinking back to my days attending St. Mary Magdalen's Catholic School, I asked Jeanette when I would have to go to Confession so I could be forgiven for my sins, in order to be "Saved." She then explained to me that I didn't need to go to *a* priest. She said that all I had to do was pray to Jesus and admit that I was a *sinner,* that I *believed* that Jesus was the *Son of God* who died and *paid the price for my sins*, and that *He rose again* from the grave and *went to Heaven,* and that I wanted Him to be *The Lord* of my life. I prayed that prayer, and I *knew* in my heart that I was forgiven for all the sins that I had committed in my life!

Jeanette told me later that it was customary for someone who has made this profession of faith to be baptized in the Church. So on April 7, 1990, at 45 years of age, I was baptized at Medical Center Baptist Church by our young pastor, David Saathoff. David was the pastor who married Jeanette and me, and I owe him a debt of gratitude.

When Jeanette and I married, Suzanne was still living at home with her mother. Apparently, my new marriage stirred up an awful lot of resentment within Joyce, and she seemed to take a lot of it out on Suzanne. Suzanne would visit and tell me what was happening at home, but I never criticized her mother. When Suzanne was getting ready to enter her Senior year in High School, she asked if she could move in with Jeanette and me, and we both said, "Sure!" so that is what she did.

John had joined the army, and in 1991 he participated in Desert Storm, assigned to an armored division. He was later honorably discharged. Cathy had been involved in a relationship and had two kids, a boy and a girl. She later remarried a good man and moved to Wimberly, Texas, where she became an EMT.

Chapter 40

"...all three were killed!"

As if Jeanette and I didn't have enough going on in our lives, we soon agreed that we didn't want to live in the city. When I first began police work in San Antonio, the rule was that city employees (Police & Fire) had to live within the city limits. But in the intervening years, that rule became unrealistic and was scrapped.

If you recall, my brother and I had bought some land together that was South of San Antonio. This was several years before Joyce and I were divorced. As part of our divorce settlement, Joyce wanted to retain a portion of that land for herself. My brother had approached me about selling my part to him, and I agreed. Several years later, Joyce finally sold Ralph her portion, too. When Ralph got control of his entire 200 acre property, he and his wife built their home and were living out there, raising their family.

Since Ralph and I (along with our sister) have always been personally close, I wanted to see if we could find something close to where he was living. Jeanette also liked the Yancey location because it was only about 35 miles from Charlotte where her sons were living.

We decided that we would concentrate our search for property around that area. Once again it seemed that the Lord was looking out for me when 200 acres came up for sale adjoining my brother's property! In addition to its location, the property had been foreclosed on by the bank, and the price was within our budget! It was meant to be, and we closed on the property in February of 1990. Now all we had to do was pay for it! My new assignment to the Traffic Bureau was going to play a significant role in paying for the property.

When I initially transferred to the Traffic Bureau I was the supervisor in charge of the DWI unit. My working hours were strictly evenings with no daily rotation of shifts. I had no desire to make this my permanent place to work. For although I was thrilled that I wasn't going to have to work "Dog Watch," I didn't envision working steady evenings with no time at home except for my days off. It was an unwritten rule that the first time an opening on one of the regular traffic shifts occurred, the DWI sergeant had first crack at the opening. I took advantage of this when an opening came up, and I was able to move over to one of the regular shifts.

Working in traffic was different from anywhere else I had been assigned. Of course we patrolled the roadways for speeders, the school zones for people speeding and failing to stop for school buses, and we worked crowd control at various events. The crowd control portion of the Traffic Bureau's responsibilities often led to major overtime assignments.

This unexpected boost to my income potential was welcomed immediately because, as a new landowner, there was no end to the demand for money needed to begin making improvements. Since Traffic was the overtime magnet of the entire Department, and I could work as many extra hours as I wanted, I quit every other overtime job I had. As I advanced in my walk with God in faith, I began to see how He was providing for us in ways that I couldn't have imagined, and that included my new assignment!

I don't mind telling you that I was devastated when I was forced to leave ROPE. One of the reasons I took it hard was because my pride had been damaged. But an even larger reason for my resentment came from the fact that I didn't want to leave the plain clothes work behind! I absolutely craved proactive police work. It was dangerous and gritty, and yet, when you made that arrest, Man, it felt so good! Even though it had cost me my marriage and hurt those around me, it was hard for me to acknowledge that I would have been better off working somewhere else.

I wish that one of my very close friends in the Department, (who also worked in Narcotics at the same time that I was assigned) had been forced to work somewhere else. He and I had worked in uniform patrol and had adjoining districts. He lived in my district, and our families socialized. He was probably one of the hardest working guys that I knew. He liked to work under cover and made a lot of good cases. He didn't want to work anywhere else other than Narcotics.

But after several years of working undercover, he was the poster boy for living the created undercover role of a "Doper." He eventually divorced, and one day died unexpectantly. At the autopsy they found traces of cocaine in his system!

The truth is that he stayed in Narcotics *too long* and lost sight of who he really was. It took everyone by surprise, myself included, and yet I can see how easy it must have been for him to fall into that trap. Looking back, Lt. Polonis did me a great favor when he decided to replace me in ROPE, and he and I later became good friends.

I am not going to bore you with details of everyday life as a uniform Traffic Supervisor, but it, too, had its moments. There were the occasional car chases and once in a while an unusual incident would occur. "Unusual" can describe a variety of situations and I have to include this one, as I think that it would rank really high on anyone's list.

We were on the daylight shift early one morning and it was the start of rush hour traffic which always led to slow-downs on the road. One of the officers was dispatched to respond to a location on his assigned expressway for a couple having sex in their car parked alongside the roadway. OKAY….

This is one of the *major* highways around San Antonio, and thousands of vehicles use it every day. I guess we would all agree that viewing a couple having sex in a parked car alongside the highway in broad daylight is not something that commuters would expect to see every day. But it seemed odd that traffic was being so noticeably impacted.

When the officer made his way through the slowing traffic jam, he could see a car pulled way to the side of the roadway. As he came closer to the car he could tell that it was a *convertible,* and he was sure of that because *the top was down!* There were also body parts visible that should have been covered with clothes*!*

Since he had to turn on his overhead emergency flashing lights, it drew even more attention to the activity taking place in the car, and traffic was coming to a standstill! To make things even worse (if that was possible) the car was parked right by a major street overpass which had also come to a complete stop.

People had been alerted to what was going on, and some were out of their cars looking down. Apparently radio stations had gotten wind of the reason for the slow down on Loop 1604, and they were broadcasting it on the air! I don't remember if the TV stations had helicopters in the air and shot video, but it made the evening news. The back log took several hours to clear up.

The other supervisors and I were still in the office, and we didn't make it out to the scene. We had assumed that it was some kids. *Wrong!* When the officer later filled us in, he told us that it was a doctor and his nurse who had partied into the morning hours, and on the way home, they were overtaken with passion and couldn't help themselves! I guess you could make the case that it was safer for them to be parked instead of driving under the influence! They could have been arrested for indecent exposure, but who hasn't been overcome with passion? We asked him what the woman looked like, and all he said was that he could understand the overcoming with passion part.

Thankfully, those types of calls were rare and didn't require a supervisor to be present (darn it!) Where a supervisor was required to respond was at all officer involved accidents, DWIs involving Police Officers, and *fatality* accidents.

A Law Enforcement officer caught driving under the influence of alcohol was probably looking at the end of his/her career. When I was the DWI supervisor, I was often called to the scene, but if I was tied up on another call, or was off duty, then one of the other traffic sergeants was called. There is no denying that in years past, if an officer was caught, and if there was no one else involved (there was no accident), he stood a good chance of just being driven home.

In that case, usually a supervisor was never notified, and the stopping officer simply called another officer, and they handled it between themselves. Understandably, things have changed, and that accommodation is no longer available! Most police cars now have dash cameras that make it hard to hide the fact that a traffic stop was made.

Another type of call where a supervisor was required to respond was when an officer was involved in an accident while driving a police car. Usually it never amounted to much unless it was a major accident (a lot of property damage or severe physical injuries suffered) which then would require an accident reconstruction team.

I can personally attest to the fact that Police Officers do have car accidents, and not just in their private cars, but in police cars, too. I was asked one time to disclose if I had a vested interest in any of the auto repair shops in San Antonio as I seemed hellbent on giving them a good deal of business. What can I say? Things happened!

Fatality accidents are the ones no one wants to respond to, either as an officer or supervisor. In San Antonio there were no shortages of fatality accidents, and I guess I made my share of them. You have to learn to harden yourself to death if you are going to be a police officer. It never becomes routine, especially when small *kids* are involved. Here was an instance where traffic death was not routine....

Joyce and I were still married, and I was working the daylight shift while assigned to ROPE. It was close to lunchtime when the Chief-of-Police who at the time was Robert Heuck, came onto the radio channel we were using, and he asked me to switch to an open channel (to have a private conversation.)

(When I went through the police academy in 1968, he was a Lieutenant who taught Report Writing. I had worked for him at various times, and he had the reputation of being a hard ass, but I always got along with Chief Heuck.) I switched over, and he asked me to contact him ASAP at Callaghan Rd., and a cross street. I knew something was wrong, but had no idea what was going on.

Callaghan is a fairly busy street, and it has a substantial hill that you climb, coming from West to East. As I topped the hill, there were police cars, ambulances, and firetrucks everywhere. I went as far down as I could and parked my car. When I got out I could see two cars that were wrecked in the intersection. I spotted the Chief nearby, and he saw me at the same time, and he motioned me over. I didn't know why, but pure dread filled my heart!

As I came up to him, he told me that *Joyce* was involved in the accident, but that *she was OK.* I recognized our blue Suburban, and the front end was really smashed up. There was a 2-door sedan to the side of the intersection, and its entire driver's side door was caved in. I asked where my wife was, and I was told that she was sitting inside one of the businesses located at the corner of the intersection.

Before I could head that way, the Chief told me that the sedan had pulled out in front of Joyce, and there were witnesses to the accident. He then added that the sedan had been occupied by three women and *all three were killed!*

I was speechless! He and I went over to the cars, and even though both cars had a lot of damage, I could not see how three people had been killed. Two fatalities had already been taken to the hospital to be officially pronounced, and the other person was still at the scene in another ambulance. The EMTs had given up trying to resuscitate her,

Since it was unusual for the Chief to make accident calls, he told me that he had been on his way to lunch, and he happened to be driving down Callaghan when he came on the scene of the accident. He stopped, and one of the officers came up to him and told him that Joyce had identified me as her husband and requested that I be notified. Since the Chief was familiar with me, he decided that he would take care of the notification.

We then walked into the shop where two or three women were attending to Joyce. She was almost hysterical because someone had already told her about the victims when she inquired about their physical condition. When she saw me, she lost it, and I couldn't blame her one bit. She wasn't hurt physically, but it took a long time to deal with the emotional side of that trauma.

It was a strange accident because there was no excessive speed, no blood to speak of, and the driver of the sedan had a clear view and should have been able to see our Suburban. The sedan was being driven by an older woman and her two married daughters were also in the front seat with their mother. It was never disclosed why all three were in the front seat, but when our much larger car struck their driver's door, all three were jerked sideways, breaking their necks.

Not long after the accident, we were served with papers notifying us that we were being sued! Luckily I had hired an accident reconstruction firm, and that was some of the best money we ever spent. Our insurance company made the families an offer which they refused, so we ended up in court.

The jury trial lasted almost a week, and they began their deliberations on Friday morning. We had gone to lunch when we were notified that the jury had reached a verdict. When everyone was back in the courtroom, the jury read their decision, and Joyce was found not guilty! The families of the victims broke down in court and complained about how unfair it all was. I can't imagine what it feels like to lose three members of your family all at once. But I remembered that our insurance company had tried to settle, and they had refused.

It was proven conclusively that the driver of the other vehicle was completely at fault, and they knew that before we went to trial. I couldn't help but feel that some greed had crept in and that played a part of their decisions to try and get more money than what had been offered.

Chapter 41

"A Retirement Prayer"

From the moment that we bought the property in Yancey, Texas, Jeanette and I wanted to move out there as soon as possible. There was no way we could afford to build a house, too, but someone had mentioned a "Barndominion." We started looking into this, and learned that they were talking about a *barn* that had *living quarters* all combined. It was perfect for us, and we decided to build it out of metal.

A nearby neighbor was a contractor who had experience with this type of construction, and I drew up a set of simple plans. We built it with two bedrooms and one bathroom, and the kitchen and living room were one open space. The rest of the building was barn space that had two overhead doors. We moved in the latter part of 1990, and it was exactly what we needed. Even Bruno, my German Shorthair Pointer, had a big, brand-new kennel right beside us! My daughter, Suzanne, was still living with us, so she took the second bedroom and moved in, too. She commuted to San Antonio, taking a couple of college courses and working a part-time job.

I started commuting from Yancey to San Antonio myself, every day going to work. It worked out great that Jeanette was in-between jobs when we moved in. Once we started living there, it became so obvious that we were in the country! There were no immediate neighbors, and it would actually get dark at night because city lights were absent. IT WAS WONDERFUL!!!

When I was on the daylight shift, I would have to leave the house around 6:00 AM. As I stepped out one morning to prepare to leave, the smell of the earth and the grass hit me. I heard a bird or two starting to stir, and I was taken back to the Van Damme farm of so many years ago in my past! There I was, standing outside waiting for the sky to lighten up, and I had to laugh because those darn farmers had gotten to me! (Thank you, Leona & Emile!)

Jeanette had gotten a job at the Food Stamp Office in Hondo, Texas which was about 20 miles north of us. When they discovered that she had her college degree, she switched over to the Child Protective Services department which worked out of the same office, but paid her a better salary. With the cases she was working in Child Protective, and some of the crazy stuff that would come up in my job, our pillow talk could get quite interesting at times!

I have to share a funny story that actually happened to Jeanette and me when we first started building the barn. When the concrete guys were building the slab for the barn, I also had them form up the slab for Bruno's dog run right beside the house. It was great to have it done at the same time so he could move in when we did. The plumbers had installed a hose bib between the barn and the kennel that we would be using to clean the kennels.

They had framed in the barn and had the dog kennels partially completed when Jeanette and I decided that just the two of us would drive out on a Saturday afternoon and spend the night sleeping on cots. We wanted to experience the seclusion of "Our Place" and be away from everyone!

Well we did that, and that evening we hooked up a hose to the hose bib and attached a garden sprayer to the hose and tied that to an overhead pipe in the kennel, and we took a shower! We had so much fun that we did that several times in the next few weeks.

I mentioned that we had no close neighbors, but a divorced guy lived alone on a place his father owned. It was probably about three quarters of a mile from our place, and you could see his house if you looked out across the country. Well, this guy would show up at our place almost as soon as we got there, and he acted like he knew we had arrived. This was weird because our barn was a good ways off the County Road, and there was no way to see any vehicles parked there just by driving down the road. He was kind of creepy, but we figured he was just lonely. One day we had arrived, and shortly thereafter, he drove up again and got out of his truck.

My wife could stand it no longer! She asked him how he managed to come by as if he knew we were there! Then he proceeded to tell us his secret: he had a telescope that he would look through! And from his house he could easily see to our *barn*, **and**........the dog kennels! That ended the outdoor showers. I should have kicked his butt.

Since Jeanette and I now lived next to Ralph and his family, my mother and father would come out from San Antonio to visit and spend time with us both. I know they enjoyed their visits to the country, and it was great to spend the time with them. My brother would get the majority of their attention because he and Carolyn had two young kids. It was all good.

My sister had been married and divorced and was now married again. She and her husband were living in Arkansas. My parents would occasionally drive there to visit her, but that was a long trip, so at their advancing ages, they didn't travel there too often any more. This will remind you that we all need to cherish those times we spend with family because we don't know when our time is done.

On the third day of March, 1991, at around 2:30 in the morning, our phone rang, and my father told me that my mother had suffered a massive heart attack, and that they were at the Methodist Hospital. He was going to call my brother next, and told me that I should get there as quick as I could.

Jeanette and I threw on clothes, and hurried toward town. When we got there, and I saw my father, I knew she was gone! He was holding it together, but not by much. Apparently it was severe enough that when she had sat up in bed (which woke my father up,) she gasped once, and fell back. She never regained consciousness.

We were in a private family waiting room there, and a few minutes after I arrived, a nurse came in to tell us that if we wanted to see her, we could go in. I went in by myself, and hugged her and cried my heart out. She was never a woman that carried her emotions on her sleeve, but I know she loved her children and rather than talk about it, she just did all she could for us! Her most intimate action toward me, and I know that my brother and sister would agree with this, too, was making the sign of the Cross on my forehead and asking the Angels to protect me! *Mom, I guess they usually answered your prayer!*

My brother and his family showed up, and Ralph also took some private time with her, and then everyone else went in to see her. I felt sorry for my sister since there was no way that she could get there as soon as she would have liked. After she did arrive several days later, my sister and I were talking, and I told her how grateful I was that the evening before mom died, Jeanette and I had stopped by their house for a visit with them. When we were there, everything seemed fine.

Unknown to me I struck a nerve when I mentioned this to my sister, and she started crying. She told me that the night before mom died, she had this powerful urge to call her. Because it was somewhat late, Jeanine decided to wait until the next morning. Once in a while Jeanine will mention to me that she still regrets not making that call.

The death of my mother was one of the hardest things I have ever had to deal with in my life. I was fortunate to have her for seventy-two years, but I wasn't ready for her to go! A heart attack wasn't a surprise since she had experienced by-pass surgery several years earlier, she was overweight, and she wasn't a vigorous exerciser. As a matter of fact my father had also had by-pass surgery, and they both were on high blood pressure medicine.

I mentioned that my mother and father didn't go to church. Even when we were growing up they didn't attend at all other than going on an occasional holiday. We never prayed before meals, and the few times that God came up in a discussion, my parents both acknowledged that God existed, but that was about the extent of any talk about religion at our house.

At the time of mom's death, I had already accepted Jesus into my life and asked Him for forgiveness of my sins. I was "saved," and my sins were forgiven when He shed His blood for me on the Cross. As a result of that, I know that when I die, *I am going to heaven!*

In the time following her funeral, I would still become emotional thinking of my Mother. I know that's not unusual, but I started to realize that I was worried if *Mom* was in heaven! I sincerely believe that we will be reunited with our loved ones when we get to heaven. I know that I am going to be there, but I kept worrying about *her* salvation, since she and I had never talked about it.

Several months after the funeral, my father asked my brother, sister, and I to come to the house and pick out some things that had belonged to our mother which were special to each of us. He was starting to make plans to sell the house and move to Hondo, Texas, which would put him so much closer to where my brother and I lived.

We picked some things that held special memories, and I went into their bedroom where my mother's clothes were laying on the bed. I looked at them and then glanced into their closet, and I saw her brown corduroy coat hanging on the clothes rod. I really only wanted that coat! It was the one she wore constantly when the weather was cool, and I felt it was a part of her that I wanted near to me. It was sort of like a security blanket! No one argued about the coat, and I took it home with me. It was summertime, so I hung the coat in my closet where I could see it, and just seeing it was comforting to me.

Since my sister had come down from Arkansas for the services, she was staying with my father for a few days longer, and she was going through Mom's personal things. As she was going through one of the drawers in Mom's dresser, she found a folded note under some clothes. When she read the note, she knew that I would want to see it. The next time she and I got together, she gave me the note.

I unfolded the paper and recognized her handwriting. She had only gone to school in Belgium for three years, and that was extent of her formal education, so her writing was very distinct.

At the top of the page, she wrote "A Retirement Prayer," and then she wrote:

"Dear heavenly Father, as I enter my retirement years, help me to see not an ending, but a new beginning. For now I have more of the precious gift of time. Time to feel the morning breeze. To experience a blooming wildflower or a graceful bird in flight. Time to explore talents and all kinds of interests. Time to be with people I care about and to meet new people as well. But most important of all, dear Father, time to spend in fellowship with You, talking with You, and reading Your Holy Word. Grant that I may be blessed with health and with a desire to use my wisdom and experience to help others grow. May these years truly be the most golden of my life, and May they be dedicated to Your glory. Amen."

When I finished reading the note, I was crying, and I was thanking God for allowing us to find it. I knew in my heart that she will be waiting for me when I get to Heaven! From that time on, I stopped grieving, and I began to enjoy other memories I had of my mother. I don't think that she constructed that poem herself; she probably copied it from something she had seen. All I know is that she took the time to write it herself and kept it near.

I held on to that coat for several years until one day, my wife said she knew a woman who really needed a coat, and we gave it to that person. So Mom continued to bless someone that she never knew!

Chapter 42

"We decided that we would raise cattle."

Life goes on. And between my job in the Traffic Bureau and beginning to work on our ranch, idle time wasn't something that I was familiar with. Our two hundred acres were a little much to be considered as just a beautiful lawn, so we had to decide what we wanted to do with the land. Farming was out because I remembered all too well those 4:30 AM wake-up calls at the Van Dammes' farm!

Ralph and I had each decided that we would raise cattle. I found out that before we could raise anything, all of our exterior fences would need to be rebuilt. Building an exterior fence around two hundred acres is a lot of fencing…I mean **a LOT** *of fencing!* I was inclined to put up a 5-strand barbed wire fence, but before I could put up a new fence, I would have to take down the old, barbed wire one! The problem with taking down the old, barbed wire was that the old fence lines were overgrown and entangled with brush, trees, and cactus… lots of cactus.

Since Jeanette and I were both the sole employer and employee of this operation, I could pretty well name my own hours. When I worked the day shift, I would get home around 3:30 or 4:00, change clothes and really go to work on the ranch. Then, when working the evening shift, I would be up early and work on the ranch until it was time to get ready to go into town. This was a team effort, and my wife would help me as she was able. She has always had an eye for straight lines, and she would line me up as I drove those darn steel posts into the ground.

It took months to complete the job, but when I finished that fence, the neighbors would drive by just to see the improvements! I had undergone some personal improvements myself during this time due to all the hard, physical work. It had allowed me to regain a better physical shape, and I was now almost as fit as I was when I completed at the Police Academy training in Wilmington.

Our place had an old, decrepit set of cattle pens standing in the northeast corner, and we reluctantly had to use them for several years to work the cattle. The phrase "working the cattle" describes penning the cattle, running them through a squeeze chute to see if they were pregnant, or administering medication to control the parasites. An exit chute allowed us to run them into a trailer for shipment to the vet or to the Sale Barn. Jeanette and I worked our cattle by ourselves most of the time, but there were times Ralph would help us (and we would return the favor when it was time to work his cattle.) Jeanette and I were both forced to run and jump up on that old fence numerous times (to get away from an ornery cow or bull.) I knew it was time to make some improvements there because it was only a matter of time before one of us would be hurt in those old pens.

When I replaced those pens with a new set, I built it out of the welded pipe. You would have thought I had given my wife, a Mercedes Benz! If you have never raised large animals, there is no way you can appreciate how important it is to have safe handling facilities when attending to them.

Even though Jeanette's father, who had died before I came to know her, raised cattle and farmed peanuts, she would be the first to tell you that she knew nothing about actually raising animals. And I knew even less than she did! We were successful for one reason: an old Yancey rancher named George Wilson befriended my brother and me.

George raised cross-bred cattle on his ranch near Yancey, and he was well known in many ranching communities in South Texas. The little town of Yancey was basically a small hub where the country people could come in to get their mail, shop at the country store, get a cup of coffee, and exchange gossip. Since my brother and I had bought land from people who had lived there for years, we were looked upon as strangers who would have to be given time to see if we could fit in. I guess we were the subject of a lot of the gossip, but when we bought our first cows from George we took a big step in declaring that we were going to be part of the community.

That country store had a large table at the rear and a big coffee pot. Every morning several of the ranchers would begin their day around that table. If I chanced to go into the store around that time of the day, I would get the questioning looks and not much else. It took time, but eventually Ralph and I and our families were accepted. And the ranchers loved hearing My Old Man tell his jokes and tales about Belgium. He was still always smiling, and he maintained his accent; after all these years in America, but he could speak perfect English.

When Jeanette and I first moved to Yancey we continued to attend Medical Center Baptist Church on Wurzbach Street in San Antonio. We drove into San Antonio every Sunday for three years. I was already driving in every day during the week, too, so it was getting too much after a while. One Sunday, we decided to visit the First Baptist Church in Yancey, and we were made to feel so welcome that we decided that we needed to join that congregation, which we did. This tightened our bond to the community even more, and it remained our church home for the remaining 22 years that Jeanette and I lived there.

Suzanne was still living with us when we first settled into our "Barn," and she got a job working for an attorney in San Antonio. She traded in the car we had bought for her for a Miata, a little red sports car convertible. One morning she was driving away from the house to go to work, and she was still on the dirt road before she reached the highway, when a huge wild hog stepped out from the brush in front her car and stopped! I knew we had wild hogs around, but she described this one as being "bigger than her car!" Well, her car wasn't very big, but it still must have been a big hog. Big or not, it made an impression on Suzanne, and it wasn't long before she told us that she wanted to move into town.

I loved having her with us, but I worried because she had to spend so much time on the road driving back and forth to her job. Besides working, she was putting herself through college, so she had a full plate herself. I am proud of all three of my kids because they have never avoided their responsibilities and have always worked hard and taken care of themselves, and later, their families.

My German Shepherd dogs had died from old age while I still lived in San Antonio. In the early 1980s my brother and I had met a contractor in town through a mutual friend who was an avid quail hunter. But his passion was hunting with dogs, but not just any dogs. He loved German Shorthairs!

For the uninformed, quail hunters are clannish about the method used to hunt these birds and that includes the breed of sporting dog considered the best! Since neither Ralph nor I had ever hunted quail with dogs, we had to take the word of our friend, and Ralph was the first to get a male German Shorthair dog. He turned out to be a very good dog, and after hunting with him a few times I was hooked.

One day I was told that someone had a female Shorthair that they could no longer keep, and they wanted to give her to someone that would care for her. She didn't have hunting experience, but she was a beautiful dog and an excellent example of the breed. It wasn't long before we let my brother's male breed with my female, and we were in the dog business!

I raised two litters, and out of the second litter, I got my once-in-a-lifetime quail hunting dog! I called him Bruno. After my male German Shepherd dog, Bruno was the best dog I ever had. With help from my brother, I started training Bruno. I found out quickly that his natural inbred hunting instincts were so strong; all I needed to do was introduce him to what we were going to be hunting which were quail!

You have to understand that a hunting dog will hunt just about anything; it doesn't matter to the dog what kind of animal or bird it is. This became painfully clear one day when I had Bruno out in a pasture letting him hunt. He was still young, so we worked on basics when he put his nose to the ground and took off.

Moments later, he was behind a dead tree that had fallen over and was rooting around, obviously very excited. I started walking over to where he was when he yanked his head up above the trunk of the tree, and he had a skunk in his jaws! *Oh, crap!!* He was *so proud* of himself, and just like I had been teaching him to do, he was bringing his prize over to give it to me! The skunk was still squirming, so

266

Bruno bit down harder, which killed the skunk, but then the skunk got his revenge because he did what the skunks do!

I was yelling for Bruno to stop, but he wanted me to have a close look at the critter. I couldn't run because that would have turned the whole thing into a game, so I stood there, cringing. As he got closer to me, I guess the smell was even getting to him because he dropped the skunk. He started rolling on the ground, and Man, that smell was awful! To make matters worse, we had driven over in my Jeep. It wasn't a convertible, and even with all the windows down and the back hatch open, I was retching all the way to the house.

When I got home, I tied Bruno to a tree in the front yard and started washing him down with soap. Wrong! I thought about it for a second, and remembered that someone had said to use tomato juice, and that would kill the smell. I went into the house, got a can of that, and washed him down. After rinsing him off for probably 15 minutes, I gave up! I guess the smell wasn't as bad by then, but I think my sense of smell was toast! My family wasn't happy with me but Bruno showed no signs of remorse!

Bruno and I had several good hunting seasons, but more important than the hunting, he was my constant companion when I was home. When I had to put him down due to a bacterial infection, it was one of the saddest days of my life. Even though I later tried owning another dog, it just never worked out, and I have never owned another dog since Bruno.

Chapter 43

"It seemed that *our* cows were better looking than Willard's cows...."

Thankfully, the guy with the telescope was the only weird neighbor we had to deal with when we lived in Yancey. One of our best neighbors was a gentleman named David Bomba. He and his wife, Shirley, lived on about 500 acres that had the Hondo Creek running through part of their ranch. Like our friend, George Wilson, David had grown up in Yancey, and he was a good source of information for a city slicker like me.

Jeanette and I share a favorite memory of David and Shirley: It was a steamy, Sunday afternoon, and it had been raining for several days, giving us concern that one of our nearby creeks might be close to flooding. Although we were safe since our home was built on top of a hill, we had grown concerned for the Bombas. We were concerned, not only for their personal welfare, but also for their ability to safely evacuate and "get out in time." When we arrived at their home, they were sitting on their front porch ...drinking Sweet Tea, eating Homemade Vanilla Ice Cream! They insisted that we join them, which we did!

They didn't seem too concerned about watching the Hondo Creek come out of its banks and start creeping toward their pecan orchard which was about 50 yards away from their home! David assured us that the flooding would stop short of their house, and thankfully, he was right. It was an awesome sight to watch big trees floating across what was normally a pasture and grass fields! They had experienced this event numerous times while living there and were not concerned one bit. Sure enough; two days later you would never have known of all that water. Only some dead tree limbs were left in the fields.

In the 24 years that we lived there, we saw "the Hondo" flooding several times ourselves. Unfortunately, we were also living there when a man lost his life by ignoring the barricades: he drove his car into the flooding water while trying to cross the Hondo Bridge.

Another notable neighbor was a rancher named Willard Wilson. His wife Evelyn made some of the best homemade donuts in that part of the country! Willard was a character and considered himself to be the resident lawman. He was a small, skinny cowboy who would tell you all you needed to know about how cowboying was done 50, 60 years ago. He and George Wilson were cousins, and it didn't take long to find out that there were numerous Wilsons in that area, and they were all related. Willard was quite a bit older than me, and he came down with cancer and died not long after we moved out there.

He and Evelyn had three grown sons, and Willard owned around 1500 acres. After he died, the land was divided between their boys, but Evelyn kept her cows which were a source of income for her, and she continued to live on the ranch. The sons would handle the cattle for their mother, but they didn't live there full-time anymore, and this became a problem for all of us.

Part of the Wilson's land joined ours at the back of our place. We had purchased cows and had our black Angus bull with our cows. The Wilsons would rotate their red Santa Gertrudis bull with their different cows in different pastures within their ranch, so at times, their bull and our bull would be across the fence from each other. Remember that old saying about "grass being greener on the other side of the fence?" Well, it seemed that our cows were better looking than Willard's cows, so his bull would often jump the fence into our place, wanting to socialize! Our bull didn't feel the need to share, so the fight would be on.

Willard's bull was bigger and size matters when it comes to bulls (in more ways than one,) so my bull was limping when I got home one afternoon. It was easy to find the culprit (and the winner of the fights) because several feet of my fence were on the ground, the big red bull was on my property, and he had gathered up my cows and was introducing himself!

I took the whole bunch of them down to my cattle pens, and separated Willard's bull into the "Chute Pen." I called Evelyn and told her what had happened, and she immediately called one of her sons who came over, backed their trailer up to the shoot, and loaded up their bull to take him back home. My bull was eventually healed of his crippled leg, and bumps and bruises. I repaired my fence and chalked the whole thing up to ranching stories. Three weeks later, the same thing happened: fence down, red bull in my pasture, and every animal bawling, but my bull was smart enough this time to remember the last butt kicking, so he wasn't hurt.

I penned the bull again, called Evelyn, and she called one of her sons who came, and took the bull back home. This time, I was assured that they would move the bull to a different pasture. It was probably about a month later when…yep, the SOB (Sorry Old Bull) was back! This time, my bull had tried to take him on again, but he had lost the fight again and was all crippled up again! I was pissed off!

I knew it wasn't Evelyn's fault, so I calmed myself down before I called her. When she answered the phone and heard it was me, she immediately became guarded. I just started the conversation right out, and I told her I had a business proposition for her. She said, "Oh?" and I told her I wanted to buy her bull! She said nothing for a minute, and then she asked me what was wrong. I told her that of course, her bull was back, my fence was down, and my bull was hurt. Now, I wanted to buy her bull, but she asked me why I wanted to do that.

Still remaining calm, and not raising my voice, I told her that since the bull was already on my place, if she would sell him to me, I was going to get my hunting rifle and kill him! She started to say something, but I kept going. I then told her that after I shot him, I was going to get me something cold to drink, take my lawn chair out to where I could see his carcass, and watch the buzzards and coyotes eat him! I finished by telling her that *one way* or the *other* that bull was *never* going to enter my property again, and if he *did,* he was not leaving!

(Silence from the other end of the line!) Finally, she pleaded with me not to kill him, but that she would send her son over immediately. I told her I knew that it wasn't her fault, but I had reached the limits of my patience.

It wasn't long before two of her boys showed up with their trailer. By now everybody (including the bull) knew the routine. Once we got him loaded the boys came over and told me that I had really upset their mother. I didn't say anything, so another one asked me if I was really going to shoot the bull.

I told them that there wouldn't be another call from me regarding this bull. And then I added that this bull would *never* see my cattle pens again. I guess they believed me because I was told later that they had taken the bull to the sale barn, and he was no longer in my part of the country. Amazingly, our friendship remained.

Chapter 44

"…my cows took the place of Valium for me."

There were two other Sergeants that worked with me on our traffic shift. One, like me, had a group of officers that worked out of cars and patrolled the highways. The third one supervised a group of motorcycle officers. These guys handled the school zones as they could easily sit (hide) on the street looking for school zone violators. They also handled a lot of special assignments, but they were not used to work the highways, if at all possible, for safety reasons.

The motorcycle Sergeant was a guy named David Head, and he and I became good friends. David was an extremely neat person, not only in his personal appearance, but his working space. The term compulsive (or anal) comes to mind. We all had our desks and filing cabinets and the desks were backed up against a wall, and we had shelves over the desks on the wall. We kept various items on the shelves, but David had one shelf where he kept his Knick- knacks. Little motorcycles, figurines, and other whatnots… they were all lined up just so!

I would watch him as he would come in at the beginning of our shift, and he would invariably take time to check out his shelf. Once in a while, he would adjust something if it didn't seem quite right. I couldn't let this go, so just to see how sharp he really was, I waited until he left for the day, and I went over and moved one of the figures *just a teeny bit*! The next day we all came in, and Dave was at his desk and got around to checking the shelf, and…I am a son-of-a-gun! He adjusted the figure that I had moved! I knew right then that this had potential.

I waited a few days and messed with the shelf again, and sure enough, Dave spotted it. This was too good! Over the next few weeks I would mess with it until Dave finally figured out that someone was deliberately moving his stuff around! Well, my feelings were seriously hurt that he immediately accused me of being the person responsible. I tried as hard as I could to keep the smirk from my face, but I couldn't do it, I was busted!

The other Sergeant was John Hickman, and his desire was to take over the motorcycle job if David left. He was a veteran like me, and had flown helicopters in Vietnam. We all worked for a Lieutenant named Steve Baum, and I couldn't have asked for a better group to work with. I was also blessed with having good patrolmen, for the most part, to supervise. As always there were one or two that made you earn your money, but thankfully they were in the minority.

Even though my traffic assignment wasn't nearly as stressful as Narcotics, ROPE, and even times on patrol, there were still those days when I would get home from working the day shift and need to unwind.

I had bought a "Ranger" ATV to use on our place, and it soon became indispensable in doing numerous tasks around the place, including feeding, moving, and herding the cattle from pasture to pasture. It was a little noisy, but the cattle had become quite used to it, and they would run toward us when they heard its noise, always thinking they were going get some cattle cubes. Many days, after arriving back home from working the day shift, I would change out of my uniform and into my civilian clothes, I would grab something to drink, grab the Little Mrs., and drive the ATV out to the fields where our cows were grazing and just park! They were quite gentle and used to me, so they would just keep doing what they were doing. The only noises to be heard were them chewing or moving around as they grazed. I have told numerous people that my cows took the place of Valium for me! It was a good life.

You might recall my mentioning that every year San Antonio holds a celebration known as Fiesta. It is always held in April and lasts for about three weeks. The highlights of the celebration are two very large parades. One takes place during the day, known as The Battle of Flowers, and the other one is a night parade, known as the Fiesta Flambeau. Crowd estimates place the number of people attending each parade at well over *100,000* people! Besides the parades, there is a carnival with all types of rides, and there are numerous other events spread over the three weeks that are held at various other locations throughout the city.

Fiesta is a prime time for officers to make a lot of money working overtime assignments. For the Traffic Bureau, this is also a time to cash in, but it's also one of the busiest times of the year. For most of the big events, we were required to provide traffic control so that vehicles and pedestrians could still move through the area. This meant that on the busiest days, everyone was required to work, even if it was your day off.

The parades are one of the most anticipated events of Fiesta! Even Police Officers assigned to the parade route will get caught up with marching bands and beautiful floats. It's a family time, and people are allowed to start picking a spot along the parade route a day or two in advance. The seasoned parade watchers all have their favorite spots, and they use them year after year. During the 34 years that I was a Police Officer, the parades have only been cancelled once.

In 1979, at about 1:00 PM, the Battle of Flowers parade was underway when Ira Attebury began shooting at the parade watchers. He had parked a motor home at Grayson & Broadway along the parade route, and he was shooting from out of those windows inside the RV. Six Police Officers were wounded, two civilians were killed, and 51 people were injured. A SWAT team eventually made entry to the motor home, and Attebury was killed. (You can Google "Fiesta Parade Sniper 1979" for the entire story.)

My assignments for parades in previous years had mostly been walking a block of the parade route to make sure the street remained clear, with no one getting in the way of the bands and floats. For this parade I was assigned to a car, riding with three other guys. It was our job to respond to disturbances along the parade route. When the call came out for the shooting, and moments later the dispatcher announcing that officers and civilians were shot, we, along with just about everyone else, hurried that way.

274

We were not far from the location, but it was impossible to get close because the crowds were running away and had the street blocked. To add to the panic, the shooting was ongoing, and due to the tall buildings, businesses, and all the hard surfaces, it was hard to pinpoint the location exactly. We had to try to direct people to safety as we parked the car, and we proceeded on foot. "Communication is Key," and it's impossible to overstate the importance of the role that our dispatchers played that day. (That can also be said of them throughout my entire law enforcement career.)

The shooting lasted for approximately 30 minutes, and it ended when our SWAT team managed to launch tear gas canisters into the RV and confront the shooter. He died, and it's still unsure whether he killed *himself* or was shot by an officer. Further investigation revealed that this man was a WWII veteran, had been briefly committed to a mental hospital, and was high on *PCP* (a hallucinogenic street drug) at the time of the incident. Try as we might, in police work (and in this World, for that matter) things will happen that cannot be anticipated!

As with everything, the passage of time seems to help us accept past events in our lives, good or bad. The Fiesta Parade sniper incident faded, as did the pain of my divorce. Eventually, Joyce and I were respectfully able to attend social events that involved our kids, and the same was true for Jeanette and her family. Since Suzanne was now living in San Antonio, her bedroom was now available, so Jeanette's sons would occasionally come over and stay the night.

The apartment side of our "Barn" was around 650 square feet. This wasn't a lot of room, and Jeanette and I were ready to enlarge our space. Since expanding the Barndominium wasn't an option, we started to work on plans for a home. House construction started the latter part of 1993, and our house was finished in August of 1994. We had it built right across the driveway from the barn so that the barn/apartment could be used for guests that could stay over, have some privacy, and yet join us in the main house for meals and visiting. That was the plan, but it was almost not realized because of an offer Jeanette wanted to extend to my father.

When my father made the decision to sell his house after my mother died, Jeanette had approached me and suggested that he could move into our Barndo- minium. It had been many years since I had lived in close proximity to my father.

I realize that time has a way of reconciling things that occur in our past, but I was now having some flashbacks about my past interactions with my father. I had stopped calling him "My Old Man" a long time ago. Once in a while though, he and I would get into a disagreement, and it still seemed to escalate into a heated argument before I could stop myself. I guess it's common for fathers to always think of their sons as maybe grown up…but *not quite*!

After giving it some more thought, I talked to my father about the offer. He was excited and came out to talk to Jeanette and me as he wanted to talk to her personally to see if she was really on board with the offer. We were sitting at the kitchen table in the apartment, and things were going well. He pulled out his pack of cigarettes and was going to light one up when Jeanette stopped him, and told him we didn't allow smoking in the house. Things stopped going well!

A few days later he called me, and told me that it would probably be better if he found a place of his own to live in *Hondo*, and that is what he did. It turned out to be the best decision for all concerned. He found a small house in town for rent, and the family next door became close friends to him, and they looked after him when he started getting sick. They would call us when they noticed something wrong and keep us informed when needed.

In December of 1995 my father started having trouble breathing, so we took him to the Hondo hospital to have him checked out. They ran tests, and we were told that his emphysema was very serious, and there was nothing that could be done to cure him. They put him on oxygen and sent him home.

His neighbors would check on him almost every day and my brother and I and our wives would also go by as often as our jobs permitted. We had notified my sister, and she came down from Arkansas and was spending time with him, too. When they put him on oxygen full time, he seemed to improve, so we felt that the immediate crisis was over. Jeanine went back home to Arkansas, and we resumed more of our normal routine. Toward the end of December, he started to get worse, and it was back to the doctor. After the doctor checked him out, we were told that he was in a state of decline, and it was speeding up.

In 1995 the hospital in Hondo was still locally owned (they were later bought by one of the big hospital groups out of San Antonio,) and they were run from the hometown perspective. If he had still been living in San Antonio, my father would have been placed in Hospice, but Hondo assigned him a bed in the hospital. They explained to us that he could stay there as long as they didn't need the bed. My wife had been talking to him about his relationship with God, and he was kind enough to listen to her.

Around the first week of January of 1996, the hospital called us and told us that we should come over as my father had taken a turn for the worse. His organs were beginning to shut down, and it was just a matter of time. Ralph and I and our wives made it to the hospital and went into his room. He was fighting for every breath, but his heart was beating strong. We stayed for several hours, and nothing changed.

The nurses told us to go home as it seemed that he was stable. They told us that they would call if something changed. The following morning we went back to the hospital, and when we reached the nurses station, they told us to go on into his room. When we walked in, I couldn't believe my eyes. He was sitting up in bed with a food tray, and he was mad! Someone asked him what was wrong, and he told us that he wasn't supposed to be there any longer. He had been ready to die and should be gone by now!

How do you respond to that? For the next few days he did well and during that time my wife had an opportunity to talk to him about Jesus, and he accepted Him as his Lord and Savior! God kept him alive so that he could be saved!

A few days after that, he began to worsen, and he didn't respond to us or the staff. My sister had driven down again from Arkansas, and she, my brother, and Jeanette and I were all sitting around his bed when on January 12, 1996, he stopped breathing. Maybe since my mother's death was so unexpected, it hit me very hard, but when my father passed, I was able to handle it much better.

He was never good with money as he felt that the money he made was there to spend. A credit card was just a little more money to spend. When he died, his estate consisted of just a couple of hundred dollars in a checking account. Several months prior, I had contacted Master Card because they had raised his credit limit, but I wanted them to return it to the lowest amount. Even though I was paying the bills, I didn't have legal authority, so they refused. Not long after his death, they sent their monthly bill out to us, and it showed that he was carrying a balance of around three thousand dollars. He had been putting his medications and essential daily needs on the card.

We ignored it until we received a late notice, and then another late notice, and finally, the dreaded collection notice. I finally talked to someone who called from the collection agency, and I had to keep from laughing out loud. They were talking to me in their threatening manner that seems to be their trademark and the agent finally told me that they needed to talk to him. I told the guy that this was going to be a problem, and he wanted to know why. When I told him of his passing, the guy replied that "Someone was going to have to pay it!" Yeah, right!

My Old Man got the last laugh as there was nothing in the bank to pay it with, and I admit that it made feel good because they wouldn't have suffered the loss if they had done what I asked a few months back. The only thing he had of value was a car, and a few months prior he had given it to his neighbors for their genuine help and kindness shown toward him.

Chapter 45

"...she asked me if I wanted to partner up..."

During the time when my father was moving to Hondo, I had decided that I wanted to get my bachelor's degree. There were several reasons why, one of them being that the Department had begun paying a monthly bonus for those having an Associates, Bachelors, or Masters. Also, I would be the first in our family to have a college degree!

Once again, the Lord was already putting things in place that would help me to accomplish that goal. Steve Baum, my lieutenant in traffic, was going to school for his bachelor's degree, and he had encouraged me to start with mine. It was tough coordinating my hours, but I got started. While this was going on, the Captain's exam was announced; Lt. Baum took the test, and he did extremely well. He was promoted, and he was assigned to the Chief's Office as the new Executive Officer.

Not long after he moved up, he called me one day and told me that there was going to be an opening for a Sergeant that would be working for him, and he wanted me to take it. It was going to be in plain clothes, strictly eight to five with Saturday and Sundays off. I wasn't just flattered, but it would turn out to be a perfect fit for my going to school, so naturally I took it. I was located in the Chief's Office, but was actually the Assistant to the Executive Officer (Lt. Baum.)

I knew most of the people there personally, including the Chief, so I enjoyed going to work. This job was about as far removed from real policing that I ever held, but it rounded out my police career. I had the opportunity to see what was involved in establishing a working relationship between the Department and the citizens that we were sworn to serve.

Wayland Baptist University was the college I chose to obtain The Degree. Its campus was on the northside of San Antonio, and I was going on Tuesdays and Thursdays from 6 to 10 PM. Its hours were set up for working people, so the student population had a good mix of older and younger people as opposed to the more traditional colleges/universities. Wayland was also a logical choice because they accepted my prior college courses I had taken under the GI Bill when I first joined the Police Department.

That mix of younger and older (at age 52, I was the old guy in the class) came into play for me in a rather humbling, embarrassing way one evening during an elective health class. At the end of the previous session, the instructor had told us to bring gym clothes that would allow us to get on an exercise mat on the floor. In the class, there was a woman in her early thirties who was absolutely drop dead gorgeous! She sat a couple of desks over from me, and every other male (except me) who had hit puberty, had tried to get close, but she stayed to herself.

I am not saying that I didn't take a second look, but my life now had changed, and with God's strength, I was determined to not repeat the mistakes of my past! Anyway, it came time to pick a partner and move to the mats, and she came over to me and asked if I wanted to partner up! I said, "Sure," and I admit that I was probably grinning when I saw some of the "younger" studs glaring.

We were going to practice stretches. So, one of us would get on the mat, and their partner would then help to extend or stabilize the other while the stretching was done. When she finished, I got down to take my turn for the stretch and everything was going fine until the third stretch. This involved bringing my legs up one at a time while lying on my back and bringing the leg back to me as far as I could. This is where the partner could gently exert some pressure. I was close to maxing out the stretch when I felt a slight pressure form in my stomach, and…I farted!!! Oh My God!

Here I was, 52 years old, and I turned red probably from my ears to my toes. Even though there was heavy breathing as people strained, everyone recognized that sound! My beautiful partner then let go of my ankle and looked at me, and I guess I had a look on my face that indicated that I could not *believe what had happened* and, combined with my shade of red, she lost it, and fell down, and started laughing!

Well the Hell; what could I do? I started laughing, and in no time, most everybody else was, too! How sad life must be for people who never find a reason to smile or laugh out loud until they cry? I don't remember my classmate's name, but she is a joyful part of my story.

I was able to get my Associates' in 1997, and my Bachelors' in 1998. As if I didn't have enough going on during this two-year period, they announced a Lieutenants exam. I was successful and promoted on 3/27/97.

Chapter 46

"Was this guy going to show up with a Mohawk? A ring in his nose?..."

Suzanne began dating a guy, and their relationship became serious enough that she wanted Jeanette and I to meet him. We set a day for the following week for them to come out to our new home in Yancey. Cathy and John had both already met the fella, and he struck them as a nice guy.

A few days prior to Suzanne coming out, I got a call from Cathy. After the normal greetings, she told me that Suzanne was very nervous about her boyfriend meeting me. I told Cathy that I remembered being nervous before my first meeting with parents of girlfriends when I was in high school, but Suzanne would just have to deal with it. Cathy then went on to tell me that he was a little different from what I would expect him to be like. Hmm? When I started pressing her about details, all she would say was that I should keep an open m*ind*! If Cathy's intention had been to smooth the way for our first meeting with a serious boyfriend, she failed miserably! Was this guy going to show up with a Mohawk? A ring in his nose? Tattoos on his face? Then, I began to think that maybe Cathy was just messing with me, Good Grief!

On the day they arrived, I was dreading opening the door. When they came in, I hugged Suzanne, but I was checking out the guy. Nothing visible, he wasn't a bad looking guy, his name was Anthony McCray, and we got along great. As the evening ended, Suzanne had gotten over the jitters, and it was a fun evening.

I guess it was a couple of days later when Suzanne and I talked, and I told her about Cathy's call and that I wasn't sure what kind of guy she was going to show up with. She then admitted that she had been really nervous because she hadn't been sure how I was going to react to her bringing over a black man. I could tell that there was more she wanted to say, but she was hesitating. Finally, she told me that she really loved Anthony, and that they were making plans to marry. How did I feel about that?

I had always considered John and Cathy as my kids. I had even adopted them, and I had given them the Jacobs name. My brother and his wife could not have children, so they had adopted a boy and girl. My sister never had children, so Suzanne was the only grandchild that represented the Jacobs bloodline. I then told Suzanne that first and foremost I wanted her to be happy, and I wanted her future husband to treat her with respect. I also wanted him to have a job and pull his share of the family and household workload.

As to the fact that Anthony was part black: Suzanne told me that she had been worried about my reaction to Anthony because she remembered that often after I had come home from work, I had often denigrated Blacks. I reminded Suzanne that the Blacks that I was critical of were engaged in criminal activity. As long as Anthony was a law-abiding citizen, I assured her that he did not have anything to worry about me.

Suzanne and Anthony were married on 9/11/1999, and they made a beautiful couple. I don't remember when exactly, but as a young woman, Suzanne had been diagnosed with Endometriosis. The doctor had told her that she would probably not be able to conceive, so it was a pleasant surprise when she found that she was pregnant. Mason Jacob McCray was born in 2000, and he was a healthy 9 + lbs.

It had been a while since we had welcomed a new grandchild as both Cathy and John had their babies during the 1980s. This meant that Mason was spoiled by everyone, including his momma. Joyce also enjoyed being a grandmother ("Bama") and was a large part of their lives. I know that I am prejudiced, but all of my grandchildren are good looking little people! (At least they were; there are some I have not seen in a long time!)

Unfortunately the marriage between Suzanne and Anthony wasn't a long one. They divorced in 2002. It is always hard, but as I am well aware of, it's even harder when there are kids involved. Despite Suzanne's initial fears about how I would get along with

Anthony, he and I talked now and then, and I was very aware of how dear he held his wife and son. I hold no animosity toward him. He continued to stay very close to Mason and meet his financial responsibilities for his son.

A couple of years later, Suzanne introduced me to a young man named Joe Piotrowski. It took a while for him to convince her to marry him, but she finally agreed. After he and I got to know one another, he asked me one day where Suzanne had gotten her temper. I initially told him that it had to be her mother, but I finally had to own up! Everyone that knows Suzanne and knows me will observe immediately that she is my daughter if based on nothing but temperament!

I taught all three of my kids that they had to be self-sufficient. I wanted my daughters to be able to support themselves and not have to rely on someone else for their survival. I had seen too many women trapped in an abusive relationship because they had no means to provide for themselves. Cathy and Suzanne took that to heart. (I suspect that there are days that both of my sons-in-law wish I had not been quite so forceful in driving that point home.)

When Suzanne and Joe got together, we received another miracle when they had a son. Aiden Alexander Piotrowski was born on January 9, 2006. He also weighed 9 + pounds, and Suzanne was grateful that he came early since she didn't need him any bigger! Speaking of bigger, at the time of this writing (2023) Mason is 22 years old and is around 6ft, 7 inches tall; Aiden at age 17 is 5ft, 10 inches tall. They are different in a lot of other ways too!

Chapter 47

"...be careful what you ask for..."

Over the years the Department switched from working out of a downtown central station to working out of sub-stations in the North, South, East, and West areas of the city. Rotating shifts were replaced with permanent shifts so now "Dog Watch" was staffed with people who wanted to work those hours.

When I was promoted to Lieutenant in 1997, I was still working in the Chief's office, and that is where all the transfers are ultimately approved. I was asked where I would like to work as there were going to be several openings in the uniform patrol division. I requested my old patrol stomping grounds on the Southside of San Antonio, and I was granted my request. I was also granted the afternoon (3-11PM) shift.

Each sub-station was run by a Captain who oversaw three Lieutenants who each had four Sergeants. The Sergeants supervised a group of patrolmen/women. I knew the Captain I would be working for, and I felt that we would be able to get along well. I also knew one of the Sergeants from my days in Task Force. I got everything I had asked and prayed for, and I couldn't have been happier!

(Remember the old adage about being careful what you ask for?) It didn't take long for me to realize that one of my Sergeants was going to be a major problem that would have to be dealt with. The Lieutenant that had occu*pied* this slot had been promoted to Captain, creating the vacancy that I was set to fill. While they waited for the new lieutenant to arrive (me,) the "senior" Sergeant was allowed to run the shift. I am not sure how much time had passed before I arrived, but it was apparently long enough for this Sergeant to convince himself that they didn't need a new Lieutenant.

Isn't it amazing that sometimes the biggest screwups seem to convince themselves that they are smarter than anyone else? That was the case with this guy! He had been kicked out of a plain clothes unit because he was incompetent and lazy, and he appeared to be just showing up to put in his time.

When I reported to the shift, I had around 29 years on the Department, so I had heard his name mentioned, and it had always been in a negative context. Still, I knew he was part of the package, so I was determined to give him, like everyone else, a clean slate and a chance to prove himself as worthy for the job. My good intentions were rewarded with backstabbing which manifested itself with outright lies to the people on my shift, and to members of the community! This guy should have spent his miserable life living in the dust like the *snake* that he was. I am not going to devote time and paper to this person other than to say that I made his life miserable enough that he decided to retire! The Police Department became better the day he left!

A San Antonio Police Officer must have a minimum of twenty years on the force to retire. Retirement salary is based on a percentage of your salary when you retire, and there is a formula that is used to arrive at the correct number for every individual. With 29 years on, I had already been looking into when I could optimize my retirement, and it became clear that I should put in 34 years. This would have me leaving the Department sometime in 2003. I was OK with the idea that my final 5 years would be spent on patrol, after all that is where I started!

Once again, God had a different plan. I had been on patrol for not quite a year when a Lieutenant slot opened up in Traffic! Tom Polonis from my ROPE encounters, had made Captain, and he was in charge of the Traffic Bureau. My good friend David Head had also been made Captain. They knew each other, and when the talk came up about filling the Lieutenant's slot, David suggested that I would be a good man to fill it. Tom remembered our previous association of when he moved me out of ROPE, and he asked David if he thought that I would consider it since I would be working for him.

Well, Tom called and we talked, and it was a done deal! It was my last assignment, and I could not have planned it better myself.

Tom and I became good friends in ways I could never have anticipated. I have always liked woodworking, and it turned out that Tom liked it as well. I had that Barn in Yancey and had a few tools, but I wanted some serious woodworking stuff. Tom was also putting together a small shop, and we discovered that we were looking for some of the same tools. He had a brother who was also into that hobby, and he was much more advanced than either one of us, so he steered us to the better-quality products. Tom was good at shopping for price, and I was good at spending money, which I did…a lot!

Traffic still commanded a lot of overtime, and the Lieutenants received their share. A lot of that was mandatory, but no one had to twist my arm to do more. The overtime pay made it possible for Jeanette and I to complete projects on our ranch, outfit my shop, and live comfortably.

A notable source of overtime was devoted to the Protection details that we would participate in when VIPs came to visit San Antonio. I am not talking about an actor or some other self-proclaimed celebrity; I am talking about *the President or Vice-President* of our country! If you live in Washington, DC, you would be used to limos blocking streets. We here in San Antonio were not used to how a visit would impact large parts of our city. Traffic was tasked with the jobs of escorting the Limo with motorcycles, blocking cross streets, etc.

With that type of visit, there were several days if not weeks that would be devoted to planning and meeting with the VIP staff and the Secret Service. Since we had to adapt our work schedule to the VIP, overtime was inevitable.

These visits were never routine, so each one brought new challenges. Then when you factored in the memory of Dallas in 1963, there was always a certain amount of stress. There was a benefit that I want to mention, besides the overtime. I got to personally meet two Presidents and their wives when they came to San Antonio. The first was President Ronald Reagan and his wife Nancy, and the second was President George H. Bush and his wife Barbara.

287

The brief time that I was in the holding room with the Reagans, there was no doubt that Mrs. Reagan was herself a force to be reckoned with. I was part of a group of Security People who were with him as he waited to go on stage and deliver a speech. He came out of the dressing room with a suit on, and when she saw it, she told him, "No Ronnie, wear the other one!" The future president of our country turned around, went back in, and put on the other suit. She was right, and he looked great, and he was later elected! President Bush and his wife Barbara were some of the nicest people I met, and their Security Details were the first to tell you that, too.

Chapter 48

"...Jeanette had her third grandchild."

While I had been going to college, Jeanette's sons were doing the same. Doug was Jeanette's oldest son, and he had graduated from high school in 1993. He went to Hillsboro Jr. College for the first two years, and in 1995, he transferred to McNeese University on a rodeo scholarship in Lake Charles, Louisiana. He graduated from McNeese in 1998, and he got a job on a big ranch around Charlotte, riding horses and working cattle.

Ben was the younger brother, and when he graduated from high school, he, too, was given a rodeo scholarship to attend McNeese. He graduated with his degree and went to work in north Texas for the Painted Horse Association. When you see so many kids today who are totally lost and unprepared to participate in society, Jeanette and I know how blessed we are, because all of our kids are to this day all self-sufficient and responsible adults.

There is a big age difference between Doug and Ben and John and Cathy. But the age difference is not nearly as wide between the boys and Suzanne. Doug is only 2 years younger, and Ben, 5 years younger. This meant that John and Cathy started having kids 8 years or so *before* Doug and Ben did. This also meant that there wasn't a lot of interaction between them, and not just because of the age difference, but also their lifestyles. Doug and Ben are happy as country boys, and John and Cathy (*and Suzanne*) are primarily city kids.

Jeanette enjoyed being around my kids and grandkids, but there was no doubt that she was anxious to see her boys marry and produce children of their own. Both boys would bring over girlfriends from time to time. After they left, we would grade them as to suitability, and we had no problem deciding which one would be best for each boy. We found out that there would be no rushing the process, and it worked out as it should, without our help!

I officially retired from the police department in May of 2003. Jeanette continued to work for Child Protective Services out of Hondo until she retired 2 years later. Around the time I retired, Doug's girlfriend, Amy Rogers, whom he had met during his one and only semester at Sam Houston State University in Huntsville, TX were getting more serious about their relationship. We had met Amy, and we both liked her because she was one of those "What you see is what you get!" kind-of-people. Of course her good looks didn't hurt either, but most importantly she was good to Doug, and she was fun to be around! This time it seemed our approval was also in line with Doug's thoughts, and he proposed to Amy!

They were married on May 1, 2004, at the First Baptist Church in Charlotte, Texas. This was the church that Doug and Ben had grown up in, and after the ceremony, a reception and dance was held at the show barn in nearby Pleasanton, Texas. It was a wonderful time, and the event was even more special for Doug because both of his grandmothers were able to attend.

Like a lot of young people newly married, it takes some time to settle into what may become a career choice, working at something that you could see yourself doing for the long haul. Amy had her degree by then, too, and they knew someone that was involved in Catastrophe Insurance Claims and investigative work. When Hurricane Katrina hit the Gulf of Mexico, they quit what they were doing, and signed on to work claims. They were able to work as a team which gave them time together even though the circumstances of the tragedies of New Orleans were very difficult to be around.

This turned out to be a very lucrative job for them, and they spent several months responding to the aftermath of various storms and the subsequent Mold Remediation that followed. They also did Mold cases in Los Angeles and northern California. But Doug had never lost his passion for horses and Amy had also been raised around them and had competed in barrel racing events. Amy grew up 3 – 4 hours North of San Antonio in a small town called Forney. This was considered horse country, and they decided to see if they could find some acreage to buy.

Land was (and is) in big demand, but they found 75 acres for sale located south of the town of Stephenville, and they bought it. They began improving the property by building a horse barn with stalls and living quarters all under one roof. They owned a large travel trailer that they used when responding to storm locations, and they lived in that until the barn was completed. While living around Stephenville, Amy got pregnant, and Reese Lee Schrutka was born on March 23, 2007.

Jeanette had her first granddaughter and between Jeanette and Marty (Amy's mom,) Reese didn't want for attention! I guess it wasn't the right time for Doug to establish himself in the horse training business because they decided to sell part of their land that included the barn/house. It sold with no problem, and they kept a large part of the remaining acreage.

It must have been the right move because a position became available for a horse trainer on a brand-new horse facility just south of Hondo. Doug interviewed and was given the job as the primary horse trainer. Doug would be handling the 2 year old young horses to prepare them for further training as they matured. There were many benefits that came with the job including a house on the property, but as far as Jeanette was concerned, her first grandchild lived just 15 minutes from Yancey!

The three to four years that Doug worked at the ranch in Hondo allowed us to get close to him and his family. On March 31, 2011, Amy give birth to her second daughter at the hospital in Hondo. We were all in attendance when Rainy Lee Schrutka made her appearance, and Jeanette now had her third grandchild.

I said *third* grandchild because while Doug and Amy were establishing themselves, Ben had graduated from McNeese, and he eventually took a job with the Farm Bureau Insurance Company at their branch office in Uvalde, Texas. He met Misty Perkins, and their relationship blossomed and became long term when they married on April 4, 2009.

Misty's mother and grandmother lived nearby in Utopia, Texas. Oma was not in the best of health, so Ben and Misty decided to make Uvalde their permanent home. Misty got pregnant after a time, and she gave birth to what would be Jeanette's second granddaughter on April 15, 2010. They named her Sydney Lee Schrutka and even though Doug and Ben's father wanted a grandson, the girls were meant to be! When Rainy was born, she would be the last of the grandchildren for both Jeanette and me. Reese is now 15, Sydney is 12, and Rainy is 11 years old.

Chapter 49

"It became a lake…"

While I was working, I didn't dwell on nor long for the day that I would retire. The idea of retirement didn't set in until I had to go to the Pension Office a month in advance and give them the actual date I wanted to retire. Once you gave them your date, the paperwork was set in motion, and when you signed your name, there was no going back.

May 1, 2003, I officially became a full-time civilian and walked out of the downtown Police Station for the last time. Our ranch and cattle eagerly welcomed my full-time attention, and I must confess that I wasn't moping around wishing I could put on a uniform again and strap on a gun! Over the years while I was working, I would occasionally hear of a Police Officer who had retired and sat on his front porch, watched the cars go by, and died within just a year or two. More than one of them decided to use a pistol to speed up the process. One of those was my ex-partner from my days in Narcotics.

That was never going to be my problem. That's not to say that I didn't have problems, because three months after I retired, I was diagnosed with Prostate Cancer! Jeanette and I sat down with my Urologist, and he laid out our options. He was not just my doctor; he was also a good friend, and he ended his talk by telling us that he would perform any of the treatments he had outlined, except one. He said he would not continue to be my doctor if I chose to do nothing.

I had turned 59 years old two months before, and we decided that removing the prostate was the best option so that is what we did. Now 18 years later, with God's Grace, I am still kicking… just not as high as I once could! I was surprised with the cancer diagnoses because I knew of no one in my family that had experienced it. Talking with my doctor one day, I told him that, and he laughed and said that if a man lived long enough he would eventually get prostate cancer! Funny, but I don't remember that making me feel any better.

Jeanette liked to fish, and I had fished all of my life, so when she shared with me one day that it would be neat if we could have a fishing tank/pond, I was interested. Between us, we knew enough people with good ideas, and it wasn't long before we came up with a plan to build a tank. A year prior we had a water- well drilled on our place, and we had struck very deep, good water. We would use this water to keep the tank full.

As with a lot of things, the small tank grew to almost one and a half acres when it was finished, and it became a lake! There were many things that our ranch provided for our personal enjoyment but the fishing "lake" not only blessed us, but a lot of other people as well. We used just the right formula in stocking it with Large-mouth Bass and big Sun Perch. We would also add fish pellets, live minnows, and huge 3-4" bullfrog tadpoles from time to time to give the fish a little extra to eat. The fish would gobble up those tadpoles like a kid eats M & M's! On the occasions that we added the crystal clear well water into the tank, it spewed up from the 4" vertical pipe about 12 inches, and Man, it was cold! And it was also too clear. Several times we added pond dye to the water. This gave the fish dark blue "cover" so they wouldn't be spied by big birds and herons. And it was beautiful!

Some of our grandkids caught their first fish there, and we hosted church picnics, and allowed them to fish. There were countless kids who were introduced to fishing at our lake. But one of our fondest friends was our preacher from our little Yancey Baptist church, Lenard Dossey, and he loved to fish. He had some young kids, and they would come out with him, and he probably fished as often as anyone ever did.

I mentioned *kids* fishing but there were some *old timers* that also enjoyed our place. One of them was Jeanette's relatives, her mom's baby sister, "Aunt Mardelle." She was in her early eighties when her kids brought her out to visit, and it so happened that we had some other people there, so everyone had a line in the water. Suddenly, Mardelle announced that she had a big fish on the line, and sure enough, when she brought the fish in, it was a five-and-a-half-pound bass! That was the biggest fish we had caught since we stocked the lake!

Well we took pictures, and everyone congratulated Mardelle, and then I told her that we would be putting the fish back in the water. Mardelle looked at me, and said, "No way; I am eating my fish!" I told her that I wanted him to get bigger, and she told me that he was big enough for her. It's a good thing I was bigger and younger, and I already had the fish in my hand because she was ready to fight me for that fish! But he went back into the water. Mardelle later reminded me of that fish whenever we got together, and I would make the mistake of mentioning *fishing*!

There was always something to do on the ranch, and when I had nothing pressing, my brother would be doing something on his place next door, and I would help him. In the summer of 2006, I was helping him with some fence work, and it was hot! We were digging fence post holes and taking turns with the posthole digger. After digging literally hundreds of holes building my own fences, I was very familiar with the process.

But this day, I had to stop almost as soon as it was my turn to dig. I would rest for 5 minutes, and dig for 1 or 2 minutes and have to stop. I knew something was wrong, and I couldn't ignore the signs any longer. An appointment with my Cardiologist confirmed my worst fears, I had a blocked artery! After a battery of tests, it was determined that he would put in two stents.

The day of the procedure my wife drove me to the hospital, and they got started. Patients are awake while this is going on, and my doctor would give me updates as he worked. In no time, the first stent was in place, and they began on number 2. Five minutes into the next one though, I could tell from the conversations between my doctor and those assisting that things were not going well. Fifteen minutes…twenty minutes…twenty-five minutes and my doctor was sweating. Not good!

Finally he announced that they were coming out, and he turned to me and said, "Norbert, I am so sorry, but I couldn't get the second one placed." I could tell he was exhausted, and I told him that it was no big deal, he had given it his best. Then he said, "You don't understand, we are going to have to contact a Heart Surgeon and operate." I said that I guess we could set up something in the next couple of weeks, and he dropped the bomb. "Norbert," he said, "You're not leaving this hospital because I don't know if you would make it home with that blockage." Well, don't sugarcoat it on my account, Doc!

Two days later, I was prepped (which means I looked like a plucked chicken as they shaved me from my neck down to the tops of my toes) and ready to follow my mother and father into the experience of Heart By-Pass Surgery! A lot of my family was there, and we had a chance to pray before I was wheeled away. I joked with the people who were situating me on the operating table, and the next time I woke up, I was in the ICU surrounded by tubes, noise making machines, and busy nurses.

I was informed that they had by-passed *not one,* but four major arteries! I got my monies worth, though, and the surgery was a total success. I mention tubes, and these included one slender one coming from the top of my shoulder into my chest, and two bigger ones on each side of my chest. These were an aggravation, but I was told that they would be removed before I left the ICU and sent to a private room.

One morning the nurse came in and had me get up and sit in a chair, and she told me that the tubes were coming out. Praise the Lord! I asked her if that would be painful, and she told me that they were going to give me a shot before they took them out.

A little later my surgeon came in, pulled up a chair in front of me, and began looking over my incision. We talked about how good everything looked. I was agreeing when he asked me if I was ready to get those tubes out. I said, "Heck, yeah," and while he started to take the tape off that was holding the top one in place, I mentioned that I had not yet received the promised shot. He said something along the lines that I would hardly notice it. Next thing I know, he is pulling out about 8-10 inches of tubing! That wasn't too bad.

Then he started removing the tape from the two in the front of my chest. As I said, these were much larger, and I could see that they were much easier to handle as he fiddled around. He got the tape off the both of them, had me take a deep breath, and he yanked out the first one! Holy shit! That hurt! And as I started to groan, he pulled out the second one, and I yelled, "You Son-of-a-bitch!" He started grinning, and told me that he got that a lot, but that I was going to start feeling much bet*ter*. It took a while, but he was right, the Sneaky So & So!

My recovery was complete, and I made up my mind that I was not going to change my active lifestyle. I know I drove my wife and Cardiologist *crazy* when I started doing all the things that I had done before the surgery, but I wasn't going to live like an invalid. Jeanette snitched me off when I had my follow-up appointments, but everyone soon realized and resigned to the fact that this was the way it was going to be, and they gave up hounding me to slow down.

Chapter 50

"Why did you do a stupid thing like that?"

I mentioned Jeanette's Aunt Mardelle in the previous chapter with the fish story. Jeanette's mother's youngest sister might have weighed 120 pounds whereas Jeanette's mother was a larger woman. Mrs. Cox and Mardy Odom became two of my favorite people. They were both serious card players and I liked playing cards with them even though you had to watch them closely. Not saying they would cheat, but....

I could not have asked for a better mother-in-law and knowing her provided in-sight into Jeanette's character that I would otherwise not have been aware of. It was well known and documented that Mrs. Cox (that was what I always called her) was a practical joker that knew no bounds. This explained the misery that I endured on every April first (better known as April Fool Day.) I don't know how I could manage to forget every previous year's prank, but every year I was sure to get wet from the handle of the kitchen sink sprayer being held open with a rubber band. I would annually find myself sliding off the toilet seat due to a liberal application of Vaseline. On my truck's radio… all the stations would be switched to Spanish ones. I would find dried pinto beans in my service hat when I got to work. And any number of other things.

In 2015 though, Jeanette outdid herself, and I readily admit that she was deserving of an award. It was April first and as usual, I was clueless. I got up that morning to go to the bathroom, and with a small sense of urgency, plopped down on the toilet. As I began to settle, something was signaling in my mind that *all was not right*. I tensed as I tried to replay what I thought my mind had registered, and I jumped up from the toilet. I looked in the toilet, and a very large, blackish creature was in the water with pinchers raised! I had no idea what I was looking at!

(Remember My Old Man and the Tarantula spider?) Well, this now required backup…*immediately*, so I called for Jeanette. As she

298

came in, she asked what was going on, and I pointed to the toilet. She walked over and said, "So what's wrong?" I asked her if she was **crazy**, and I looked into the bowl, and there was ***nothing***! I described what I had seen, then realized that the thing might have crawled out, and I started backing up.

This was a small bathroom space, but I looked around, and I couldn't see it anywhere on the floor. When I looked in the bowl again, it had come out of the discharge hole at the bottom of the bowl. This time Jeanette saw it, and (so innocently) asked me what it was. Feeling that it probably couldn't get out, I studied it and finally determined *it was a **crawfish***! And a pretty darn big one, too! Now I am wondering how in the heck it came up through our plumbing.

Each time I stooped down, it would raise its pinchers and back further into the flushing hole. She advised me to just flush it down the toilet, but I didn't want to do that because I wasn't sure if that would get rid of it. She asked me what the big deal was, and I told her that *"my stuff"* was dangling down there, and if that thing grabbed me with one of those pinchers, it would all be over, for sure!

I finally managed to catch the thing with a small strainer and got it out. I was puzzled to no end, trying to figure out how that thing had travelled all the way to our commode. She was still trying to convince me that it must have come up from our public sewer system!

A few ***years later*** I was telling a friend of ours about our unwelcome visitor when I happened to look at Jeanette, and I saw that smirk! I knew that I had been had once again. She confessed that on the day prior to April Fool Day that year, she had gone to our local HEB grocery store, and that they had just received a new shipment of live crawfish, so she bought one, stashed him in a zip-lock bag, and hid him away until the perfect time came the next day to introduce him to her husband!

Her mother would have been proud. Unfortunately, Mrs. Cox passed in 2010. When it came time for the service, it was a celebration of a life well lived! There were some tears, but mostly it was people remembering someone who brought smiles to a lot of people she met along the way.

I have mentioned that one of the main reasons I loved living on our small ranch was the lack of close neighbors. This changed when in 2009 a family from San Antonio bought some acreage across the road from us. The place had been the original home-place of David Bomba's parents many years ago. And although there had been attempts to remodel the old house (which sat across from our front gate,) family members could not agree on how to settle the estate, so they put it up for sale.

I had seen cars and people walking around there but didn't realize that it had sold until the new neighbors began moving in. One day I was in my "ranch buggy" (ATV) pulling out of my front gate when I saw several people in the neighbor's front yard; I drove in and introduced myself. I met Rob and Ann Karns and their junior high school aged son, William ("Will.") Rob was active military, and he was part of the Air Force Band of the West at Lackland Air Force Base in San Antonio. Ann had been in the military when they first met, but now she was a stay-at-home mom who was homeschooling Will.

Even though I was curious as to what kind of neighbors they would be, I was immediately impressed with their excitement about being out "in the country." As they settled in, they impressed me even further because they were not shy about asking for advice! I remembered how much George Wilson and David Bomba had helped us when we first moved out "to the country," and I was happy to help all I could.

One of the Karns' first purchases (that I was aware of) was Guinea Hens. They are a funny-looking bird about the size of a chicken with *a* long neck, and they are known as a *farmers watchdog*. When Guineas are surprised, they can make some ungodly racket! They prefer to walk fast but can fly if they feel the need to do so. They also constantly make clacking noises as they forage for food in the ground.

It was their constant noise that made me aware of their presence one morning around daylight. I had been asleep when a strange, loud noise woke me up. Our bedroom window was off the front porch, and these noises came from the porch. I got up and peeked out the window, and there were about 20 Guineas on our porch and in the front yard. I put on some clothes and sneaked around to the front of the house, but when the birds saw me, all hell broke loose!

You have never heard such a racket as they squawked, cried, flew, and ran down our driveway toward the front gate and back to their house! We had a long driveway primarily gravel with grass on either side, and the Guineas had made their way up towards our house eating bugs! The next day, Jeanette heard the squawking coming up our drive again, and she ran them off by hollering and chasing them off with a wild mop, waving them high up in the air! Interestingly, there is always one Guinea in the back of the bunch who continues to yell-out as a lookout! They didn't come back the next day.

I got used to them visiting now and then, but apparently, predators are fond of Guinea meat, so their numbers started dwindling before long. I think the Karns started with about 20 birds, and in no time they were down to about 4 that managed to avoid being the guests of honor at supper. When I say predators, we had a variety that ran from owls to raccoons, to foxes and bobcats… even the occasional *mountain lion*. I saw a mountain lion on our place at three different times over the 25 years that we lived there.

Since Rob was still on active duty, he would be required to go to the base in San Antonio every day during the week, and he would occasionally have to fly with the band to perform at various functions out of town. The Karns became close friends of ours, so when Rob was gone, Jeanette and I would be available to help Ann and Will if the need arose. I found out that Rob wasn't the only musician in the family. Ann also played the clarinet, and Will played a big Double Base and some kind of tuba.

It turned out that Will was exceptionally good on the Double Base, and he began to focus his studies and practices on that instrument. Will was really good because he was practicing 8 hours a day! This was in addition to doing his home schoolwork! He became good enough that after his graduation from high school, he was accepted in the Music Department of Baylor University in Waco, Texas! He continued to strive for a scholarship to the prestigious Curtiss School of Music in Philadelphia. He was able to get that scholarship, went to school there for the next 2 years, and graduated from there with his degree in Music. We all felt that a major Orchestra would pick him up, but Covid arrived and put those dreams on hold.

While Will was still home, his mother wasn't shy about volunteering to help me as I worked on various projects around the ranch. She expressed to me her only concern: that his hands could not suffer any catastrophic injury! One day he was helping me as I was digging post holes, and we were using a long steel bar to loosen up the dirt. My bar was heavy, had one beveled end and a round sharp point on the other end. He was taking a turn using it, and as he brought the bar up and then brought it down, he stuck the sharp end into the top of his boot!

We both looked at his foot, and I was dreading taking off his boot. He convinced me to leave the boot on and it seemed OK, so we kept going. We finished for the day, and I took him home, and he was limping as we walked in. His mother noticed and asked him what was wrong. He told her what he had done, to which she replied, "Why did you do a stupid thing like that?" I had a Mom flashback of my own! I was trying to apologize, but Ann told me that his toe was a long way from his hands, so it was no big deal. She told us both that he would be ready to go the next morning. What could I say? He was ready to go the next morning!

I could not have asked for better neighbors. They turned out to be very hardworking people, and not too long after they moved in, Rob retired from the Air Force. They made the decision to make their farm self-sustaining, and they never stopped improving and innovating. Today, they have a beautiful *Lavender Farm* where they host tours, sell garden plants, and operate a new Tea Room during the season. They have *chickens,* a *donkey*, and *goats*, and I recently learned that they have added *Alpacas* to the mix. Will is 23 now. He made a personal decision *not to take* the Covid-19 vaccine shots last year, and it has cost him several offers to become employed by large, major orchestras in America. I give him credit for standing by his beliefs, and I know that for now, he is right where God wants him to be.

Chapter 51

"Just like that, the Jacobs brothers had vacated Yancey."

My brother's kids were out of high school, and his son had been accepted into the Naval Academy in Annapolis, Maryland. Ralph had retired from the police department in May of 2005 (the same month that Jeanette had retired from Social Services) and was working at the sale barn in Hondo.

Ralph and Carolyn had some close friends that had built on a golf course named Briggs Ranch which is located outside of Castroville, Texas; about 30 miles west of San Antonio, and Ralph found a lot that he liked at the same subdivision. They ended up buying the lot and started talking about selling out at Yancey and moving there.

A Farm/Ranch real estate agency was handling the marketing of their property in Yancey, and it was drawing a lot of interest, but no serious buyer. One day Ralph called and told me that his agent wanted to talk to me about a deal that had been proposed. The agent came out and told Jeanette and me that he had a serious buyer for Ralph's ranch, but the buyer wanted more property and wondered if we would agree to sell ours, too.

I was taken by surprise as I had not considered selling and moving. I told the agent that *we* would talk about it and let him know within a few days. Around this same time, Doug and Amy and the girls had left the horse training job in Hondo. They had moved back to Stephenville to build their own horse facility on their remaining land and to go into business for themselves.

With them gone and the prospect of new people replacing my brother as neighbors, we decided that we would sell if the money was right. Funny how things work out. The "deal" that we were initially approached about fell through, but by then, Jeanette and I had gotten the urge to sell, so we put our property on the market.

Within a month we had a buyer, and we closed on April 14, 2014. Ralph's place sold a couple of months after ours, and just like that, the Jacobs brothers had vacated Yancey. *God blessed* all the hard work that Ralph, Jeanette, and I had poured into our places, and we were well rewarded. The most difficult part was telling the Karns family goodbye.

Now we had to scramble for someplace to stay. Jeanette and I had always been fond of the Texas Hill Country, so we rented a house in Kerrville which we used as a home base while we began looking for something permanent. We both had a "must have" list of things that would have to be present for us to buy our new home. First on Jeanette's list was a place near good medical facilities and running a close second she wanted to have friends she could socialize with. Our years in the country were fine while we were both working, but she didn't want to be quite as isolated as we had been.

I could appreciate her concerns, but I didn't want to live in a subdivision where I could hear the neighbor flush his toilet. My absolute "must have" had to include *a* shop where I could put all of my woodworking tools, and a place where I could find time to be by myself. It took several months, but we found the place that filled all our wants and needs.

The *Falling Water* subdivision is on Hwy. 87, 5 miles north of Comfort, Texas, "on the way to Fredericksburg." It is made up of about 100 lots that range in acreage from two-and a half to around 10 acres. We bought 6.5 acres, and we built a new house with a detached shop. We lived in Kerrville for about a year and had a wonderful landlord and great neighbors there. When our new home was completed in 2016, we moved in, and we were met by numerous fellow residents who stopped by to welcome us to the community.

When you look off the front porch of our home, it wouldn't be hard to convince yourself that you are somewhere in the mountains of Colorado. The neighbors are not right next to us, but they are nearby. There are strong social groups within the neighborhood with similar histories and varied interests. We are located within a hub that is surrounded by Kerrville, Fredericksburg, and Boerne, and we are about 35 miles north of San Antonio. Good medical attention is available within a 20-minute drive. There is abundant wildlife which requires harvesting as dictated by a state biologist, and we can still see the stars at night! In other words, I can't think of any place that we could have found that would be any better for us to live. To this day, I still walk out my front door and stand amazed at the view we have of our surrounding hills. I wish that our parents were still alive to enjoy the blessings that God has granted us.

One day a short time after we had bought our property in Falling Water, my brother and I were talking, and I told him about our lot. They were working on plans to build a house on the lot he had bought in Briggs Ranch, but he was curious and wanted to see our property. They met with us one day, and they, too, fell in love with the area.

It wasn't long before they found a lot on top of a high hill, and they decided to buy it! They ended up building a house, and unfortunately, just as they were ready to begin moving in, it burned to the ground! A plumber had walked away from welding on a copper connection, and during the night, the nearby wood ignited, flared up, and caught the house on fire. Fortunately, the builder had adequate insurance, and they had to completely rebuild the house. When it was all said and done, my brother and sister-in-law ended up with a beautiful home and once again we are living within seeing distance of each other's houses.

Chapter 52

"Not quite the end!"

Well, it's been a journey, and I appreciate you coming along for the ride. From that day in 2014 when I got under Rainy's bed until today, February 2023, as I am writing this last chapter, I am thankful that I had the opportunity to complete what I started.

In the Old Testament of the Bible there is a book titled 2 Samuel. It is an account of the life of King David and his relationship with God. In Chapter 7: v.18, David asks this question of God, "Who am I, O Lord God? And what is my house that You have brought me this far?" I have asked God that very question numerous times myself. Since you have just read an account of my life, I don't have to tell you that there were *many times* that I didn't behave as the man I should have been. There were numerous times that I could easily have been killed. I encountered some of the horrible misery of this world, was shot at on six different occasions, had numerous accidents, and yet, here I am.

During my 34 years in Law Enforcement, 22 officers I knew lost their lives serving the citizens of San Antonio. I mentioned Barney Salazar, but there were many more, especially if you add in those who survived their wounds. Time and again, I thought I was lucky when things turned out for the best.

In spite of our mistakes in our first marriages, our children have raised good kids themselves. They are not perfect (as none of us are,) but they are doing their very best. My wife and I have both been granted forgiveness and second chances to live a Godly life, and I thank God for her. We have also been given second chances when it comes to being around our kids and grandkids, and you could say again that I am lucky. At one time, I would have agreed with you and proudly bragged that I was one lucky Son-of-a-Gun. But not anymore!

Since accepting Jesus as my Lord and Savior, I know that luck has nothing to do with the life I have been granted. Even when I wanted nothing to do with God, He had a purpose for me to accomplish while I am here on earth, so He has kept me around. I have surely not completed His mission for me, but I try to respond to circumstances *as* I think He would want me t*o*.

I will never be perfect (here, my wife is probably saying, "Amen,") but I will not stop trying. The good thing is that God wants to have a relationship with all *of* us just as we are. Accept His free gift of salvation, and let Him guide your steps. I know for a fact that He will be there for you when you stumble. (I have given him lots of practice!)

It's not up to me to write the ending for this book since I don't know when that will come. I know the number of my days was determined before I was even born, so why should I spend time worrying about it? Some people would give anything to be able to foretell the future. *Why?* Don't we have enough on our plate to worry about today?

I think that if we spend too much time looking toward the future, we could easily miss the opportunity of "getting under the bed" and finding the hidden treasure of sharing something special today! Enjoy the journey. After all, we are all Sojourners until we are called Home.

Not quite the end!

Acknowledgments

When I started on this journey, I made a commitment to finish this account if God were willing. God was willing, but I never realized it would take more than His willingness and my stubborn resolve to finish what I started. As in anything worthwhile, the finished product you hold in your hand is the result of multiple people willing to give of their time and expertise.

Mark Trapino not only encouraged me to write it, but then he took the time to read through it and make suggestions that enhanced the readability of the book. My wife Jeanette applied her knowledge of English grammar and made sure that it would conform to the basic rules of sentence structure and convey what I meant to say.

To Rudy French, my Canadian fishing guide. You were an inspiration as you have written several books and yet continue your missionary work showing me that when we let God direct our steps HE will provide the time and tools to complete that good work he has chosen for us.

To the many people who have crossed my path and have knowingly or unknowingly affected my life as it's reflected within the pages of this book...thank you. I hope that, more often than not, I treated you with respect. I ask for forgiveness from those whom I might have hurt in one form or another. I am human, but I strive to be better each day. Thank you all for making this book a reality.

Milton Keynes UK
Ingram Content Group UK Ltd.
UKHW020756080823
426520UK00015B/786